JEWISH SUNDAY SCHOOLS

NORTH AMERICAN RELIGIONS

Series Editors: Tracy Fessenden (Arizona State University), Laura Levitt (Temple University), and David Harrington Watt (Haverford College).

Since its inception, the North American Religions book series has steadily disseminated gracefully written, pathbreaking explorations of religion in North America. Books in the series move among the discourses of ethnographic, textual, and historical analysis and across a range of topics, including sound, story, food, nature, healing, crime, and pilgrimage. In so doing they bring religion into view as a style and form of belonging, a set of tools for living with and in relations of power, a mode of cultural production and reproduction, and a vast repertory of the imagination. Whatever their focus, books in the series remain attentive to the shifting and contingent ways in which religious phenomena are named, organized, and contested. They bring fluency in the best of contemporary theoretical and historical scholarship to bear on the study of religion in North America. The series focuses primarily, but not exclusively, on religion in the United States in the twentieth and twenty-first centuries.

Books in the series

Ava Chamberlain, *The Notorious Elizabeth Tuttle: Marriage, Murder, and Madness in the Family of Jonathan Edwards*

Terry Rey and Alex Stepick, *Crossing the Water and Keeping the Faith: Haitian Religion in Miami*

Isaac Weiner, *Religion Out Loud: Religious Sound, Public Space, and American Pluralism*

Hillary Kaell, *Walking Where Jesus Walked: American Christians and Holy Land Pilgrimage*

Brett Hendrickson, *Border Medicine: A Transcultural History of Mexican American Curanderismo*

Jodi Eichler-Levine, *Suffer the Little Children: Uses of the Past in Jewish and African American Children's Literature*

Annie Blazer, *Playing for God: Evangelical Women and the Unintended Consequences of Sports Ministry*

Elizabeth Pérez, *Religion in the Kitchen: Cooking, Talking, and the Making of Black Atlantic Traditions*

Kerry Mitchell, *Spirituality and the State: Managing Nature and Experience in America's National Parks*

Finbarr Curtis, *The Production of American Religious Freedom*

M. Cooper Harriss, *Ralph Ellison's Invisible Theology*

Ari Y. Kelman, *Shout to the Lord: Making Worship Music in Evangelical America*

Joshua Dubler and Isaac Weiner, *Religion, Law, USA*

Shari Rabin, *Jews on the Frontier: Religion and Mobility in Nineteenth-Century America*

Elizabeth Fenton, *Old Canaan in a New World: Native Americans and the Lost Tribes of Israel*

Alyssa Maldonado-Estrada, *Lifeblood of the Parish: Men and Catholic Devotion in Williamsburg, Brooklyn*

Caleb Iyer Elfenbein, *Fear in Our Hearts: What Islamophobia Tells Us about America*

Rachel B. Gross, *Beyond the Synagogue: Jewish Nostalgia as Religious Practice*

Jenna Supp-Montgomerie, *When the Medium Was the Mission: The Atlantic Telegraph and the Religious Origins of Network Culture*

Philippa Koch, *The Course of God's Providence: Religion, Health, and the Body in Early America*

Jennifer Scheper Hughes, *The Church of the Dead: The Epidemic of 1576 and the Birth of Christianity in the Americas*

Sylvester A. Johnson and Tisa Wenger, *Religion and US Empire: Critical New Histories*

Deborah Dash Moore, *Vernacular Religion: Collected Essays of Leonard Norman Primiano*

Katrina Daly Thompson, *Muslims on the Margins: Creating Queer Religious Community in North America*

Laura Yares, *Jewish Sunday Schools: Teaching Religion in Nineteenth-Century America*

Jewish Sunday Schools

Teaching Religion in Nineteenth-Century America

Laura Yares

NEW YORK UNIVERSITY PRESS

New York

NEW YORK UNIVERSITY PRESS
New York
www.nyupress.org

Library of Congress Cataloging-in-Publication Data
Names: Yares, Laura, author.
Title: Jewish Sunday schools : teaching religion in nineteenth-century America /
Laura Yares.
Description: New York : New York University Press, [2023]. | Series: North American
religions | Includes bibliographical references and index.
Identifiers: LCCN 2022040806 | ISBN 9781479822270 (hardback) |
ISBN 9781479822287 (ebook) | ISBN 9781479822300 (ebook other)
Subjects: LCSH: Jewish religious education of children—United States—History—19th
century. | Reform Judaism—United States—History—19th century. | Women educators—
United States—History—19th century. | Jewish women—Religious life—United States—
History—19th century. | United States—Ethnic relations.
Classification: LCC BM103 .Y37 2023 | DDC 296.6/80830973—dc23/eng/20220825
LC record available at https://lccn.loc.gov/2022040806

New York University Press books are printed on acid-free paper, and their binding materials
are chosen for strength and durability. We strive to use environmentally responsible
suppliers and materials to the greatest extent possible in publishing our books.

Manufactured in the United States of America

10 9 8 7 6 5 4 3 2 1

Also available as an ebook

CONTENTS

List of Figures	ix
Introduction: Making Jewish Education Religious	1
1. Jewish Women on the Educational Frontier	21
2. Catechisms, Masculinity, and Rational Jewish Religion	48
3. How Do You Solve a Problem Like Shavuot?	71
4. Expanding the Educational Marketplace	98
5. Religious Education as Americanization	128
6. From Theology to Religion	145
Conclusion: Is Judaism a Religion?	167
Acknowledgments	175
Notes	179
Bibliography	217
Index	239
About the Author	251

LIST OF FIGURES

Figure 1.1. Teachers at Beth El Religious School 37

Figure 2.1. George Jacobs, *Catechism for Elementary Instruction in the Hebrew Faith* 62

Figure 3.1. The interior of Kahal Kadosh Beth Elohim 87

Figure 3.2. Eoff Street Temple 89

Figure 4.1. Confirmation certificate published by the Bloch Publishing Company 110

Figure 4.2. Confirmation medal awarded to Herbert A. Moses 113

Figure 4.3. *Bird's Eye View of Samaria* 123

Figure 4.4. *Jews of Jerusalem at Abraham's Vineyard* 124

Figure 5.1. Children at a pageant held at the Sunday school of Temple Beth Israel 133

Introduction

Making Jewish Education Religious

Isaac Mayer Wise, a twenty-seven-year-old Jewish immigrant from the Bohemian village of Steingrub, arrived in the United States in 1846. Wise was a promising young scholar. At age nine he had left his family home and traveled more than three hundred miles to study at *yeshiva* in Prague. He would later enroll at the city's university to complete secular studies as well. Wise began his career as a teacher in Bavaria before deciding to join a tide of Jews from across Western Europe who were leaving behind the Old World for the New.[1] Arriving in New York in July 1846, he soon learned that America's new Jewish communities were in sore need of rabbis and teachers. By October Wise had secured a position at Congregation Beth El in Albany. His duties included sole responsibility for the congregation's school, where he taught both secular and Judaic subjects each day from 9:00 a.m. to noon and again from 1:00 to 4:00 p.m., earning nine dollars a year for every child enrolled.[2] A year after his arrival in Albany, he wrote a letter to the Leipzig newspaper *Allgemeine Zeitung Des Judenthums* in which he described the "fine progress" of German American Jewry in all matters—with the exception of Jewish education. In only some communities like his own, he lamented, "the Chazan [cantor] teaches Hebrew reading and has the children read a little in various catechisms, and frequently the miracle occurs that a boy learns to render the Neginah (chant) and a few chapters of *Chumash* (Torah) into German." In other congregations, Wise lamented, "they have introduced a phantom affair called a Sunday School. There religious instruction for children is imparted each Sabbath or Sunday by good-hearted young women. What fruits these few hours can bring forth hardly necessitates further description."[3]

The Sunday schools that Wise decried bore little resemblance to the education that he had received as a boy in Bohemia and in Prague or to the school that he led in Albany. Students came for only a few hours on a Sunday or Saturday morning rather than each day during the week, and they were taught only Judaic subjects, with no secular curriculum. The Jewish instruction was altogether different from Wise's experience too. In American Jewish Sunday schools, the Bible was typically taught in English instead of Hebrew. Its rabbinic commentaries were absent from the curriculum, as was the Talmud, the voluminous compendium of halacha (Jewish law) that was the backbone of yeshiva education in Europe. Perhaps the most jarring difference, however, was that the instructors of the school were not rabbis or experienced educators like Wise. They were "good-hearted young women" who brought vivacious spirit but little Jewish educational training to the task of teaching their young charges.

The Jewish Sunday school in America redefined the nature and purpose of Jewish education. During the nineteenth century, it also served as a site for American Jews to reimagine Judaism itself. This book tells that story. It begins on March 4, 1838, with the opening of the first Sunday school for Jewish children in Philadelphia. Ringing the opening bell was Rebecca Gratz, a pioneering US-born Jewish woman who had dedicated her life to philanthropic work among Philadelphia's needy.[4] Gratz's Hebrew Sunday School offered its students a religious education modeled on the Sunday schools attended by their Christian peers. Jewish children playing on the streets of Philadelphia had become easy prey for enthusiastic missionaries who would lure recruits to their Bible classes with promises of prizes and trinkets.[5] Gratz's school offered its pupils a safe place to spend their Sunday mornings and a basic primer in Judaism that she hoped would equip them with sufficient Jewish knowledge to rebut the claims of predatory missionaries. Gratz eschewed the curriculum of traditional European Jewish education in favor of introductory Jewish catechisms, prayers in English, and simple home rituals for celebrating the Jewish holidays. Teaching the Chumash (Pentateuch) in Hebrew or the intense legal disputations of the Talmud was unrealistic for a once-a-week school, and the women who volunteered as teachers had not received training in such subjects either. At the Hebrew Sunday School in Philadelphia, Jewish children were instructed in concise lessons steeped in the values of nineteenth-century bourgeois female religiosity—piety, benevolence, and virtuous conduct. As a catechism memorized by children in Gratz's Sunday school explained, the essential teaching of all religion, including Judaism, was "faith, hope and charity."[6] Meeting on Sunday mornings when Christians would be attending the schools of their own denominations, the Hebrew Sunday School taught Jewish children that their tradition had a repository of spiritual and moral lessons that was more than equal to those boasted by the Presbyterians, Methodists, Episcopalians, and Baptists down the street.

Gratz was not a proponent of the Jewish Reform movement, nor was she an advocate for the dismantling of traditional Jewish scholarship. Her goal was not a revolution in Jewish learning but a pragmatic institution that could equip Jewish children with sufficient knowledge to defend themselves against predatory evangelists and kindle their enthusiasm for Judaism. Isaac Leeser, hazan of Gratz's home synagogue, the traditional Sephardic Congregation Mikveh Israel, was one of the Sunday school's staunchest supporters.[7] Even though the educational curriculum of the Jewish Sunday school was limited, Leeser reasoned, it at least offered some semblance of Jewish training for children who were otherwise far removed from organized Jewish life. When he visited Cincinnati in 1851, he was dismayed to find many critics of the enterprise that Gratz had pioneered. "Now we perfectly agree with those who object to the movement, that religious instruction should not be confined to one day out of seven, but should be a daily exercise," he conceded in a travel diary published in his newspaper, the *Occident and American Jewish Advocate*. Yet "Jewish children do not attend, as a rule, Jewish schools, even where such are established. . . . The fact cannot be disputed. We therefore ask our friends: 'will you place any hinderance in the way of this enterprise, by which, should you succeed in breaking it up, you could to a surety deprive many of the only chances they will even have to obtain the least knowledge of religion? The case may be deplorable. It in fact is so; but let us not reject the only remedy we have at hand, in the hope that, if children once tasted the waters of life, they will thirst for more.'"[8]

Leeser's sentiments were shared by Jewish communities across the country that recognized that the Sunday school offered a pragmatic and affordable model for Jewish education. During the nineteenth century, Jewish Sunday schools were established across the United States, Canada, and the Caribbean. They were founded by philanthropic groups, established synagogues, by small Jewish communities on the frontier of American Judaism, and under the auspices of charitable organizations set up to serve new immigrants. Many schools were organized by female superintendents, and throughout the nineteenth century they were served by volunteer female teachers. The Sunday school thus offered critical opportunities for communal leadership to women who wanted to play public roles in their local Jewish communities.[9] The Sunday school would ultimately become synonymous with the Reform movement, yet in their formative period Sunday schools were founded by communities that proclaimed fidelity to traditional Judaism, as well as those inclined toward modernity and change. Some convened on Saturdays, some on Sundays, and some during the week as well. Some were called Sunday school, while others were titled "Religious School" or "Sabbath School." The principle that they shared was the foundational philosophy that Judaism could be taught and learned as a religious tradition—a vocabulary and an ideology adapted from Protestant Christianity. Sunday school textbooks focused on defining Jewish beliefs, explaining Jewish home rituals, and constructing boundaries between Judaism and other traditions. The confirmation ceremony that was adopted by most Sunday schools as a coming-of-age ceremony celebrated Jewish children who "confirmed" their commitments to creedal principles they had learned in Jewish catechisms. The Sunday school thus served as a critical mechanism through which the idea of Judaism as a religion—imagined in the overtly Protestant terms of private leisure-time faith commitments—was implanted across the grassroots frontier of American Judaism.

By the 1880s the Sunday school had become the regnant institution for Jewish learning in America. Isaac Mayer Wise ultimately became its ardent supporter, having become convinced that it offered a practical and financially expedient solution to the task of equipping students who spent their weekdays in public schools with an introductory Jewish education. Demarcating religious instruction to Sunday mornings, he reasoned, also served as a rationale to encourage the removal of Christian influences in the weekday public schools. "It is our settled opinion here," Wise wrote in an 1870 report for the US commissioner of education, "that the education of the young is the business of the State, and the religious instruction, to which we add the Hebrew, is the duty of the religious bodies. Neither ought to interfere with the other. The secular branches belong to the public schools, religion in the Sabbath schools."[10]

During the twenty-five years that had elapsed since his arrival in New York, Wise had become a leading voice within the American Jewish Reform movement, a radical reimagining of Jewish practice imported from Europe. The reformers defined Judaism as a system of religious ideas, a set of beliefs rather than an ethnic, legal, cultural, or political community.[11] For American Reform Jews, the Sunday school's curriculum offered an educational instantiation of their own philosophy of Judaism, one that proclaimed, in the words of their 1885 Pittsburgh Platform, that Jews were "no longer a nation, but a religious community" who recognized the Bible as their "most potent instrument of religious and moral instruction."[12] As Reform Judaism ascended in America during the middle decades of the nineteenth century, the Sabbath school became its principal educational organization. When educator Harry Bricker conducted a survey of Jewish education in Chicago in 1940, he described the city's once-a-week Sunday or Sabbath schools as the invention of "reform Jews, with their German background and their conception of Judaism as a religion."[13] If traditional systems of Jewish education seemed to the reformers to bolster anti-Semitic canards that Judaism offered nothing more than dry legalism, the Sunday school proclaimed that Judaism was a repository of refined theological truths. Jewish religious training could mirror Protestant Christian education, emphasizing the Bible, morality, theology, and ethics.

The Sunday school remained the dominant model for Jewish education in America through the turn of the twentieth century, when it was displaced by new institutions imported from overseas. A wave of Jewish immigrants arriving in America from eastern Europe between 1881 and 1924 led to the proliferation of a diverse array of educational institutions that reflected the immigrants' various cultural and religious ideologies, including cheders offering elementary instruction in Hebrew and Jewish subjects; Talmud Torahs providing lessons to older students; schools focused on Yiddish culture; and Jewish socialist education offered by organizations like the Arbeiter Ring.[14] In 1910 concerned philanthropists created a central agency to establish order out of the chaos. The New York Bureau of Jewish Education hoped to set up a centralized administrative, pedagogical, and financial apparatus for the array of Jewish schools that had been created by new Jewish immigrants in New York City, with the ultimate aim of revolutionizing Jewish education in America writ large. The bureau was led by Samson Benderly, an enthusiastic young educator from Safed, Palestine, who had forged an innovative community model for Jewish schooling in Baltimore that infused spoken Hebrew into the curriculum. As Benderly's chief historian, Jonathan Krasner, has chronicled, Benderly and his protégés at the New York Bureau imagined they would bring about a "Jewish national and cultural renaissance" by transforming Sunday school into Hebrew school.[15] Benderly rejected the Sunday school's curriculum for Jewish learning and advocated for a more intensive multiday model that emphasized Hebrew language instruction, seeking to induct children into a cultural world rather than into a set of religious ideas. Benderly famously described the Sunday school as a "shandeh school"—a disgrace school—and pilloried its graduates as "otherwise intelligent men" who "know nothing of Judaism."[16]

Historians of American Judaism have largely replicated Benderly's appraisal, maintaining that the curriculum of the nineteenth-century Sunday school was static and its failings were endemic until Benderly and his "boys" arrived to deepen, intensify, and improve the sorry state of American Jewish learning.[17] The nineteenth-century Sunday school, created by Gratz and dominant until Benderly, has largely been ignored within American Jewish historiography, dismissed as feminized, sentimental, and saccharine; led by untrained female teachers overly concerned with teaching blasé lessons on morality; and devoid of efforts toward pedagogical innovation and change.[18] The reality, as this book will demonstrate, was more complex. Sunday school teachers and administrators grappled with questions of pedagogy and curriculum as they sought to engage children in a Jewish educational experience that could persuade the next generation to remain Jewish in America, despite the compelling attractions of the Christian mainstream. What is more, the Sunday school had an enduring effect on the organization of Jewish education in the United States. Its legacies are evident in the continuing American Jewish predisposition for public school education complemented by "religious school" in leisure time, even if the particularities of the curricula used in the nineteenth century were ultimately supplanted by new models introduced in the twentieth century and beyond. Per-

haps even more critically, however, the women—and men—who shep-
herded Jewish education during the nineteenth century did important
and influential work that extended far beyond the classrooms in which
they worked. We cannot understand the nineteenth-century American
Jewish experience, and the mechanisms American Jews used to sustain
Judaism in an overwhelmingly Protestant context, without looking at
the development of the Jewish Sunday school.

This book examines the seventy years of educational efforts, from the
opening of the Hebrew Sunday School in Philadelphia in 1838 to the
founding of the New York Bureau of Jewish Education in 1910, to illuminate the various ways that American Jews with investments in the
Sunday school navigated the evolving ramifications of defining Jewish
education as religious education. They were influenced by new ideas
about religion within contemporary American popular culture, as Jews
and Christians alike encountered an increasingly expansive landscape
of conceptual vocabularies for defining religion and for articulating
religious "truths." To observe that the American Jewish Sunday school
taught Judaism as a religious tradition modeled on American Protestantism demarcates a critical point of distinction between the Sunday
school and other models of Jewish education.[19] Yet it tells only part of
the story. When American Jews defined Jewish education in terms of religion, they adopted a category that was dynamic rather than stable, constructed rather than absolute. As the American Jewish Sunday school
evolved during the nineteenth century, changing ideas about what religion was and how it should be practiced proved pivotal to the process.

The Invention of Jewish Religion

Though it may seem intuitive to assume that Judaism belongs naturally
in the category of religion, that it is one of the major world religions,
the appellation is not native to a Jewish context. *Religion*, a term that
eludes precise etymological definition, is a cultural construct, historically inseparable from its origins within Western Christianity. Critical
histories of the category of religion published since the early 1990s have
illustrated the various ways that the concept is mired within the hermeneutics of European Protestantism. Definitions of religion in Western
contexts have therefore habitually emphasized faith and theology rather

than experiences embedded in culture and community, things set apart rather than lived and embodied.[20] According to Tomoko Masuzawa, Russell McCutcheon, Timothy Fitzgerald, and Talal Asad, applying the category of religion thus inevitably represents an imposition of Protestant hermeneutics upon non-Christian traditions.[21] Indeed, the limitations of the concept of religion are rendered especially apparent in the case of Judaism, where perceptions of ethnic identity, community, and peoplehood have historically been as central to Jewish self-identity as faith and theology. "Judaism the religion, in North America, Europe, Latin America, the South Pacific and South Africa," historian Jacob Neusner argued, "finds itself wrapped around by Jewishness, the ethnic identity of persons who derive from Jewish parents and deem 'being Jewish' to bear meaning in their familial and social life and cultural world. The beliefs and practices, if any, of Jews do not by themselves form data for the description of Judaism."[22]

Yet during modernity Jews and Judaism became irrevocably entangled within the discourse of religion, a category that was both applied to Jews by nation-states and claimed by Jews seeking citizenship within them. In his 1783 defense of Judaism, "Jerusalem," philosopher Moses Mendelssohn argued that the primary role of halacha (Jewish law) was to define the religious responsibilities that were incumbent on Jews alone. Utilizing Mendelssohn's conceptual logic, defining Judaism as a privatized set of faith commitments became part of a coterie of arguments that attempted to establish a rationale for change in the political status of Jews living in modern Europe toward full and equal rights.[23] Judaism as a religion in the context of the Haskalah (Jewish enlightenment) of the late eighteenth and nineteenth centuries was promoted as a private identity compatible with full participation in public life, a mediation of Judaism that promised that a Jew could be a "man in the street and a Jew in the home."[24] In concert with these political rationales for naming Judaism as a religion, a theological agenda was advanced by self-proclaimed Reform thinkers who proposed the reconfiguration of Judaism along the lines of what they understood to be modern rational religion: lived not through the practice of "Oriental" ceremonies and rituals but by cultivating Judaism's distinctive position on spirituality, morality, and ethics.[25] The application of the mantle of religion to Judaism is therefore not only a story about the imposition of a Christian category upon Jews. It is also a story of Jews who actively chose to adopt, for political, social, and theological ends, a construct mired within Protestant hermeneutics.[26]

For Jews in colonial America, defining Judaism as a religion served important practical and legal purposes. Laws vested in Protestant Christianity excluded Jews from a variety of rights and responsibilities, from the ability to vote to the eligibility to hold public office.[27] With American independence came commitments to the separation of church and state, and when the new president, George Washington, visited Newport, Rhode Island, in 1790, he assured Moses Seixas of the Hebrew Congregation of Newport that the new republic was founded on the commitment to religious liberty. Anti-Jewish discrimination did not disappear, yet in the years to come American Jews could protest anti-Jewish discrimination on the basis that Judaism was indeed a religious tradition: exercising the First Amendment principle that government could make no law restricting religion or prohibiting the exercise thereof. Jews used the rationale that Judaism was a religion to protest blue laws that prohibited Jews from conducting business on Sunday, arguing that their own Sabbath, observed on Saturday, was the equivalent of Christianity's holy day.[28] Though attendance at synagogue and participation in prayer and ritual were only some of the ways that Jews in early America engaged with Jewishness, defining Judaism in religious terms offered an important recourse for Jews to assert their rights as American citizens.[29] In the nineteenth century the expansive growth of the Reform movement offered American Judaism an ideological expression of Jewish religion, with the Reform movement's distinctive emphasis on Judaism's theological attributes rather than its cultural or ethnic dimensions.

Within the historiography of American Judaism, however, analysis of Jewish entanglements with the category of religion have focused less on the nineteenth century and more closely on the experiences of Jewish suburbanites during the second half of the twentieth century. According to this narrative, while Jews defined Judaism as a religion for important legal ends before the twentieth century, as well as in theological terms under the auspices of the American Reform movement, it was during the 1950s and 1960s that Judaism truly became an American religion. In the decades that followed World War II, Jews flocked to America's burgeoning suburbs, constructing Jewish enclaves rooted predominantly in the religious domains of synagogue and the nuclear family rather than in the ethnic and cultural Jewish spaces of urban downtowns. Just as postwar Christians expressed their religious belonging through membership in churches, suburban Jews chose to demonstrate allegiance to Judaism through the distinctive mechanisms of synagogue, the celebration of religious holidays, and commitments to the religious education of children.[30] Historians have described the postwar embrace of synagogue-centered Jewish religion as an attempt to conform to the dominant pattern of suburban life and as a rejection of Judaism's ethnic dimensions among Jews who aspired to inclusion in middle-class America.[31]

This teleological rendering of Judaism finally becoming a religion in the context of postwar suburbia offers an overly narrow accounting of American Jewish engagements with ideas of religion. It overlooks the ways that American Jews navigated definitions of Jewish religion in other historical and ideological contexts. It also evades the constructed and dynamic nature of the idea of religion itself. As historian of religion Jonathan Z. Smith succinctly observed, religion is an anthropological, not a theological, category.[32] It is a socially constructed concept that reflects the cultural mores of the various environments in which it has been articulated and deployed. In the twentieth century, Jewish entanglements with the category of religion were shaped by Cold War rhetoric that equated membership in religious institutions with American patriotism. In other periods the valence of religion and religious belonging has been marked by different cultural associations and an evolving set of images and ideas.[33]

During the nineteenth century, articulations of Judaism as a religion were inflected by a distinctive and dynamic set of ideologies that emerged across a rapidly changing conceptual landscape. Bourgeois Victorian America embraced German theologian Friedrich Schleiermacher's notion that religion was primarily a matter of feeling and sentiment. In sermons, religious discourse, and popular literature, women were extolled for their fidelity and piety by virtue of their innate capacity for emotion, as religion became intertwined with feminine domestic piety, anchored in the institution of the sentimental family. Simultaneously, philosophical constructions of "good" religion with rationality made religion synonymous with masculinity, and barriers to women's officiating as clergy established that religious knowledge was the preserve of men alone. In nineteenth-century America being religious was judged essential to proper citizenship. Yet by the later decades of the century, the legitimacy of religious truth claims had been challenged by new ideological currents that included Darwinism, free thought, and the historical critical study of the Bible. In universities the comparative study of religion was emerging as a field of inquiry obsessed with the primitive and the original, focused on mapping the development of religion from its first beginnings to forms that the discipline's largely Christian progenitors judged to represent sophisticated modern piety. As these histories of religion became popular and were studied in reading circles and literary societies, they seemed to offer scientific evidence for a hierarchy that had never been far below the surface of American culture: one that proclaimed white Anglo Protestantism to be culturally superior to other ethnic and religious groups. Meanwhile, universalist movements such as transcendentalism and Ethical Culture espoused the fundamental equality of all religions, a philosophy that the Parliament of World Religions celebrated with great aplomb at the 1893 World's Columbian Exposition in Chicago.

The Jewish Sunday school offers a site to examine how Jews negotiated the shifting semantics of nineteenth-century religion and to explore how these negotiations shaped the development of Jewish life in America. Beyond the treatises of modern Jewish thought, and the platforms and statements issued by major denominations, education reveals how evolving ideas about religion were negotiated on the ground. Education was pivotal to the ways that Jews encountered and navigated modernity, and the history of Jewish education offers important insights into the ways that Jewish learning served as a mechanism for transmitting values relevant to local and historical contexts. Education highlights the syntheses that Jews have created between Judaism and the majority populations in which Jews have lived."[1] In Europe educational settings offered sites for modernizing European Jews to explore expressions of Jewishness that emphasized Hebrew and Yiddish, ideologies of Jewish nationalism, and the reconciliation of Jewish tradition with the cultures and values of local nation-states. In nineteenth-century America the project of adapting Jewish education to modernity broadly eschewed overtly political frameworks in favor of a pedagogical synthesis that emphasized the theological rapprochement of Judaism and Christianity. It stressed the idea that Judaism was a religion that could be taught and learned in Sunday school.

Women's Religion

This book proceeds from the assumption that there is value in studying the history of Jewish education beyond the search for instructional exemplars. Educational sources are important for understanding the Jewish past, irrespective of their relative merits as paradigms for Jewish pedagogy. Historians have heaped derision on the American Jewish Sunday school mostly because they have been preoccupied with the question of whether it represented "good Jewish education," capable of imparting literacy in Jewish subjects and producing graduates who would prioritize membership in Jewish institutions and affiliations with the Jewish community. Yet evaluating the Sunday school solely in terms of its ability to ensure Jewish continuity is a limited criterion by which to judge its curriculum and cultural influence. What is more, this approach has largely made women responsible for the Sunday school's failings.[35] Both contemporary critics of the Sunday school as well as later historians have argued that the presence of volunteer female teachers, and the focus on subjects associated with women's spirituality, offer evidence of the Sunday school's lack of Jewish rigor. The Sunday school has been judged as limited and wanting because its teachers were women and its curriculum was shaped by women's religion.

Women were instrumental to the American Jewish Sunday school movement. They founded schools across the country, and throughout the nineteenth century they served as teachers in Sunday school classrooms. In 1909 Bernard Cronson and Mordecai M. Kaplan conducted a broad survey of Jewish educational institutions in New York City. After critically comparing the various curricula and pedagogies of the city's Sunday schools, they determined that no two schools were alike. Nevertheless, some broad defining characteristics did demarcate Sunday schools from other Jewish educational institutions. Sunday schools organized by Reform congregations were attended for the most part by the children of their members and typically met once a week. This was the primary distinction that separated Sunday schools and the Hebrew schools organized by Orthodox and Conservative congregations, which typically offered instruction two to five times a week in addition to Sunday mornings. Sunday schools were also incorporated into "mission schools" and community schools founded by sisterhoods and the National Council of Jewish Women; these schools offered vocational and secular training alongside Sunday morning classes in religion. However, the primary characteristic that distinguished Sunday schools from all other educational institutions was that their teachers typically were female volunteers. In Conservative and Orthodox congregational schools, cheders, and weekday Talmud Torahs, paid male instructors dominated the educational scene.[36] A national survey conducted by the Union of American Hebrew Congregations in 1924 found that 73 percent of teachers in Reform Sunday schools were female and only 27 percent were male.[37]

For contemporary critics the prevalence of female teachers symbolized the Sunday school's principal failing. Critics dismissed the Sunday school curriculum as nothing more than female domestic religiosity in a Jewish key and belittled women volunteers for their ignorance of Hebrew and classical Jewish texts. These critics, mostly men, had personal investments in professionalizing the field of Jewish education that did little to endear them to the untrained female volunteers who taught in Sunday schools. They were rabbis struggling to maintain congregational afternoon and day schools, as well as new immigrants seeking to use expertise gained in European yeshivas to make a living as teachers and tutors in America. The usurpation of Jewish education by women who brought little Jewish educational expertise to their work seemed, to these critics, to represent nothing more than the dilution of Jewish schooling into a mold shaped by public Protestantism. Historians of American Judaism have largely replicated these critiques, arguing that the Jewish Sunday school perpetuated the feminization of Jewish education by affording women a platform to teach spirituality and morality, topics that in contemporary Protestantism were considered central to women's religiosity.[38]

There is an overt gendering at work in this historiographic narrative: that nineteenth-century Jewish Sunday school education was limited principally because it was conducted by women and proceeded from women's distinctive religious concerns. As religious studies scholar

Sarah Imhoff has observed, historians who have argued for the so-called feminization of American Jewish life in the nineteenth century have typically neglected to coherently define feminization as an analytical category. Feminization as a result of the increased visibility of women's bodies has been conflated with feminization construed by the presence of qualities associated with women. The two dynamics are interrelated, but they are not the same.[39] In the case of the Jewish Sunday school, the feminization narrative has obscured the presence of male bodies. The Sunday school was pioneering in its extension of Jewish education to girls, yet there is little evidence to suggest that most contemporary parents therefore saw Sunday schools as institutions for their daughters and not for their sons. The rosters of some schools certainly featured fewer boys, particularly in New York toward the end of the nineteenth century as a result of the availability of new Jewish educational options open only to male students. Yet on balance most Sunday schools did not lean overwhelmingly female. In 1889 a national survey by the Union of American Hebrew Congregations found that 48.7 percent of students in Reform Sunday schools were boys, and 51.7 percent were girls. By 1924 those percentages had changed only slightly: 46.4 percent of students were male and 53.5 percent were female.[40]

What is more, while it is certainly true that female volunteers played outsize roles as founders of Sunday schools and as teachers in Sunday school classrooms, when Jewish Sunday schools were created under the auspices of congregations, rabbis (all men) were typically appointed as superintendents. They supervised volunteer female teachers, taught older grades, and officiated at confirmations. Congregational educational boards could circumscribe rabbinic leadership, yet men also dominated these boards. On a national level men founded and dominated a growing panoply of rabbinical and communal organizations, including the Union of American Hebrew Congregations, Central Conference of American Rabbis, and Jewish Chautauqua Society, organizations that attempted to align local Sunday schools with national standards that these organizations took it upon themselves to devise. Within a generation of the founding of the first Hebrew Sunday school, women had been displaced from the administrative leadership of the Jewish Sunday school movement, although their volunteer labor remained vital to its viability as a financial model for American Jewish education.

Male voices dominate the records of nineteenth-century congregational Sunday schools. The historiographical trope that Sunday schools
perpetuated the feminization of Jewish education ignores the presence
of men in leadership roles and fails to account for the influence that they
had upon curricula and instruction. Furthermore, it erases the ways that
Sunday schools also served as sites for Jewish men to navigate conceptions of masculinity and male authority in the context of Jewish education. As this book demonstrates, while the Sunday school undoubtedly
provided an important vehicle for women to explore new vistas of female public Jewish identity, involvement in the Sunday school also offered men opportunities to explore new methods of articulating Jewish
expertise in a setting that severed the historic connection between the
male educator and his knowledge of Jewish law.

This book therefore complicates the narrative that the religious program of the Sunday school represented the feminization of Jewish education in nineteenth-century America. It situates the dismissive equation
of the Sunday school and feminine religion within broader discursive
frameworks that governed gender and religion in the nineteenth century
and beyond. Recognizing that gender is a constituent of a politicized set
of discourses that center frameworks of power, this book investigates
the ways that femininity and masculinity, and female and male bodies, were described in the context of the Sunday school in relation to
emerging ideas about what Jewish religion was, and in relation to claims
about who had the authority to teach. By moving beyond the paradigm
that the Sunday school represented "feminine religion," this book opens
space to explore how associations of gendered religion were attributed
to men and to women in educational settings. It also highlights other
professionalized roles that women played in the Sunday school context,
as public school teachers who brought pedagogical expertise into Jewish
classrooms, and as activists for educational causes. Women dominated
American public school education during the nineteenth century, and
Jewish women who trained as teachers brought the knowledge they had
gained in normal schools and other educational programs to their Jewish communities by volunteering in Sunday schools. Here too they often
struggled to assert expertise and leadership in institutions that were led
by rabbis and male educational boards. As this book demonstrates, the
idea of Jewish religion and Jewish religious education assumed gendered

dynamics that were as much about power and authority as they were about the content of the Sunday school curriculum.

Sources and Outline

This book argues that Sunday schools were central to efforts to describe and define Judaism as a religion in nineteenth-century America. It explores the diverse methods that the Sunday school movement utilized to offer an approach to Jewish education that explicitly emphasized faith and theology, ethics, and morals. It does not claim to offer a history of the Sunday school movement, in the sense that it does not chart the evolution of its institutions or its curricula chronologically. Anchored in the field of religious studies, the book explores key aspects of the Sunday school and its negotiation of American Jewish religion thematically, within a loosely chronological structure. Similarly, while much of the activity of Sunday schools takes place within the nineteenth-century Reform movement, this book does not offer a denominational history of Reform Sunday schools. American Jewish Sunday schools were not inevitably Reform institutions, even though they did ultimately become a Reform institution. Following Cronson and Kaplan's typology, this book focuses on settings that described the curricular object of Jewish education as "religious education," that met once or twice a week, and in which women played active roles.[41]

While the lived experiences of children and teachers in Sunday schools, as preserved in workbooks, diaries, and memoirs are integral to the story told here, this book does not attempt to reconstruct the Sunday school through their eyes. It analyzes a range of settings instrumental to the production of discourse about American Jewish religion in the context of Sunday school education, including, but not limited to, students and teachers in the classroom. Inevitably a central challenge for a study of the nineteenth-century Jewish Sunday school is the unfortunate historiographical truth that relatively few archival records speak to the classroom experiences of students and teachers, which were rarely deemed sufficiently important to record.[42] In the minutes of congregational boards and education committees, as Gerda Lerman astutely observed, "the women who had done all the work . . . if they appeared in the record at all, would be visible only as a ladies auxiliary group or as unpaid, unrecognized volunteers."[43] The American Jewish press recorded the important efforts of women to found Sunday schools in the midnineteenth century, while the proliferation of women's auxiliary societies and sisterhoods of personal service beginning in the 1890s attest to the important impact that women had on American Jewish Sunday schools at the end of the century, improving classroom conditions and founding schools to serve new immigrants as women assumed more conscious roles as public activists for education. Yet rarely did synagogues and communal organizations keep detailed records of what happened in the classroom or document the processes of teaching and learning that students experienced.

Studying the negotiation of American Jewish religion in the context of education encourages us to go beyond the high roads of the platforms and statements proclaimed by national leaders and down the byways of local congregations, amateur teachers, and periodicals with short publication lives and small circulations. This book draws on a range of archival sources, including congregational records, prescriptive materials, first-person narratives, pedagogical literature, and reports about education in the American Jewish press. It uses congregational records to analyze the creation and implementation of Sunday schools in local contexts. It surveys prescriptive and pedagogical materials published by national organizations such as the Union of American Hebrew Congregations and the Jewish Chautauqua Society, as well as the textbooks, catechisms, and pamphlets produced by local educators for use in their own classrooms. It also closely examines the material and consumer cultures created to enhance Jewish learning by appealing to the senses, as educators began to emphasize that Jewish education should be an affective, as well as a cognitive, endeavor.[44] The form, distribution, and function of commercial goods created for the purposes of Jewish learning offers a vibrant illustration of the various ways that American Jews took their cues from the material inventories of American Christianity as they sought to make American Jewish education attractive to upwardly mobile and assimilating American Jews.

Together, local and national sources tell a textured story about the Sunday school and its evolving attempts to define Jewish education as religious education during the nineteenth century. Chapter 1 explores associations between the Sunday school and so-called women's religion.

Gratz's curriculum relied on sentimental piety anchored in moral lessons from Bible stories, hymns, and household rituals. Yet in the second half of the century, control of the curriculum within congregational Sunday schools was broadly assumed by men, and rabbis increasingly called upon women to embrace their domestic responsibilities as "mothers in Israel." Chapter 1 illustrates that although the first paradigmatic Jewish Sunday school made feminine piety central to its curriculum for Jewish religious education, as the Sunday school spread beyond Philadelphia, it became ensnared in multivalent, ambivalent, and contradictory rhetoric about the role of women and the feminine in the public leadership of American Jewish religion.

Chapter 2 focuses on catechisms, brief question-and-answer précises of Jewish theology that were popular in American Jewish Sunday school classrooms across the country. Nineteenth-century Jewish catechisms customarily opened by asking, "What is religion?" They reveal not only that defining Judaism as a religion was one of the central curricular preoccupations of Sunday school education but also that during the nineteenth century American Jews defined religion using a diverse and evolving set of conceptual vocabularies. Catechisms were also especially gendered educational texts. Almost all the catechisms used in nineteenth-century Sunday schools were written by men and defined religion in proximity to the male-coded categories of reason and rationalism. The catechism illustrates that from the outset of the Sunday school movement, ideas of religious education as feminine were offset by the presence of textbooks that defined religion in terms that were coded overtly as male.

The confirmation ceremony was the principal religious ritual of the nineteenth-century Sunday school, a grand end-of-year spectacle that celebrated graduates who confirmed their belief in Judaism's cardinal theological principles. Held each year on Shavuot, confirmation also provided a mechanism for modernizing nineteenth-century American Jews to evade their increasing discomfort with a holiday that historically celebrated the revelation of the Torah to Moses. Chapter 3 investigates how Jewish Sunday schools used confirmation to elevate the Bible within modern American Judaism while also wrestling with the challenges of nineteenth-century scholarship for defining the Torah as Judaism's principal religious scripture. This chapter explores the use of material display, ritual theater, and the material culture of flowers in the performance and invention of a new religious ritual for Jewish coming of age.

The focus on the material dimensions of the American Jewish Sunday school continues in chapter 4, which analyzes the emergence of pedagogies designed to blend the didactic and the cerebral with material goods that engaged the senses and sentiments as educators recognized that children needed to be engaged experientially. This chapter explores how Sunday schools taught Judaism as a religion not only through theology but also through commercial goods, including magazines, prizes, and educational aids.

The American Jewish landscape was altered dramatically by the arrival of approximately two million Jews from eastern Europe and Russia between 1880 and 1924. Chapter 5 examines new initiatives, led by American Jewish women, to provide Sunday school education to the children of the new arrivals. Women became activists for education at the end of the century, as they formed synagogue sisterhoods, founded mission schools and free schools to serve new immigrants, and established national representation with the creation of the National Council of Jewish Women. These efforts intertwined Jewish religious education and American cultural assimilation, stylizing Jewish religious learning as a mechanism for inculcating American values as well as Jewish ones.

Though the Jewish Sunday school had, during the nineteenth century, been successful both in establishing itself as a nationwide institution and in attracting children to its classrooms, its graduates seemed consistently reluctant to join a synagogue as adults. The final chapter analyzes the complex ways that authors of educational texts and pedagogical materials in the Reform movement began to reimagine the child as the twentieth century dawned. As Sunday school educators confronted their failure to retain children as adult members of the synagogue, rabbis and educators began increasingly to reframe the Sunday school as an education in spirituality rather than in Jewish religious knowledge, and to imagine the Jewish child as a soul to be nurtured.

Throughout these six chapters, this book demonstrates that Jewish Sunday schools fostered innovation and sustained reflection on Gratz's model for Jewish religious learning in America during the nineteenth century. The critique of a successor generation of educators, broadly assumed within American Jewish historiography to be accurate, has painted the Sunday school as a one-dimensional set of lessons in female and saccharine spirituality. On closer inspection, however, most nineteenth-century Sunday schools in fact departed significantly from the curriculum instituted in Philadelphia. Though Sunday schools remained committed to the principle that Judaism should primarily be taught and learned as a religious tradition, they also served as a site for educators at local and national levels to navigate shifting ideas about religion, gender, critical Bible scholarship, the anthropology of the Jewish child, and the purposes of education as an enterprise. From 1838 through the beginning of the twentieth century, teachers in Sunday schools created and re-created curricula in response to shifting intellectual and social dynamics, and they confronted their students with a dynamic set of lessons about how to practice Judaism as a modern American religion.

The story of nineteenth-century American Jewish Sunday schools is not one of educational success but of educational struggle. The Jews that most schools sought to engage were largely children of mobile new immigrants who maintained various degrees of sympathy toward Judaism but did not necessarily yearn to express those sentiments by becoming affiliates of institutions. Across the Americas, Sunday schools sought to make Jewish education relevant to the lives of modern American Jews by refashioning it as religious education, with varying degrees of success. When we take nineteenth-century Sunday schools seriously, we find that they offer a vibrant set of case studies for examining the negotiation of religion as an applied category in modern Jewish life, as well for exploring the ways that nineteenth-century Jews confronted the ramifications of defining Judaism in religious terms for the transmission of Judaism and Jewishness in America.

1

Jewish Women on the Educational Frontier

On March 4, 1838, the first Sunday school for Jewish children in America opened its doors at 97 Walnut Street in Philadelphia.[1] Presiding over the assembling children was Rebecca Gratz, the school's founder.[2] March 4 was an auspicious date: it also marked Gratz's fifty-seventh birthday. Born in 1781 to a family of merchants who had amassed a fortune from shipping and trading in the American West, Gratz had grown up among Philadelphia's wealthy elite. Although she socialized freely with Christians, she came from a family of observant Jews, scions of the city's traditional Sephardic Congregation Mikveh Israel. Gratz, who was not married, had dedicated her life to her family and to charity work on behalf of women and children. In 1838 she turned her benevolent efforts to Jewish education and gathered a group of women to found the Hebrew Sunday School Society of Philadelphia for the Instruction of Children Belonging to the Jewish Faith. Fifty children arrived that morning to see what the new school had to offer.[3] Four objects that Gratz placed on a table beside her hinted at an answer: a Bible containing both Old and New Testaments, a copy of Watt's *Christian Hymns*, a handbell, and a penny box "for the poor of Jerusalem."[4]

Gratz's Hebrew Sunday School was open to "any Israelite," with the aim of "giving a sound religious instruction to the Jewish children of Philadelphia." Children whose families could afford to pay contributed two dollars per year, or twenty dollars for life, to attend its Sunday morning classes.[5] Unlike other contemporary schools for Jewish children, the Sunday school did not aspire to offer a full day of instruction, to teach secular alongside Judaic subjects, or even to train students in Hebrew for the purposes of reading the siddur (prayer book). In Philadelphia, as in other cities where Jews had established communities, Jewish day schools offered secular and Judaic instruction to American Jewish youth.[6] Some were organized by congregations, others were private day or boarding schools created by enterprising Jewish teachers. Congregational schools and a few community Talmud Torahs offered afternoon instruction in the Hebrew language and in classical Jewish texts, while wealthy parents could also opt for a private tutor in the home.[7] In almost all cases the educators were men who had received at least some training in Hebrew and Jewish subjects in Europe and who looked to Jewish education as a means to make a living in America.

Across the spectrum these schools were beset with challenges. Classes were large and corporal punishment was rife. At Congregation Rodeph Shalom in Philadelphia, children were expected to attend the congregational school each weekday afternoon, on Shabbat, and on Sunday mornings. With more than eighty students enrolled in its two afternoon classes, and one instructor for both groups, the school was chaotic. When one teacher announced his resignation to the synagogue board, he complained that it was impossible to teach when students spent class sessions setting off firecrackers. By the time he managed to restore order, it would be time for dismissal.[8] In other schools it was teachers rather than students who disrupted the educational proceedings. Teachers were often itinerant hazanim (cantors) with inconsistent training in either Jewish studies or education. At Adas Israel Congregation in Washington, DC, the weekday Hebrew school was closed when it was discovered that Hazan Joseph A. Cohen was late to lessons, sometimes did not show up at all, and was mistreating the children with physical punishments. Cohen was persuaded to resign, and the school ceased operation for the next two years.[9]

The challenges were financial as well as administrative. For many Jewish parents the cost of Jewish education, even at the relatively affordable congregational schools, extended far beyond their financial means. As dissenting members of Kahal Kadosh Beth Elohim in Charleston, South Carolina, noted in 1824, "It is not everyone who has the means . . . to acquire a knowledge of the Hebrew language and consequently to become enlightened in the principles of Judaism."[10] Tuition paid instructor salaries, a considerable expense, even if teachers themselves often complained that they were poorly compensated for their expertise. Yet the fees were challenging for parents with irregular income, and schools often teetered on the brink of financial disaster. Congregational school boards maintained long lists of students who were either "half pay" or attending the school as "free scholars," creating a revenue deficit that the members of the congregation ultimately would be looked upon to cover. Early in his tenure as hazan of Congregation Mikveh Israel in Philadelphia, Isaac Leeser found cause to write regularly to the community's parnas (lay leader) to seek financial support for the congregation's day school. Writing in 1835 that affluent parents had been "very backward in offering [to enroll] their children," preferring more elite educational institutions, he confessed that he had admitted students who could not afford to pay tuition, and he hoped the community would support them.[11] With the increasing availability of free public education, which expanded across the northeastern United States beginning in the 1840s, calls to Jewish parents to enroll their children in expensive Jewish institutions fell increasingly on deaf ears. The public schools offered free access to education and the opportunity to become proficient in the English language, facilitating children's future employment prospects and seeming to signal that Jewish parents were committed to immersing their children in American culture.[12]

The American Jewish community expanded exponentially beginning in the midnineteenth century, and with it grew the population of Jewish children for whom access to Jewish education would depend on the charity of their more established coreligionists. Whereas only two to three thousand Jews settled in America before 1800, between 1820 and 1880 approximately 150,000 to 200,000 Jewish migrants arrived in the United States.[13] The number of congregational communities grew in tandem with the rise in the Jewish population and the increasing diversity of its liturgical customs, and by 1877 there were at least 277 synagogues spread across the country.[14] Yet relatively few American Jews joined a synagogue or prayed daily with a minyan (quorum).[15] Recent Jewish immigrants were mobile rather than settled, and synagogue attendance was only one mechanism for maintaining and establishing Jewish ties.[16] For new immigrant families scarce financial resources often were an insurmountable barrier to joining congregations and obtaining access to religious education for children. Children often helped to support their families by engaging in paid employment, piecework, and caring for younger siblings during the week, with few opportunities to attend day schools or supplementary Jewish schools held on weekday afternoons.[17]

An uneducated Jewish population not only posed a threat to the stability of Judaism in America but also made children susceptible to

Christian evangelism. Beginning in the 1790s, proponents of the Second Great Awakening had popularized a dire theological warning about the damnation of the unsaved and expounded upon the need for total immersion in the gospel. Missionaries described their evangelizing not only as a benevolent service to the unenlightened but also as the cornerstone of a broader crusade to Christianize the nation.[18] The mission of saving lost souls was taken into the emerging public institutions of nineteenth-century America, as organizations, including the American Education Society (founded in 1815), American Bible Society (founded in 1816), American Sunday School Union (founded in 1824), and American Tract Society (founded in 1825), sought to build a public American Protestantism. Leeser wrote trenchantly in the *Occident and American Jewish Advocate*, the newspaper he founded and served as editor, about the dangers of missionary activity in the nation's public schools. "We are in great error," Leeser warned his readers in 1843, "if we suppose that Christian teachers do not endeavour [sic] to influence actively the sentiments of their Jewish pupils; there are some, at least, who take especial pains to warp the mind and to implant the peculiar tenets of Christianity clandestinely."[19]

In a January 1838 letter to her great-niece, Miriam Moses Cohen, Rebecca Gratz wrote that she had begun to formulate plans for a Hebrew Sunday school that might "block the power of Christian evangelists."[20] Gratz's solution was simple. Take Jewish children off the streets on Sunday mornings by enrolling them in low-cost Jewish Sunday schools of their own and in those few short hours equip them with enough foundational training in Jewish religion that they might be able to defend themselves against claims of Christian supersessionism.[21] Gratz's Hebrew Sunday School offered a pragmatic Jewish educational alternative for children of limited financial means. Unlike schools that operated under congregational auspices, Gratz's did not discriminate against children whose parents were not synagogue members, and it did not require congregational dues for children to attend. The Sunday school was open to all Jewish children, male and female, irrespective of their financial status, their synagogue affiliations, or lack thereof. Although Gratz and many of the women who worked alongside her were affiliated with local Sephardic Congregation Mikveh Israel, most of the students were Ashkenazi. The Sunday school thus offered, at least in principle, lessons that transcended the agendas of nascent American Jewish denominationalism.

The model that Gratz devised was borrowed from Protestant Christianity. Indeed, it was no coincidence that Philadelphia was the site of the national headquarters of the Protestant Sunday school movement.[22] At the Hebrew Sunday School in Philadelphia, children learned that Judaism was a religion according to the terms of mainstream American Protestantism: defined by faith, family, and moral virtue. "The whole spirit of religion," wrote Gratz in a letter to her brother Benjamin, "is to make men merciful, humble and just."[23] Instead of halacha (Jewish law), Hebrew, or liturgy, the Sunday school emphasized that Judaism had a system of ethics and theological principles based on a biblical tradition that children could learn about in English, through catechisms, rhymes, and simple prayers. Like Protestant Christianity, the Hebrew Sunday School stressed individualistic belief as the core animating principle of religious life. From 1838 to 1900 the lessons taught by the first American Jewish Sunday school emphasized stories from the Hebrew scriptures, the Ten Commandments, Jewish ideas about life after death, home rituals, and devotion to God.[24] Judaism, students would learn, demanded reverence for the Bible, charity, upright moral conduct, and faith in God, just like Christianity did.

The curriculum that the Sunday school implemented was not only an attempt to replicate Judaism in a bourgeois Protestant key. It also represented the upper limits of the training in Jewish subjects that its volunteer female teachers themselves had received. Gratz could read little Hebrew, and as a woman she could play no leadership role in the traditional synagogue services that she attended at Mikveh Israel. Her Jewish education was limited to a smattering of lessons from private tutors, alongside Bible stories and instruction from female relatives in Sabbath, holiday, and life-cycle rituals. Male children who attended cheders, congregational schools, or Talmud Torahs would receive at least mechanical instruction in Hebrew and in the liturgy of the Jewish prayer service, and perhaps they would be introduced to the study of the Bible and its commentaries in preparation for bar mitzvah. Female children, on the other hand, typically received Judaic instruction only in the home, with a curriculum defined by the capacity and the interests of their parents. Home rituals were emphasized; formal instruction in Hebrew or Jewish texts was rare. The subjects that the Hebrew Sunday School eliminated were not only those that represented the furthest points of demarcation between Judaism and Christianity. They also pointed to the curricular differences in the Jewish educational training of men and women.[25]

Yet while Gratz may have had little formal training in Jewish subjects, in the broader context of midnineteenth-century American popular culture, women were assumed to have special disposition to matters of religion.[26] In the late eighteenth century, Protestant theologian Friedrich Schleiermacher had proposed that the experience of the divine was fundamentally an emotive endeavor, dependent on feelings like awe, reverence, and gratitude.[27] Protestants influenced by Schleiermacher maintained that because women possessed a particular capacity for these sentiments, they maintained a special aptitude for religion irrespective of any formal theological training they may have received. European Protestants who emphasized the sentimental dispositions of women described the religious education of children as an extension of women's special proclivities for domestic piety and the natural instincts that women were popularly believed to possess for nurturing the young. In America the cult of true womanhood that proliferated within popular American literature in the early decades of the nineteenth century celebrated women's special capacity for sentimental religion and extolled morality, spirituality, and affect as religious qualities that women possessed in abundance. Popular periodicals like *Godey's Lady's Book*, first published in 1830, exhorted its readers to consider the importance of domestic virtue and reminded women that their particular mission in life was to cultivate religious sentiment at home and abroad.[28] Jews in both Europe and the United States were influenced by these cultural trends.[29] As historian Paula Hyman observed, one of the hallmarks of assimilation among modernizing European Jews was the transfer of responsibility for children's religious education from Jewish fathers to Jewish mothers, mirroring the public cultures of European Protestantism.[30]

None of the women who volunteered as teachers in Gratz's Hebrew Sunday School could bring expertise in Judaic subjects to their work in the classroom. Yet, like their Christian counterparts, the women who joined Gratz on that first Sunday morning saw benevolent service to the cause of education as a project particularly appropriate for women and an important intervention in the future of their religious community.[31]

Immersed in contemporary cultural mores that extolled women as paradigmatic religious educators, for Rebecca Gratz and her colleagues teaching was a form of benevolent service rather than the end result of sustained scholarship. It modeled the activities that Victorian America expected of genteel women—cultivation of the virtues of religion among the next generation and dedication to charitable endeavors. The teachers in the Hebrew Sunday School in Philadelphia instituted a curriculum that defined Judaism according to attributes associated with the religious proclivities of women in nineteenth-century America, emphasizing faith and theology rather than Hebrew and halacha. They eliminated much that was canonical in the traditional curriculum of Jewish education, yet the institutions in which that curriculum had traditionally been taught were historically limited to men and boys and foreclosed to Gratz and her colleagues when they were children. The Hebrew Sunday School in Philadelphia subverted traditional Jewish paradigms about the relationship of gender and Jewish educational expertise but affirmed contemporary cultural assumptions about the role that women were supposed to play in nurturing the young in spiritual affairs. Rather than Talmud, the Hebrew Sunday School emphasized devotional study of the Bible, a text associated with women in both traditional frameworks of Jewish education and the Protestant cultural mores of Victorian America. The curriculum of the Hebrew Sunday School signified the Americanization of its Jewish founders as they reimagined Jewish learning within contemporary frameworks for women's religiosity.

An American Movement

News of Gratz's initiative spread quickly, and within two years three more schools were founded by women active in benevolent work within their own communities. Just a few months after Gratz opened the Philadelphia school, Sally Lopez of Kahal Kadosh Beth Elohim in Charleston, South Carolina, assisted by Sarah Moise and "other ladies of the congregation," created a Sunday school. Reportedly, Lopez replicated Gratz's lessons, which Gratz would copy and send to Charleston each week.[32] A third school, the Association for the Moral and Religious Instruction of Children of the Jewish Faith, was created under the auspices of New York Congregation Shearith Israel later that year; it offered classes for poor Jewish children each Sunday, regardless of synagogue membership. Inspired by the "ladies of the Jewish persuasion of Philadelphia," the school was led by a female superintendent, and twenty women volunteered as teachers.[33] In 1839 a Sunday school was founded in Richmond, Virginia, under the auspices of the Ladies Auxiliary of Congregation Beth Shalome, led by Emma Mordecai.[34] Education was the Mordecai family business. Born in North Carolina in 1812, Emma's father, Jacob, ran a girls' boarding school, the Warrenton Female Academy, where Emma was educated and spent her formative years. Jacob Mordecai experienced uneven luck with his business ventures, moving from town to town periodically during his adult life as he pursued new opportunities. Emma seems to have inherited some of her father's resourcefulness in business matters. As superintendent of the Beth Shalome religious school, she organized elaborate annual fundraising balls that brought Richmond's Jews and gentiles together for an evening of entertainment in support of Jewish education.[35]

The Jewish Sunday school movement took root across the emerging denominational spectrum of American Judaism. Gratz's school was a community institution, functionally independent of any congregation, although the leaders of Gratz's own synagogue, Mikveh Israel, were frequent visitors. In Charleston, Beth Elohim was the principal seat of the emerging American Reform movement. However, another Charleston congregation, Shearith Israel, which had split from Beth Elohim in the aftermath of its moves toward Reform and maintained traditional Spanish Portuguese customs recruited sixty women in 1844 to organize a rival Sunday school for "impressing upon the tender minds of their pupils the *orthodox* tenets of our religion."[36] Richmond's congregation, Beth Shalome, similarly followed the traditional Spanish-Portuguese rite until its merger with Reform Congregation Beth Ahabah in 1898. Sunday schools that were founded after 1838 and beyond Philadelphia largely departed from the community-wide model championed by Gratz in favor of congregational schools aligned with the various ideological and denominational philosophies of their communities, from Orthodox to Reform.

Following the models pioneered by women in Philadelphia, Charleston, New York, and Richmond, Sunday schools were founded in Jewish communities across the country. Pragmatic, affordable, and requiring little commitment from students or from volunteer teachers, the Sunday school seemed to offer a realistic model for Jewish education in America. The voluntarist character of American life, its preference for congregational autonomy, and the absence of recognized sources of communal authority created an environment of unprecedented latitude for Jewish communities. The Sunday school offered an affordable model for Jewish education and a compelling contemporary technology for engaging the next generation with a curriculum that demonstrated that Jews did not have to look to Christianity to find a set of religious truths that chimed with the spirit of the age. The Sunday school taught its students that Judaism was a religion with a set of theological traditions that, while distinctive, cohered with American cultural norms.

At the forefront of these early efforts, organizing schools in their local communities and serving as volunteer teachers, were women with personal financial resources that enabled them to dedicate time and energy to philanthropic projects. Influenced by the movement of upper-class American women into organizational roles in communal philanthropy, beginning in the 1820s wealthy American Jewish women founded hundreds of women's auxiliaries and benevolent charitable organizations.[37] They became active in general causes through membership in ladies' circles and councils, and in Jewish philanthropy as members of female Hebrew benevolent societies. They were motivated to do charitable work among their coreligionists by both the mandate of Jewish religious tradition that "all Israel is responsible for one another" and the necessity of providing safe alternatives to the Protestant religious groups that would proselytize the Jewish poor who depended on their charity.[38] Some women balanced their work as teachers, committee members, and clubwomen with their responsibilities as wives and mothers. Others, like Gratz, never married, devoting their lives to their charitable endeavors as a maternal project of a different kind.[39] Midnineteenth-century Jewish women's benevolent organizations raised funds for their charitable projects in part by charging membership dues, inevitably limiting their ranks to women who had the financial means to participate. When the women of Temple Beth El in Detroit formed the Ladies Society for the Support of Hebrew Widows and Orphans in Michigan in 1863, annual membership dues were set at a minimum of four dollars.[40] Poor women and recent immigrants were more likely to be recipients of charity than organizers of it. They were contributors to the family economy, leaving little time for clubs and society activities.[41]

Affluent Jewish women involved in benevolent work founded Sunday schools in cities that were home to extensive systems of Jewish communal infrastructure, as well as in frontier communities with few Jewish resources. In 1844 Boanna Wolff traveled from her home in Philadelphia to visit her sister in Columbia, South Carolina. Dismayed by the dearth of Jewish communal institutions in the city, Wolff immediately settled there and resolved to "set about the formation of a Sunday school." By the end of 1844 the school had enrolled twenty-six children who had become "quite proficient in their lessons" under the tutelage of Wolff and teachers Julia Mordecai, Cecelia Marks, and Eliza Marks.[42] Born in Alabama, Wolff had befriended Isaac Leeser and Rebecca Gratz while living in Philadelphia and saw in Columbia an opportunity to re-create the model Gratz had so successfully planted in Pennsylvania. Wolff's efforts in Columbia also epitomized advice proffered by another female pioneer of religious education, Catherine Ward Beecher, who had instructed Christian women to civilize the American West by volunteering as teachers on the frontier and by marrying and raising families in their new communities. Beecher is unlikely to have considered Jewish education a civilizing force—her 1835 essay included a tirade against "degraded foreigners" who were pouring into the nation, a category that undoubtedly included Jews—yet Wolff's life offered a model illustration of Beecher's premise. Wolff resigned from the Sunday school upon her marriage to Elias P. Levy in 1846 and remained in the South, where she continued to volunteer in benevolent activities while also raising children.[43]

The formation of a Sunday school in Columbia presaged the establishment of the city's first synagogue. Shortly after Wolff opened her school, Columbia's Hebrew Benevolent Society contributed funds to build a permanent physical space to house the community's religious instruction. When the building opened in late 1846, a congregation calling itself Shearith Israel (the remnant of Israel) began to meet on the upper floor of its new quarters.[44] A similar trajectory accompanied the Sunday school in Augusta, Georgia. Sarah Ann Moise, a former teacher in the Charleston Sunday school, opened a school for the Jewish youth of Augusta in 1846. Assisted by one other female teacher, the school began with a dedicated group of ten students. By 1848, however, the school had garnered such popularity that the community mobilized to organize a congregation. "The establishment of a Hebrew Sunday school," a correspondent wrote to the *Occident* to inform the paper of the new congregation, "paved the way to this gratifying result. . . . To those ladies who have originated and have since presided over this valuable institution, the meed of praise must be awarded."[45] In other contexts the erection of a synagogue building paved the way for a Sunday school that would be established under the congregation's auspices. The Portuguese community of New Orleans consecrated its synagogue, Nefutsoth Yehudah, in 1850. The edifice was a former Episcopalian church purchased and renovated as a gift to the community by philanthropist Judah Touro. By the end of the year a Sunday school open to all children in the community had been organized by the women of Nefutsoth Yehudah Congregation to meet in the new building.

The women who successfully founded Sunday schools were skilled in community organizing for charitable causes. These women had to marshal extensive resources to implement a Jewish educational program that was open to children regardless of their ability to pay. They needed to recruit teachers who could volunteer rather than demand compensation, and solicit financial commitments from community benefactors to support their institutions. When he died in 1854, Touro left a bequest of $2,500 to the Nefutsoth Yehudah Sunday school as a token of his esteem for Rebecca Florance, who led the efforts to create the community's Sunday school.[46] Yet when the achievements of women who founded Sunday schools were recounted in the midcentury American Jewish press, reports tended to emphasize that their efforts were extensions of their inherently spiritual natures rather than evidence of their administrative prowess. When Sally Lopez retired in 1843 from her position as principal of the Sunday school that she had founded at Beth Elohim in Charleston, the address given in her honor mentioned no details of her efforts to organize the institution, create curricula, and recruit students but instead meditated on her commitment to the cause of true Jewish womanhood and "spirit of Jewish benevolence." In leaving her post, the panegyric concluded, her name "is identified with all that is pure and delicate in Jewish love, and all that is high and generous in Jewish devotion."[47] Two years later, when a correspondent to the *Occident and*

American Jewish Advocate wrote rapturously about the annual examination held by the Sunday school of Charleston's Orthodox Congregation Shearith Israel, he described the achievements of the children as evidence of the vitality of American Judaism, a result he attributed to the women who organized and taught in the school. "We have here in this city," the correspondent reported, "the daughters of Israel waging an interminable war against immorality and irreligion by imbuing the tender minds of our youth with a knowledge of our ancient faith and a practice of its divine precepts. We begin to feel and recognise [*sic*] the true social position of woman; and the existence of this institution has so beautifully developed her latent resources, her zeal and perseverance, that with a heart gushing with grateful emotions (as a parent of one of the pupils), we exclaim, 'Powerful and beautiful is thy influence, O woman!'"[48]

Such effusive praise of American Jewish women and their efforts to found Sunday schools was not, however, unanimous. Critics of the movement denounced the once-a-week schools as offering little more than saccharine feminine spirituality, a pale imitation of popular Christian theological motifs in a vaguely Jewish key.[49] Sarah Nunes Carvalho rallied a group of seventeen volunteer teachers to found the Baltimore Hebrew Sunday School Society in 1857.[50] "It was a commendable thing in the ladies of Baltimore," said Isaac Leeser in his address at the school's opening, "that they had resolved to employ the day of leisure, on which the law of the land does not permit the pursuit of business, to the diffusion of knowledge on religion."[51] Within a year the school had enrolled more than thirty students, leading a correspondent for the *Occident* to conclude that its growth was "unparalleled by any Israelitisch school in America."[52] Yet Carvalho's work was ridiculed by Rabbi David Einhorn of Baltimore. Arguing that Carvalho and her team possessed little in the way of Jewish or Hebrew knowledge, he told parents that children who attended the school would be crippled by "weibliche Theologie" (women's theology). The sentiment persisted in Baltimore more than forty years later. "There is no better way to make a mockery of religion than to depend upon volunteers to carry out the religious instruction of the children," argued Rabbi Benjamin Szold to the school board of Baltimore's Orthodox Temple Oheb Shalom in 1891.[53]

Szold's dismissal of the female volunteers who taught in Baltimore's Jewish Sunday schools was motivated in no small part by the perception that they posed a threat to more intensive Jewish educational initiatives, such as the afternoon school at his own congregation, as well as to the livelihoods of male educators. Jewish education had historically been a male-dominated enterprise, with instruction in Hebrew, liturgy, and the Jewish rabbinic tradition limited to boys and men. In America as in Europe, teaching offered a means for Jewish males educated in yeshivas to make a living, whether as private tutors or as instructors in congregational afternoon schools and Talmud Torahs. They claimed educational expertise based upon their European training. When a Mr. A. Lehman arrived in Cleveland from Europe in 1847, he advertised his services in the local press with a letter from Nathan Marcus Adler, chief rabbi of the United Kingdom, verifying that he had examined Lehman in "Hebrew Language, Bible and Religion on the 4ᵗʰ day of July 1837 and that he had passed it well: that he has been teacher in that time, and that he has given entire satisfaction to his superiors."[54]

In the United States, however, the relative apathy of nineteenth-century American Jews toward intensive American Jewish education, combined with the popularity of free public schooling, threatened the stability of more traditional male-centered models of Jewish learning. Hazan Henry Loewenthal opened a school in Macon, Georgia, in 1859 but soon found cause to lament to Isaac Mayer Wise that "the school that I opened with some pride + rieguer [sic] will soon be closed for want of patronage." When a Sunday school was organized in the community, however, it soon boasted a thriving enrollment of fifty-five students.[55] It seemed incongruous to men like Loewenthal that parents would reject educators trained in the classical languages and literatures of Jewish religious tradition in favor of Sunday school classes taught by women who, by their own admission, brought little educational training to their work. Yet the part-time curriculum of weekend schools was attractive to upwardly mobile and assimilating American Jews. What is more, as the Sunday schools were staffed by volunteers rather than educators in search of a salary, they were also a cost-effective educational option for newly established Jewish communities to support.

By the 1870s Jewish weekday schools were finding it increasingly difficult to compete in an educational landscape dominated by affordable part-time institutions.[56] Congregation Emanu-El in New York created a full-time elementary school shortly after it acquired its first

building in 1848.[57] Within just six years enrollment had dropped so dramatically that a religious school, meeting only on Saturdays and Sundays, was created in its place.[58] Isaac Leeser was an erstwhile supporter
of Gratz's Sunday school initiative, but from his arrival in Philadelphia
in 1828 he had advocated with equal vigor for an institution that could
provide intensive classical and Jewish education to Jewish children in
the city. In 1851, with funds donated by Judah Touro's estate, he opened
a school for twenty-two pupils under the auspices of the Hebrew Education Society. By 1873, however, the school, mired in financial crisis and
with a declining enrollment, was forced to close its doors.[59] In Cincinnati, Congregation Bene Israel opened a day school and Talmud Torah
in 1842. By 1866 the parnas and lay leadership of the synagogue had
determined that because the day school was struggling to maintain enrollment, it should merge with two other local full-time schools. After
a six-month trial, however, the committee wrote again the parnas,
reporting, "We have very reluctantly come to the conclusion that the
object for which the union was formed has not been accomplished"—in
other words, student enrollment had not grown sufficiently. The Sabbath
school, which had been founded by Rabbi Max Lilienthal in 1855, was,
however, "in a very flourishing condition, and fully realizes all its most
ardent friends have claimed for it. We therefore recommend that the
connection with the union school be dissolved."[60]

Teachers in Israel

By the 1880s Sunday schools organized under the auspices of a congregation had become the dominant model for Jewish education in
America.[61] The Union of American Hebrew Congregations fielded a
survey of Jewish religious education in 1875 that identified seventy Sunday schools in different communities across the country.[62] A subsequent
survey conducted in 1889 determined that the number had grown to at
least two hundred.[63] Some were known as Sunday schools and others
as Sabbath schools, the latter typically indicating that the school would
meet not only on Sundays but on Saturday afternoons as well. Some,
such as Detroit's Temple Beth El, also added a session during the week;
attendance at its School of Religious Instruction, founded in 1869, was
expected for two hours on Saturdays, two hours on Sundays, and an

hour on Wednesday afternoons. This was an overly ambitious curriculum, and the Wednesday afternoon classes lasted for just two years. The board decided in 1871 that the Wednesday sessions must "regretfully be discontinued" on account of consistent lack of attendance by the students. The school accordingly changed its name to Sabbath School.[64] The adoption of a weekend curriculum was, for most congregations, a pragmatic shift. It was more affordable, and it aligned with the relationship of most midcentury Jews to institutional Judaism—demanding minimal time and effort and requiring participation only for a couple of hours each week.[65]

Though women were instrumental in founding the first Jewish Sunday schools in the United States, schools that were founded under the auspices of an established congregation typically fell under the administrative control of men. The removal of women from the center of administrative leadership within the American Jewish Sunday school mirrored a broader exclusion of women from positions of governance within philanthropy in the years following the Civil War. The professionalization of charitable efforts focused power increasingly in the hands of all-male executive boards, with women relegated to assisting rather than leading.[66] Women continued to occupy central roles in the Sunday school movement as teachers, however, particularly for younger grades. This organization mirrored a gender-oriented hierarchy that had long persisted within the nation's public schools, where women were predominantly employed as teachers of elementary grades rather than as superintendents. "Heaven has plainly appointed females as the natural instructors of young children," explained Henry Barnard, secretary of education for Connecticut in 1840, "and endowed them with those qualities of mind and disposition which preeminently fit them for such a task."[67] Barnard believed that women were equipped with affective rather than intellectual skills and therefore were best suited to instructing younger grades. But common school reformers like Barnard also understood the financial value of female teachers. Because women commanded significantly smaller salaries than their male counterparts, hiring women allowed a school to stretch its budget further, and the practice of grouping female teachers under male leaders quickly became commonplace.[68]

While Gratz and her successors retained administrative control of the independent Hebrew Sunday School in Philadelphia, when schools were founded under congregational auspices, the curriculum typically was set by rabbis or by male-dominated congregational education boards rather than by its volunteer teachers. In 1866 Congregation Emanu-El in San Francisco approved a constitution for the board of its religious school that determined that the board should "have the power and it shall be their duty, to adopt a Course of Study, and to make and enforce Rules and Regulations for the government of the School, Teachers and Pupils."[69] Congregational education boards curtailed the freedom of teachers to decide what to teach in their classrooms, and could even challenge the authority of the congregation's rabbi, who usually was appointed, at least nominally, as the head of the school. As a young girl, Rebekah Kohut taught Sunday school at another San Francisco congregation, Temple Ohabei Shalom, which her father served as rabbi. Instead of teaching catechism, the textbook mandated by the congregation's school board, she decided to teach about heroic characters from the Bible. When the chair of the school board paid a surprise visit to her classroom and found her teaching the story of Ruth, Kohut was summarily dismissed from her position, and her father was "called to account for his neglect of the school."[70]

Women who taught in American Jewish Sunday schools were, like Kohut, often young or unmarried. With leisure time to spare they were interested in contributing to their local Jewish communities, and teaching offered a public-facing role in the synagogue at a time when women were barred from ritual leadership.[71] Teaching offered a gateway for women to explore meaningful work outside the home and to build skills that they could transfer to other arenas of public life.[72] Ray Frank, who became known as the "Girl Rabbi of the Golden West," taught Sunday school in Oakland, California, where she honed the oratorical skills that she would later use to command pulpits.[73] Julia Richman explored her interests in education by teaching at the Sunday schools of Congregation Ahawath Chesed and Temple Beth El in New York. According to one of her former pupils, Richman was a beloved instructor, idolized by the girls in her class.[74] She would later become an accomplished public school teacher and ultimately the superintendent of schools for the Lower East Side. The Jewish Sunday school came of age as the field of teacher preparation in American education was beginning to take shape, with the founding of normal schools and teachers' colleges on the East

Figure 1.1. Teachers at Beth El Religious School, Detroit, Michigan, c. 1899. Courtesy of the Rabbi Leo M. Franklin Archives of Temple Beth El, Bloomfield Hills, Michigan, from the Temple Beth El Photograph collection.

Coast and in the Midwest during the 1850s and 1860s.[75] Jewish women interested in a career in teaching could cut their teeth in the Sunday school, and many, like Richman, continued to serve as Sunday school teachers alongside their weekday responsibilities in the public schools. At Temple Beth El in Detroit in 1892, four of the five female teachers who taught in the congregational Sabbath school were also teachers in local public schools. "They bring to their classrooms," observed the school's superintendent, "experience in discipline and management of pupils to such a degree that our sabbath school is a pattern of orderly conduct, considering the crowded state of some of the rooms."[76]

Teaching in Jewish Sunday schools offered women opportunities for continuing Jewish education as well as a means to provide service to their communities. Teachers were typically handpicked from among the school's graduates, making volunteering in the classroom an opportunity for continuing education once their own Sunday school program was complete. At the Hebrew Sunday School in Philadelphia, Isaac Leeser and his successor at Congregation Mikveh Israel, Sabato Morais, gave classes to the volunteer faculty to help equip them for their work as educators. These instructional sessions were replicated in other Sunday schools, particularly those organized under the auspices of congregations. Women predominantly taught younger grades, while male educators, often the congregation's rabbi, took responsibility for teaching the confirmation class and the volunteer teachers, offering instruction in Hebrew, Jewish history, and the Bible. In the latter decades of the nineteenth century, American Jewish women enthusiastically sought opportunities for Jewish study, and classes in literature and the Bible were particularly appealing to Sunday school teachers who were acutely aware of the gaps in their own religious education. "What we want," as one female teacher explained in 1896, "is to educate ourselves, so that we may bring into the homes where the children are all around us, or into the Sunday schools, the influence of that education and that study to which we are devoting ourselves."[77] Jennie Mannheimer, born in Cincinnati in 1872, began teaching at the Rockdale Temple Sabbath School when she was eighteen. In her diary entry for Saturday, October 4, 1890, she reflected on a whistlestop day teaching four different subjects to four different groups of students: Bible from 9:00 a.m. to 9:35 a.m., scripture from 9:35 to 10:10 a.m., Hebrew from 10:25 to 11:00 a.m., and Jewish history from 11:00 to 11:35 a.m. Other pages in her diary were filled with questions that she had devised to test the comprehension of students in each of her classes. Two years later she would become one of the first women to earn a bachelor's degree in Hebrew letters from the Hebrew Union College.[78]

Volunteering as a Sunday school teacher also afforded Jewish women opportunities for creative expression. Born in 1865, the same year that her synagogue, B'nai Israel, turned its congregational day school into a Sunday school, Clara Lowenberg of Natchez, Mississippi, watched her grandmother head the Ladies Hebrew Benevolent Society, her aunt teach in the Sunday school, and her grandfather serve as president of the congregation. While her biological family regularly enjoyed oysters, shrimp, and ham, Clara's stepmother was a "strict religious Portuguese Jew" and insisted the house be kept kosher and the Sabbath observed. Given all these influences, it is perhaps not surprising that Clara recalled feeling "very religious" as a child. When she came of age, she was quickly recruited to join the teachers at B'nai Israel's Sunday school, where she found that she enjoyed teaching the younger grades so much that she authored a book of Jewish stories to use in her classroom.[79]

Clara's literary activities were not unusual, as women became prodigious authors of religious literature in nineteenth-century America. Increasing literacy rates in America's growing population created a market for women's literature, and magazines and periodicals published material by women and for women that addressed women's particular concerns. Religion was a popular topic. The leitmotifs of the literature produced by American Jewish women mirrored the emphases of their Protestant counterparts, foregrounding faith, spirituality, domestic duty, and obedience. A song written by Mary Cohen, a teacher in the northern branch of the Hebrew Sunday School Society of Philadelphia, and later the superintendent of its southern Sunday school, reminded the "children of Judah" that they must cultivate manners and be as careful with their tongues as they were with their needles. But "more than all," the last stanza cautioned, "remember God, who in love gives you home and friends, offer him praise, and glad hearts raise, to the Lord who blessing sends."[80] By incorporating themes common to Christian women's religious literature, Jewish women's devotional writing offered not only a popular resource for Jewish Sunday school classrooms but was also frequently sufficiently ecumenical for publication in Christian periodicals and mainstream journals. Mary Cohen's work was frequently republished in the *Baptist Register*, while Penina Moise, the second superintendent of the Beth Elohim Hebrew Sunday School in Charleston and a prolific author of poems and hymns, was regularly published in the *Occident and American Jewish Advocate*, as well as in *Godey's Lady's Book* and the *Ladies' Home Journal*. The memorial published in the *American Jewish Yearbook* upon her death in 1905 lauded the application of her creative talents to Judaism, praising her "delight in writing sacred songs, poems and recitations for the children, exulting in all the history and traditions of her race."[81] Authors like Cohen and Moise, who had materials accepted for publication in popular periodicals, could demand monetary compensation for their work; indeed, as they became more prolific and were published in more high-profile periodicals, they could demand higher rates of compensation.

Most of the women who contributed to their local Jewish Sunday schools, however, received little remuneration for their efforts. Indeed, the Sunday school movement offered a reliable financial model for nineteenth-century Jewish education because volunteer teachers provided unpaid labor. In 1887 members of the school committee at Ahawath Chesed, a traditional congregation in New York, marveled that they were able to run a school for nearly five hundred pupils on a budget of only $650 per year, thanks to the labor of female volunteers.[82] Male instructors, on the other hand, were typically compensated, albeit at varying rates depending on the size of the school's enrollment. At Congregation Bene Israel in Cincinnati in 1870, the weekday afternoon school had a smaller enrollment—154 students—than Ahawath Chesed's, yet the total expenses of the school ran to the much higher sum of $898.92, most of which went to three paid male teachers.[83] In his state-of-the-field review of Jewish education for the 1914 *American Jewish Yearbook*, Julius Greenstone, a Conservative rabbi and instructor in Jewish education at Gratz College in Philadelphia candidly reflected on the fact that Sunday schools had been successful because of the availability of cheap or unpaid teaching staff. The Sunday school was the most enduring of the Jewish educational institutions, he explained, because it had so few overhead expenses. "It is safe to assume," he concluded, "that the average cost per capita of a Sunday School Jewish education does not exceed three dollars per year."[84]

For the majority of women who volunteered their time and talents to the cause of Jewish Sunday school education, their only remuneration was a token gift presented at the end of the school year or a scripted statement of gratitude from congregational leadership. At Congregation B'nai Israel in Galveston, Texas, in 1903, the minutes of the congregation's board recorded that "a vote of thanks was tendered to each of the Sunday school teachers and the Secretary instructed to transmit to them in suitable times the appreciation of the congregation for their services during the past year." The teachers were also given a sail for a boat that cost the congregation $7.40.[85] This seems quite the hollow gift, however, as the minutes also record that the rabbi, Dr. Henry A. Cohen, was given a boat named *Cynthia*, for which the sail was presumably intended. The relative short shrift given to these women volunteers is put into even sharper relief by the congregation's financial records, which for

1903 show that the annual operating costs of the Sabbath school totaled $109.84, far less than the $457.92 the congregation spent that year on its choir. The intellectual content of the classes at B'nai Israel's school was considered to be the domain of the rabbi; its female teachers were merely his dutiful servants. In the minutes for 1903, the school board praised Cohen for his intellect, his knowledge, and his pedagogy. The women, however, were described simply as "sweet and self-sacrificing young workers in Israel."[86]

Mothers in Israel

The work of women was essential for nineteenth-century American Jewish Sunday schools. Their volunteer labor kept expenses low. Yet the celebration of women's service in American Jewish education took on an increasingly ambivalent tone in the later decades of the nineteenth century, as American Jews began to express anxiety about the apathy of American Jews toward Judaism. Religious indifference had long been a theme within American Jewish life, yet in the second half of the century the perception that it posed a threat seemed to escalate exponentially. As Jews became increasingly comfortable in American public life, and as the Reform movement eliminated many of the practices that had set Jews apart from their Christian neighbors, rabbis opined that the very survival of Judaism in the United States seemed to be at stake. Beginning in the 1870s, Jewish apathy became a major topic of sermons and rabbinic writing.[87] Communal leaders drew upon the discourse of race to remind Jews that they were biologically and essentially different from their Christian neighbors by virtue of Jews' ethnoreligious heritage. Revival organizations like the Menorah Society, meanwhile, sought to reawaken Jewish pride and cultivate a renaissance of Jewish life through Jewish learning.[88]

In this rhetorical war against Jewish indifference to Judaism, the work of women educators was idealized as a potent weapon. Men and women who supported women's volunteer efforts as teachers stressed that women were paradigms of spirituality who could inspire a love for Judaism in the young. "Does not every true woman teach?" asked Rose Barlow, a Sunday school teacher in Detroit in 1892, in an essay for the Women's Club at Temple Beth El. "The manner and spirit with which she performs the work are an evidence and a test of her religion."[89]

When Reform rabbi Kaufman Kohler was invited to offer a prayer at the first national convention of the National Council of Jewish Women in 1896, he used the opportunity to rhapsodize about women's "more delicate and sympathetic nature" and "deeper sense for the pure." He concluded, "In this age of materialism and doubt, may the lamp of religious devotion, the fire of enthusiasm be rekindled . . . in the hands of the daughters of Israel."[90]

Yet for every advocate who exalted the public service of women as essential for the flourishing of Jewish Sunday school education, there was another who used the trope of the inherently religious Jewish woman to remind women that the home exercised a more powerful claim on her time and attention. Laments about the absence of religion in the American Jewish home became a popular topic in sermons and Jewish newspaper editorials during the closing decades of the nineteenth century, as rabbis and communal leaders lamented the apathy of American Jews toward Judaism.[91] With assimilation and modernity came declining male interest in synagogue and public prayer, and Jewish leaders in both America and Europe began to emphasize the paramount importance of Yiddishkeit (Jewish customs and practices) in the home for passing on Judaism to the next generation. "The house has little power without schooling," pronounced German Orthodox rabbi Samson Raphael Hirsch in 1837, "the school, however, has nothing without the house."[92] Hirsch's declaration transferred responsibility for the stability of Jewish religious life from male-led institutions to women, for the home was assumed to be a woman's domain in both traditional Judaism as well as in contemporary popular culture. It set up the expectation that the success or failure of Jewish schools would be determined not by the expertise of their educators or the organizational capacities of their administrators but by the presence of women in domestic settings and the strength of their commitments to Jewish home life. In the United States the idealization of the Jewish home was heightened by the proliferation of parallel rhetoric within contemporary American Protestantism, as male disinterest in attending church led ministers to emphasize that responsibility for nurturing religion lay expressly upon a mother's shoulders.[93] For the largely immigrant American Jewish community, meanwhile, nostalgia for homes and families left behind in Europe fueled the perception that hearth and home were the center of Jewish religious life and that mothers were essential to the emotional attachments their children would feel toward Judaism.

During the last decades of the nineteenth century, as they wrestled with anxieties about Jewish continuity, American rabbis, mirroring their European counterparts, argued that Sunday schools could never succeed in teaching Jewish religion in the classroom if "mothers in Israel" did not aid their efforts by cultivating domestic piety within their own families.[94] In a letter admonishing the parents of Detroit's Temple Beth El for their lack of interest in the Sabbath school in 1892, Louis Felling, the president of the congregation's education committee, concluded his missive with a reminder to mothers that the cause of Jewish education was lost if they did not create a Jewish home environment. "The good home influence should be engrafted into every child's heart," he insisted. "Do not put the entire responsibility upon the teachers, who have at the most but three hours opportunity each week to instruct them. Do not say you have not the time, it is the greatest labor of love that you can perform."[95] Writing in the *American Israelite* in 1885, Isaac Mayer Wise implored parents that a "sabbath school will labor in vain, a rabbi will labor in vain in his confirmation classes without the support given them by home training. There can be no religion in the young ones if there is none in the old ones." He proceeded to list an array of practical tips for mothers to inculcate religious sentiment in the home, such as praying with children in the morning and at night, establishing a rule that children must read a chapter of the Bible out loud before bedtime, and ensuring that there were catechisms and Bible histories around the house for children to find.[96] Without a maternal guide to create a spiritually nourishing Jewish home environment, idealistically imagined as scripture lessons before the fireplace and Sabbath candles aglow on the mantel, critics opined that it was impossible for children to gain any sense of Jewish religious connection from their Sunday school studies.[97] Arguing that the Jewish home had historically been the locus of religious devotion and that the job could not be outsourced to the Sunday school, these diatribes against the absent spirituality of the domestic sphere served to temper the enthusiasm by which rabbis greeted the service of women in benevolent causes, including teaching.[98]

American Jewish women were not oblivious to the argument that their presence in the home was essential to the continuity of Jewish life in America. Many maintained their own ambivalence about women's activities that seemed to detract from their responsibilities as wives and mothers and maintained their own nostalgia for childhood homes in which Judaism was unquestionably at the center of family life. At the 1893 World's Columbian Exposition in Chicago, as iconic a figure as Ray Frank, a woman lionized for her fiery ability to command the empty pulpits of western synagogues and fill the de facto role of the rabbi, argued that women had no need for rabbinic ordination, for their priority must be the home, "her highest ideal." She appealed to the assembled women to think of the religious spirit they created in their homes as work on behalf of the synagogue. "As mothers of Israel," she concluded, "I appeal to you to first make our homes temples. . . . If the synagogs [sic] are deserted let it be because our homes are filled. . . . Nothing can replace the duty of the mother in the home. Nothing can replace the reverence of children and the children are yours to do as you will with them."[99]

The call to mothers in Israel to commit to their domestic responsibilities was also sounded by authors and publishers of Jewish women's literature. Esther Ruskay played active public roles in various Jewish educational endeavors, including the Educational Alliance of the Lower East Side, and the Young Women's Hebrew Association. Yet she used these platforms to encourage women to make the family their primary arena of activity, publishing a volume, *Hearth and Home Essays,* in 1902 in which she argued that the most important educational institution in American Judaism was not the synagogue or the community school but a mother nurturing her children.[100] The *American Jewess,* the first English-language periodical for American Jewish women, was created by Rosa Sonneschein in 1895. It argued for expanded roles for women in the synagogue and robustly critiqued the gender inequalities faced by women in American Jewish communal life. Yet here too the trope that the most sacred duty of women was to be a mother in Israel abounded. Columns in the *American Jewess* celebrated women's achievements in benevolent work alongside odes to "ideal motherhood" that reminded women that their first duty was the raising of children.[101] Writing in August 1895 that education ought to prepare women "to be the best qualified guardian of her offspring," a woman's foremost mission, Sonneschein explained, "will forever be the propagation of the race."[102] Women like Sonneschein and Ruskay, who advocated for the expansion of women's roles in public Jewish spaces, sensed little contradiction in also arguing that a woman's primary role was to nurture Judaism in the home. They believed that because women were naturally attuned to matters of spirituality and education, their work in the public sphere represented an extension of their efforts on the domestic front. In both domains their responsibility was to inspire enthusiasm for Jewish religion among the next generation.

The Feminization of American Jewish Education

Throughout the nineteenth century, both critics and pioneers of the American Jewish Sunday school described its curriculum as one steeped in women's religion. Beginning in Philadelphia, Rebecca Gratz and her colleagues understood themselves as working in a sphere that midcentury Victorian culture had ordained for women: religious education and nurturing the young. Using their own, albeit sparse, Jewish educational training, they sought to provide children with a rudimentary primer sufficient to retain their Jewish commitments in a Christian environment that was both alluring and hostile. Advocates of the Jewish Sunday school movement commended women's volunteer teaching efforts as manifestations of their so-called natural piety. In an address surveying the various Jewish educational institutions in Philadelphia, Sabato Morais, hazan at Congregation Mikveh Israel, acknowledged, "Though not an advantage to Hebrew culture, Sunday schools, by bringing our little ones together, foster mutual attachment among all classes of Israelites, and furnish our rising generation with arms of defense against apostasy or atheism."[103] In the face of hostile proselytizing, Morais rhapsodized, "Women of Israel, whom, in the days of old, Talmudists extolled for the practice of taking their children to the school house, will gain a still higher merit, that of having disarmed the adversaries of our religion and supplied us with spiritual weapons of self-defense. May I not have spoken in vain."[104]

Yet simultaneously, the rhetorical trope that women were natural religious educators was also weaponized to remind women that motherhood and domestic religiosity should take precedence over public educational leadership roles. Encouraging women to engage in domestic educational activities, such rhetoric emphasized that real Jewish education was emotional education, not by virtue of any curriculum that women had brought into the Sunday school, but by prescribing the paradigmatically faithful female body in the home as essential for Jewish survival. It implicitly defined Jewish religious training not as a culture of male learning but as an emotive spirituality that women were uniquely able to inculcate at home. At once venerated for their affective religiosity and lionized for their benevolent service to the cause of Jewish learning in America, while also instructed to prioritize domestic instruction over their public service efforts, women were tasked with ensuring the future of Judaism in America by dedicating themselves to home and family—and lambasted when it seemed that they had failed. The label of women's religion, then, was not merely a descriptor of the Sunday school curriculum. It functioned as a rhetorical trope that was both mobilized in celebration of women's involvement in Jewish education and weaponized to protest their presence.

For historians, the trope of women's religion has offered a convenient shorthand to dismiss the labor of two generations of female volunteers in order to emphasize the more intensive and professionalized Jewish educational initiatives pioneered in the twentieth century by Samson Benderly and his "boys." The replication of the trope that the Sunday school offered "women's religion" has mostly blinded these historians, however, to the roles that men played in the nineteenth-century Sunday school movement. As the Hebrew school spread beyond Philadelphia, control of the curriculum moved out of the hands of its female founders and into the purview of male rabbis. What began as a project pioneered by women was soon supervised and organized by men. Whether rabbis or members of a congregation's school board, men took control of the Sunday school curriculum in the midnineteenth century and censured what women could teach. Men assumed administrative control of congregational Sunday schools at a national level as well. The last decades of the century saw the formation of congregational and rabbinical associations, including the Union of American Hebrew Congregations (1873), the Central Conference of American Rabbis (1883), and the Rabbinical Association of the Jewish Theological Seminary (1901). When these umbrella groups formed committees with mandates to centralize policy and pedagogy for Sunday schools, the exclusion of women from the rabbinate ensured that they were disassociated from administrative policy making and from the national effort to improve and regulate religious learning. Instructional materials created for use in Sunday school classrooms also bore the imprint of male authority. They were not an extension of "women's religion," nor were they limited to so-called sentimental women's concerns. As Sunday schools were created in cities and Jewish communities across the country, male rabbis and educators wrote textbooks to be used by their students that were later distributed by publishers with national reach. The most popular was a genre that described Jewish religion in terms associated less with spirituality and women's religion and much more closely with rationalism and masculinity. Throughout the nineteenth century, most American Jewish children learned about Jewish religion from catechisms that emphasized that Judaism was not a sentimental religion, but a rational one with a distinctive theological message.

2

Catechisms, Masculinity, and Rational Jewish Religion

In December 1881 the *American Hebrew* newspaper began to serialize a new story for children that spun a seasonally themed tale about Jewish education. In the opening chapter a group of boys received an invitation to their first Hanukkah party. Thrilled to be invited to the gathering, they quickly realized that they did not know the story of the holiday. Seeking information, their first port of call was not a textbook or volume of Jewish history. "It's evident we don't know," said one of the boys, "and it's evident we've got to know. Who has got a catechism?" The children combined their funds to purchase one, and when quizzed on the story of Hanukkah at the party each child offered a parroted repetition of the catechism's answers to questions about Hanukkah, earning a sharp rebuke from the host, who told them he was aware they had no understanding of what they were reciting. "Boys," he chastised, "I don't want you just to remember that there was a King named Antiochus and a hero named Judah. . . . What you have learned does not point out what I want by any means." He then proceeded to lecture them on what, in his estimation, the list of facts included in the catechism had failed to teach them—that Hanukkah reminds Jews of the necessity of making sacrifices for their religion.[1]

The *American Hebrew*'s story of the children reaching straight for their catechism to refresh their forgotten Hanukkah lessons, notwithstanding the intended critique of its limitations as a primer for Jewish learning, illustrated the ubiquity of the genre in nineteenth-century American Judaism. In Sunday schools catechisms were commonly used by older students preparing for confirmation in classes typically taught by the rabbi of a congregation. At first these primers were imported from Europe, but beginning in the late 1830s American rabbis and educators began to write English-language catechisms for their own classrooms, marking the beginning of an indigenous grassroots publishing market for Jewish educational materials in America.[2]

No aspect of the curriculum used within Philadelphia's Hebrew Sunday School seemed to epitomize its dependence on Protestant models for religious learning more than its use of catechisms. The catechism had been ubiquitous within Christian religious education since the sixteenth century. In the aftermath of the Protestant Reformation, question-and-answer primers provided a precise format for outlining the distinctive theological truth claims that divided the denominations of Christian Europe.[3] The catechism remained an idiosyncratic pedagogy of Christian religious learning through the modern era, and as churches established a foothold across the Atlantic, catechisms offered an efficient technology for presenting religious truth claims to children. Catechisms and question books written by American Christian educators taught the basic doctrines of their various denominational theologies, such as original sin, redemption, and the requirements of Christian moral conduct.[4] When Rebecca Gratz opened the doors to the Hebrew Sunday School in 1838, there were few Jewish resources that were suitable for its condensed curriculum or appropriate for its volunteer teachers. The Sunday school's first classes used catechisms published by Protestant churches, with references to Christian themes carefully concealed. "Many a long summer's day have I spent pasting pieces of paper over answers unsuitable for Jewish children," Rosa Mordecai, a former teacher in the school, would later recall, "and many were the fruitless efforts of those children to read through, over, or under the hidden lines."[5]

The school's volunteer teachers soon set to work on a more holistic adaptation of Christian catechisms for use in their elementary classes. Simha Peixotto published *Elementary Introduction to the Hebrew Scriptures for the Use of Hebrew Children* in 1840, and the fondly remembered *Catechism in Rhyme, or Scriptural Questions for the Use of Sunday Schools for the Instruction of Israelites*, intended for younger children and written by Simha's sister, Mrs. Eliezer [Rachel Peixotto] Pyke, followed in 1843.[6] These much beloved texts were only one degree removed, however, from the censoring efforts of Rosa Mordecai. Both catechisms used the Protestant Sunday School Union's *Child's Scripture Question Book* as a prototype, deploying substantial edits to ensure that the material was appropriate for a Jewish classroom.[7] Rachel Pyke's catechism in rhyme offered a poetic distillation of Judaism for the youngest classes in the school; she selected verses from the Protestant edition that corresponded with Jewish theology and adapted others to evade their Christological references. Its opening question and answer, "Who formed you, child, and made you live? God did my life and spirit give," were taken directly from the Protestant catechism in rhyme, whereas its exhortation "God loves an infant's praise" carefully adapted the original text's refrain of "Jesus loves an infant's praise."[8]

Catechisms were not the sole preserve of nineteenth-century Christian educators, however. They were also popular within European Jewish schools. European Jewish catechisms largely eschewed the rhyming verse embraced by the Peixotto sisters in favor of dry philosophical prose. In Germany, where catechisms were produced prolifically by adherents of the Reform movement, catechisms routinely began by philosophically defining religion as an abstract philosophical concept before proceeding to explore the topic of Judaism as a particular religious tradition. German-style Jewish catechisms typically opened with the question "What is religion?"—implicitly defining Judaism as one of many religions in the modern world. Rooted in modern Enlightenment thought, German-style catechisms sought to define Judaism by illustrating the various ways that, just like Christianity, Judaism was a rational tradition with a distinctive set of theological truth claims, rather than, as its detractors professed, a legal tradition characterized only by abstruse rituals. German catechisms emphasized that Judaism could be defined and explained philosophically and that framing Judaism in the context of the universal human phenomenon of religion should be the first lesson of the modern Jewish educational curriculum.

The German Jewish–style catechism was adopted by another supporter of Philadelphia's Hebrew Sunday School who wrote a catechism for use by the school's older students. Isaac Leeser, hazan of Gratz's home congregation, Mikveh Israel, published his catechism in 1839. Leeser's textbook was based on a paradigm by a German Reform Jew, and it incorporated the German emphasis on defining religion, and Judaism, in philosophical and rational terms. As the Sunday school spread beyond Philadelphia, and local rabbis and educators wrote catechisms for use in their own classrooms, they looked to Leeser's text as a model.[9] Catechisms written for American Jewish Sunday school classrooms across the country, in traditional congregations as well as Reform temples, followed Leeser's paradigm and made the inquiry, "What is religion?" into the foundational question of American Jewish Sunday school education.

An examination of the Jewish catechisms produced for use in Sunday schools after 1838 and beyond Philadelphia challenges the conventional historiographic framing of the Sunday school as dominated by women and by a curriculum steeped in saccharine spirituality. The German-style catechism emphasized that rationality was the primary hallmark of religion in general, and Judaism in particular, implicitly coding Jewish religion as male.[10] Reason as a value assumed a gendered intellectual and cultural cadence within modern Enlightenment thought, and when religion was defined in terms of its proximity to reason, it was defined in gendered terms as well. Real religion was rational, reasonable, and masculine. Feminine religion was sentimental and emotional, inferior, and not intellectual. When catechisms defined Judaism as rational and universal, the implicit comparison was to irrationality and to religion as defined with recourse to attributes associated with women.

In adopting the German-style catechism, with its emphasis on defining Judaism according to the male-coded categories of reason and rationalism, authors asserted a continuing role for male-gendered expertise in the education of American Jews. The limited curriculum of the Sunday school offered few opportunities for rabbis and educators trained in classical Hebrew literature to demonstrate traditional Jewish knowledge. Historically, study of the Torah and familiarity with the Jewish textual tradition had functioned as an important marker of Jewish masculinity, while exclusion from the study house was a condition of Jewish womanhood.[11] In the nineteenth century the American Jewish Sunday school severed the assumption that a Jewish teacher was someone with expertise in Hebrew texts, foregrounding Bible instruction in English by devoted female volunteers in place of the intensive study of classical Jewish literature in its original languages. Yet within this broadly woman-centered milieu, the catechism, a text predominantly written and taught by men, and that defined Judaism in philosophical terms coded as male and masculine, offered men ongoing opportunities to perform key educational roles, albeit in a new arena of Jewish content knowledge. Whereas cheders, Talmud Torahs, and yeshivas emphasized halacha (Jewish law), and schools founded by European Jewish moderns emphasized Hebrew and Yiddish language and literature, the catechisms of nineteenth-century American Jewish Sunday schools emphasized that expertise in Jewish subjects could also be demonstrated by reconciling Jewish knowledge with the universal concept of religion, and with the philosophies of modern European thought.

A Transatlantic Vehicle of Jewish Instruction

Catechisms first emerged in European Jewish education as a response to the creation and state regulation of Jewish educational systems, a consequence of increasing modernity for late eighteenth-century European Jews.[12] Catechisms offered a format for detailed yet concise explanations of Jewish theology and an effective pedagogical strategy to convey the "essentials" of Judaism in a newly modern landscape in which education in Jewish subjects had to be balanced with secular studies.[13] Catechisms represented a sharp departure from traditional modes of Jewish learning that emphasized the linguistic and methodological ability to navigate the Torah and its commentaries for the purposes of understanding Jewish law and liturgy; they also marked a departure from the pedagogy of *chavruta* learning (joint study sessions) characteristic of the yeshivas of Europe.[14] However, catechisms also stood within a long tradition of accessible, primarily theological, introductions to Judaism and Jewish thought. From Maimonides' Thirteen Principles to Bahya Ibn Paquda's *Duties of the Heart* and Moshe Chaim Luzzatto's *Derech haShem*, syntheses of Jewish theological knowledge had long been produced by Jewish authors who identified a need for introductory Jewish educational texts.[15] In the context of Western Europe, as Jews began to participate in modern educational systems in which Jewish studies represented only one of many subjects within the curriculum, catechisms introduced what their authors considered to be the essential theological elements of Judaism in the vernacular languages spoken by European Jews.[16]

Historian Jacob Petuchowski has estimated that between 1782 and 1884, Jews in Western Europe produced more than 160 catechisms that attempted to offer a systematic presentation of Judaism.[17] As these little texts made their way across the Atlantic, they forged a Jewish knowledge economy that connected the Old World with the New and shared a common solution to the problem of conveying a broad curriculum in an educational context that was limited by both time and resources. Decades before the first Hebrew Sunday school opened its doors, American Jewish educators recognized that catechisms offered a valuable tool for systematically introducing students to a comprehensive range of Jewish topics. Early nineteenth-century Jewish day schools, boarding schools, and afternoon congregational schools used imported German- and French-language catechisms produced for use in continental European Jewish education, as well as English-language catechisms from Britain. Beginning in the second decade of the nineteenth century, schools began to engage local printing houses to republish these European texts locally, to lower the costs associated with importation and to assure a greater volume of materials as the American Jewish population began to expand. The first Jewish catechism published on American soil was a reprint of a catechism written in Britain, Orthodox rabbi Jacob Cohen's *Elements of the Jewish Faith*. Printed in 1817 by the W. W. Gray Print Company in Richmond, Virginia, the catechism provided the local Jewish community, which as yet had no rabbi and no religious school for its children, with a comprehensive primer on Jewish topics.[18] "You cannot be otherwise [than] pleased with it," wrote Rachel Mordecai to her brother Sam in July 1817. "Conveying much useful information, without bigotry or illiberality, it proved that our faith was a good one."[19] European catechisms offered a systematic overview of Jewish knowledge and a pragmatic educational tool for communities in America where Jewish institutional resources remained few and far between. The Mordecai siblings were well attuned to the challenges of providing religious education to Jewish children and to the opportunities afforded by Jewish catechisms. Rachel and Sam's father, Jacob Mordecai, was the founder of a pioneering nonsectarian academy for girls in Warrenton, North Carolina. At the Mordecai academy Jewish and Christian students were encouraged to observe their faith traditions, yet to circumvent proselytizing, the school eschewed any formal religious instruction. Convinced of the merit of the work, Rachel informed her brother that their father had already ordered twenty copies of Cohen's book for distribution to the academy's Jewish pupils.[20]

European Jewish catechisms were used by students enrolled in Jewish schools from elementary grades through to confirmation classes. They typically included an overview of Jewish theology, outlined the Jewish calendar, and offered a précis of Jewish history. Catechisms teach "the theoretic part of Judaism," wrote Isaac Leeser in the *Occident and American Jewish Advocate* in 1866, "they outline the principles of the Jewish religion from a theological point of view."[21] Characteristically written in the form of prescriptive questions and answers, the teaching of catechisms typically focused on recitation with the expectation that the student would memorize each assigned response. Instruction using rote memorization was the predominant pedagogy of the modern era, and the adoption of catechisms within American Jewish education represented the incorporation of a popular mode of learning as much as a genre specific to studying theology.[22] Yet with its characteristic ability to synthesize complex information and ideas into an easily digestible set of questions and answers, as well as its long associations with Christian religious learning, the catechism, it seemed to American Jews, was particularly suited for the project of Jewish religious education. It provided a pedagogical manual for teachers, as well as a script for end-of-year ceremonies in which children would recite their catechisms in a grand display of their learning. Catechisms became popular in large part because of their use in public exams held to mark the graduation of Jewish children. When the students recited the questions and answers that they had memorized during their catechism classes, it seemed that they had developed a mastery of their content knowledge. The American Jewish press published reports on the end-of-year examinations for various Jewish schools that included glowing testimonies to the students' prowess in catechism. A report on the closing examinations of the Talmud Torah and Hebrew Institute of New York in 1844 lauded the students' recitations of their catechisms, theorizing that it was enlightening for the audience as much as for the boys themselves, providing "an indirect instruction in religion" for the parents who gathered for the ceremony, as well a demonstration of the many hours spent by the children memorizing the assigned questions and answers.[23]

The Genus and Species of American Judaism

Though catechisms had been studied by American Jewish children for generations before the founding of the first Hebrew Sunday School, it was not until 1839 that a Jewish catechism was authored for the first time on American soil. Written for use in the Hebrew Sunday School in Philadelphia and dedicated to Rebecca Gratz, Isaac Leeser's *Catechism for Younger Children* was a question-and-answer primer written in formulaic prose. Based on a German paradigm, Eduard Kley's 1814 *Catechism of the Mosaic Doctrine*, Leeser's catechism was designed for use by children aged eight to fourteen and was reprinted across at least nine editions between 1838 and 1890.[24] Leeser's catechism, rather than the texts written by the Peixotto sisters, set the tone for the majority of Jewish catechisms produced for use in American Jewish Sunday schools. Following the format common in Germany, Leeser's catechism opened by asking, "What is religion?" before proceeding to define Judaism in relation to the idea of religion as a universal human phenomenon.[25]

A central tenet of European Enlightenment thought was the idea that religion could be defined philosophically as an autonomous proposition, independent of any particular doctrinal or scriptural tradition. Modern Jewish thinkers who sought to reimagine Judaism in relation to modernity necessarily had to account for the ways that Judaism could be defined in these terms.[26] Immanuel Kant proposed that all knowledge, including religious knowledge, was grounded in the sense experience of the autonomous self and filtered through the prism of human reason.[27] Kant was equally insistent that Christianity alone provided a framework for the experience of true religion, with Judaism offering little more than desiccated legalism.[28] In 1783 Moses Mendelssohn took up the challenge of defining Judaism as a religion according to the terms established by Kant and of defending Judaism against Kant's charges.[29] In *Jerusalem: Or on Religious Power and Judaism*, Mendelssohn argued that Judaism inherently conformed to human reason and to rational morality; it was not, as his detractors suggested, dry legalism. While Judaism did maintain a legal tradition, Mendelssohn clarified, Jewish law was not a theocracy to be imposed on the non-Jewish world but private legislation binding on Jews alone. Mendelssohn's philosophical defense of Judaism as a religion that professed universal and rational truths, while also maintaining specific beliefs and practices relative to Jews, became essential to the Haskalah, the European Jewish enlightenment movement. For its proponents Mendelssohn's philosophical bifurcation of Judaism as both universal religion and a system of religiolegal obligations specific to the Jewish people justified their contention that Judaism was fully compatible with modernity; it also bolstered their demands for the extension of full citizenship to Jews within their nation-states. For German Jewish authors of catechisms who followed in Mendelssohn's footsteps, it seemed logical that Judaism should be described relative to religion as a universal phenomenon, different only by virtue of the particular doctrines and duties binding on Jews. Defining Judaism as a religion independent of halacha inscribed the idea that Judaism was, like Christianity, primarily a philosophical and ethical system rather than a judicial one.[30] If religion was a genus, then Judaism was one of many species, an incarnation of universal religion while also manifesting that phenomenon in expressly Jewish terms.

When he wrote his catechism in 1814, Eduard Kley was fully immersed in the efforts to embrace modernity promoted by European Jews. Kley was a proponent of the Reform movement in Germany and believed that Jewish education should help to acclimate Jewish children to citizenship within modern European society as well as to citizenship within the Jewish community in particular.[31] His catechism had little to say about halacha, Jewish ritual, or the Jewish calendar. It emphasized the devotional aspects of Jewish religion that could bridge Judaism and Christianity, namely the experience of worshipping the divine. In response to the opening question in his catechism, "What is religion?" Kley explained that religion is the adoration of a supreme being. In the broadest sense, he elaborated, religion is steadfast obedience to God, and to be religious means to recognize God's will, to live according to it, and to recognize God's rule over humankind.[32] For Kley religion was a set of feelings toward the divine that made its adherents into good human beings. By becoming good, he theorized, Jews would emerge as conscientious citizens of the state as well.[33]

Leeser was an erstwhile champion of traditional Judaism. Nevertheless, he chose as his model a catechism by Kley, an adherent of the Reform movement, acclaiming its pedagogical merits even while berating the author's membership in a "society of schismatics."[34] Leeser and Kley approached their catechisms from divergent denominational vantage points, but they were motivated by similar concerns. Both were apprehensive about the apathy of their fellow Jews toward Judaism and the rate of Jewish defections to Christianity. They also shared the conviction that Jewish education offered critical opportunities to demonstrate to the next generation that Judaism was compatible with participation in modern civic life. Yet, whereas Kley promoted reform as a necessary conduit to engage the apathetic Jewish modern, Leeser focused on building an infrastructure for traditional Jewish practice, believing—perhaps naively—that tradition offered a pillar of unification for American Jews.[35] Leeser took a selective approach to his adaptation of Kley's catechism. He retained Kley's division of subjects and most of his questions, but only occasionally did his answers mirror those of the German reformer's.[36]

Leeser's catechism, like Kley's, began by defining religion in general and then proceeded to describe the Jewish religion in particular. Leeser's answer to the question "What is religion?" was more direct than his predecessor's. "Religion," Leeser stated, "is the knowledge we have of God and the duties we owe in obedience to his will."[37] To believe in God is to believe that "everything I see around me, the trees, the flowers, the earth, the water, also the sun and the moon, and the thousands of stars that shine in the night sky, were made by the great creator." Leeser's operative definition of religion stressed the interdependence of God and creation. Human happiness, he maintained, is dependent upon "a correct knowledge of those actions which our creator bids us to do." To be religious, he concluded, is to "know God's directions, and to obey and live them accordingly."[38]

Leeser's definition of religion maintained the paradigm espoused by post-Kantian European Enlightenment thought, that religion was fundamentally an activity located within the sense experience of the autonomous individual. Human beings, he explained, can "sense the existence of God as it is manifested in the creation and arrangement of external nature, which we perceive by our senses." Yet Leeser also upheld revelation as a source of religious knowledge. The bedrock of Leeser's theology was his unwavering belief in the literal revelation of the Torah on Sinai and his conviction that the "spirit of the age should not dictate the reform of Jewish belief and practice."[39] The Torah, he clarified in his catechism, was "the word of God, kindly sent us from Heaven to teach us how to please God by our actions."[40] Revelation conveyed what was specific to Judaism and what was incumbent upon Jews to practice. "The Mosaic religion," Leeser explained, "was revealed by the Lord; and I esteem the same as the true, pure, and unmixed word of God."[41]

The distinction between reason and revelation that Leeser introduced in his catechism was an epistemological binary first deployed by Moses Mendelssohn to claim that Judaism was a religion in the universal sense while also claiming theologies and practices specific to Jews alone. Natural religion, Mendelssohn proposed, was observable in creation and was intelligible through the exercise of human reason—only revelation divided religions from each other. Leeser was well versed in Mendelssohn's conceptual logic; he was also at work on a translation of Mendelssohn's *Jerusalem*, a volume he ultimately published in 1852.[42] Leeser saw in Mendelssohn a paradigm of his own conviction that it was possible to maintain fidelity to traditional Judaism while also participating fully in modern life. "Our philosopher is often invoked in defense of reform," he explained in the introduction to his 1852 translation of *Jerusalem*, "when in point of fact nothing could be further from the truth . . . [Mendelssohn] had the fullest faith in the inspiration of our scriptures."[43] By making the epistemological binary of reason and revelation central to his definition of religion, Leeser, like Mendelssohn, sought to anchor Judaism within the universal phenomenon of religion without sacrificing Jewish claims for divinely ordained particularity.

By defining religion in general and Judaism in particular using the terminology of Mendelssohn and of the Haskalah, Leeser's catechism established as a core premise that Jewish education was not only training in the particular values, observances, and theologies of the Jewish people; it also was a philosophical introduction to the concept of religion as a universal dimension of human life. It established that defining religion was an elementary lesson that a Jewish Sunday school student should be expected to learn. The Hebrew Sunday School in Philadelphia was founded by a woman, led by female teachers, and its first curriculum was closely associated with female spirituality in bourgeois Christian America. Yet within this broadly woman-centered milieu, the catechism that Isaac Leeser wrote for use by older students proclaimed the fundamentals of Judaism in terms that were associated inherently with men and masculinity. The German-style catechism tied Jewish education to the central project of modern European Jewish thought, of defining religion as an experience anchored in the autonomous self. If Gratz's syllabus for the Hebrew Sunday School focused on cultivating spiritual virtues and moral conduct, Leeser's emphasized that Jewish education

must also be able to account for perhaps the most pressing Jewish philosophical question of the modern era: how Judaism could be defined as a
religion according to the frameworks established by modern European
rationalism.

A Legion of Catechisms

Catechisms offered an expedient tool for the Sunday school's condensed
curriculum, and as Sunday schools were established across the country,
catechisms became popular in classrooms far beyond Philadelphia. During the 1840s and 1850s the catechisms written by the Peixotto sisters
were commonly used in elementary classes, while Leeser's catechism
was adopted for older students.[44] In the second half of the nineteenth
century, the range of catechisms used in American Jewish Sunday school
education began to expand dramatically. New catechisms were published by congregational rabbis and local Sunday school educators as
well as by leaders within the emerging national institutions of American
Judaism. They were sponsored by local presses as well as by publishers
with national reach.[45] In 1867 a review of literature for children in the
Jewish Messenger observed that "about a dozen" catechisms had been
written in America.[46] Twenty-three years later, in 1890, Reform rabbi
David Philipson could report that the number of published catechisms
available to American Jewish educators was "legion."[47] As one editorial
in the *American Hebrew* noted, "The number of catechisms has now so
rapidly increased that Sunday School trustees find it difficult to make
selections."[48]

Catechisms became popular in American Jewish Sunday schools both
because they offered a pragmatic pedagogical tool for classes that met
for only a few hours once or twice per week, and because they were
economically expedient. Catechisms were typically published as small
pamphlets or short books, rarely more than fifty pages. Lightweight volumes typically bound within colored paper covers, catechisms were relatively inexpensive for teachers and Sunday school principals to purchase
for their classrooms. Catechisms were, however, susceptible to damage
by eager young hands. When Pyke's catechism was distributed to the
students in the Hebrew Sunday School in Philadelphia, Rosa Mordecai
recalled, the school had to apply preventative measures to protect the

school's collection and assessed a five-cent penalty charge to any child whose catechism became damaged or lost.[49]

Publishing houses quickly began to capitalize on the utility of catechisms for Jewish Sunday school education, offering new volumes for sale by the dozen and incentives for bulk purchase. An October 1880 advertisement in the *American Israelite* for educational materials published by the Jewish printing company Bloch included fifteen volumes, of which half were catechisms. Pyke's catechism was offered at a rate of one dollar per dozen, while a single copy of a translation of Henri Loeb's French catechism *Derekh HaEmunah* (Road to Faith) cost thirty cents each.[50] Even as American rabbis more attuned to the social context of American Jewry began to write catechisms specifically for local audiences, translations of European works such as Loeb's continued to be reprinted in the United States.[51] American Jews remained dependent upon rabbis trained in Europe until the last decades of the nineteenth century, so European authors were regarded as authoritative, representative of Old World expertise. "It was a real pleasure to teach from Henri Loeb's *The Road to Faith*," Rosa Mordecai recalled in 1857. It was "the best work for the purpose."[52]

Within a few years, however, American Jewish Sunday schools began to opt for catechisms written in English for a specifically American audience rather than translated European productions. Rabbis and educators seemed happy to supply them. "That the youth of our community is especially in need of religious and moral instruction seems to me a fact hardly to be disputed or doubted; and it appears equally as evident that in order to impart such instruction methodically and profitably, a manual to be used in our religious schools is indispensable," wrote Rabbi Jacob Mendes DeSolla of San Francisco in the introduction to the catechism that he published in 1871.[53] For the rabbis and educators who authored catechisms, national distribution was both a pedagogical intervention and an expedient means to augment the salaries they received in compensation for teaching and pulpit duties within their own congregations.[54] When George Jacobs, hazan of the traditional Sephardic Congregation Beth Shalome in Richmond, Virginia, published his first catechism in 1868, he believed himself to be poorly compensated by his community. Jacobs earned $1,200 per year as hazan, yet his salary had not increased since before the Civil War. In 1868 he wrote to the board of Beth Shalome to lament his financial situation, threatening to leave unless he received a raise.[55] One year later he made good on his threat, taking a new position as hazan of Beth El Emeth, a Sephardic congregation in Philadelphia. Jacobs continued to augment his salary by writing catechisms; he published a second text for older children in 1879.[56] Even after his death in 1884, his catechisms remained lucrative for his descendants. In 1895 and in 1896 Rebecca Jacobs sold two dozen copies of her father's catechism *Elementary Instruction in the Hebrew Faith* to the Sunday school of Congregation Shaaray Tefila in New York.[57] At $1.50 per dozen, each new elementary class at Shaaray Tefila meant three dollars in the Jacobses' pockets. Rebecca Jacobs was protective of the income from her father's catechisms. In 1888, four years after her father's death, she published a scathing letter in the Philadelphia *Jewish Messenger* accusing the Bloch Publishing Company of "blunted morals" for retaining the entire profit of its sales of Jacobs's catechisms and awarding none of the royalties to his heirs.[58] She was wise to guard the income from her father's works so closely. An 1896 survey by the National Council of Jewish Women of 114 Sunday schools across the country found that Jacobs's two volumes were among the four most popular catechisms used by American Jewish Sunday schools, alongside Isaac Mayer Wise's *Judaism: Its Doctrines and Duties* and Pyke's *Scriptural Questions for the Instruction of Israelites.*[59]

Catechisms were written by authors whose practice of Judaism ranged from Reform to traditional, and they were used within Jewish educational settings that spanned a wide variety of religious affiliations. Catechisms were an educational technology, and their use united rather than divided Jews across the nascent denominational spectrum.[60] Catechisms for younger children typically focused on introductory explanations of God and creation. Among catechisms for older children in confirmation classes, however, the religious proclivities of their authors, as well as the communities that they served, noticeably shaped the catechisms' form and content. Texts by authors of more Orthodox orientations typically emphasized the Jewish calendar and liturgy.[61] Jacques Judah Lyon, hazan of traditional Sephardic Congregation Shearith Israel in New York, published his catechism, *Sunday School Lessons for Young Israelites,* in 1864. It offered a translation of the Shema prayer, an explanation of the Ten Commandments and the various books of the He-

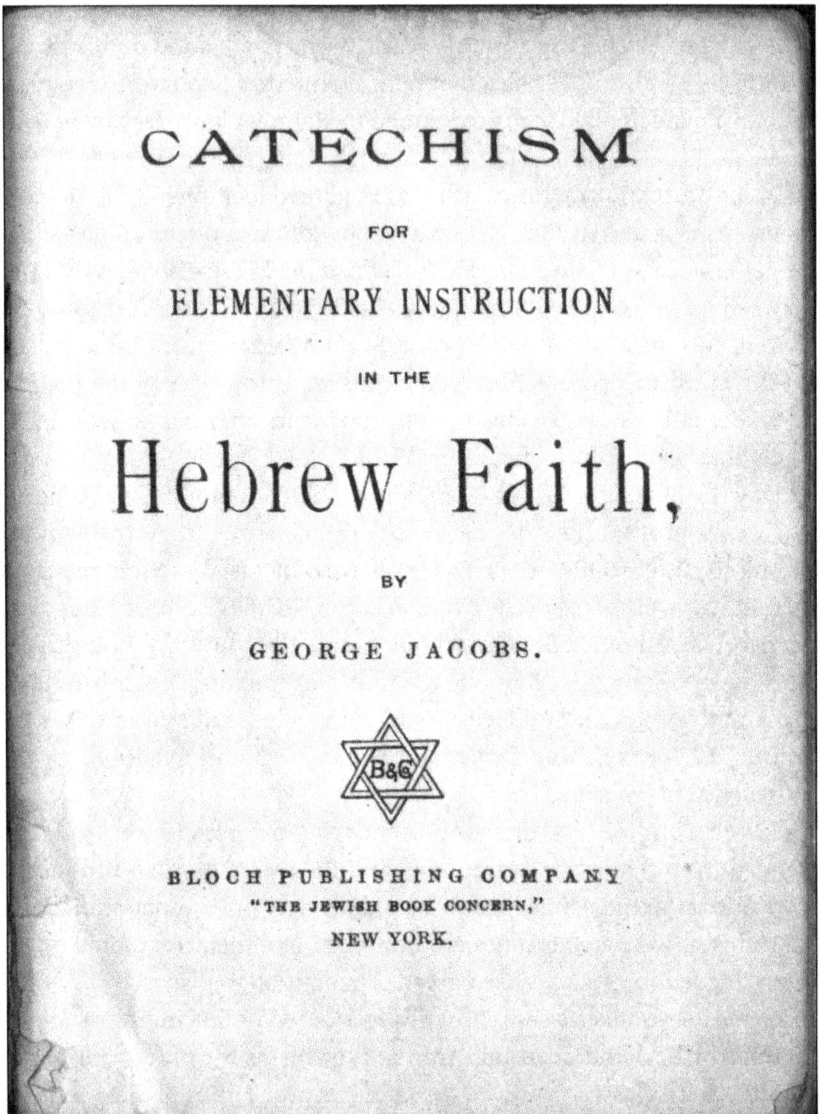

CATECHISM

FOR

ELEMENTARY INSTRUCTION

IN THE

Hebrew Faith,

BY

GEORGE JACOBS.

BLOCH PUBLISHING COMPANY
"THE JEWISH BOOK CONCERN,"
NEW YORK.

Figure 2.1. George Jacobs, *Catechism for Elementary Instruction in the Hebrew Faith* (Philadelphia: W. W. Jones: De Armond & Goodrich, 1868). Courtesy of the Klau Library, Hebrew Union College–Jewish Institute of Religion, Cincinnati, Ohio.

brew Bible, and an overview of the Jewish calendar.[62] Benjamin Szold, the Ashkenazi traditionalist rabbi of Baltimore's Temple Oheb Shalom, authored a catechism, *Reshit Da'at* (First Knowledge) in 1873.[63] Written in question-and-answer format, it focused on the covenant between God and the "Israelitisch nation"; the Hebrew calendar; and the laws of the Sabbath and holidays. It also included a section of excerpts from the morning blessings (Birchot haShachar) with English translations, blessings traditionally said before and after eating, a section of English-language hymns with sheet music, and a Hebrew primer.

Catechisms by Reform authors, on the other hand, generally embraced the German theological style. Emphasizing religious philosophy rather than calendar and liturgy, a catechism published by Rabbi Barnett Elzas of South Carolina's flagship Reform synagogue, Kahal Kadosh Beth Elohim, in 1896 contained seven sections, each treating a different philosophical idea: on religion in general; Judaism; the existence of God; revelation; reward and punishment; Israel's mission; and Israel's creed.[64] Whereas the primary focus of Szold's catechism was to give the Jewish child an understanding of Jewish liturgical time, and equip the student with foundational synagogue literacy, Elzas's catechism concentrated overwhelmingly on Jewish answers to universal theological questions and on providing the Jewish child with the vocabulary to understand fundamental philosophical distinctions between Judaism and Christianity. As Elzas freely acknowledged in his preface, "in this catechism the ceremonial part of Judaism, however interesting and important from one point of view, has been left untouched."[65] A more cautious approach was adopted by Jacob Mendes DeSolla, headmaster of the religious schools of San Francisco Congregations Emanu-El and Sherith Israel, whose catechism was published three times by Bloch between 1871 and 1890. The congregations that he served moved slowly toward Reform during the 1870s.[66] DeSolla was mindful of the diverse religious proclivities among his constituents, and his catechism navigated a careful path between tradition and Reform. The first half dealt with philosophy and theology, whereas the second was devoted to "practical religion" and included an overview of the liturgy, the injunction to refrain from work on the Sabbath, an outline of the Jewish calendar, and laws concerning diet and moral conduct. Other catechisms written for confirmation classes had failed to "stoop to the level of the comprehension of young students," DeSolla explained in the introduction. This manual would present lessons he had successfully taught in San Francisco for years.[67]

Whether Orthodox or Reform, catechisms relied on a common pedagogy: dictation and rote memorization. In Sunday school classrooms across the country, children heard catechisms read out loud and were instructed to memorize their contents. At B'nai Jehudah, a Reform congregation in Kansas City, Kansas, Rabbi Emanuel Hess introduced catechisms for students preparing for confirmation in 1872. For one hour each Saturday and two hours each Sunday, catechism was recited aloud by the teacher, and students were expected to memorize the texts word for word.[68] Catechisms that were published in pamphlet form often began life as lectures that rabbis and educators had written for their own students. These lectures were delivered orally, and students were expected to copy what they heard into their notebooks. Miriam Greenbaum, who was confirmed at the Eutaw Place Temple in Baltimore during the 1890s, filled her confirmation notebook with flowery lectures dictated by Rabbi Adolph Guttmacher.[69] Only one endearing spelling mistake—she recorded the Kedushah prayer as "Holly, holly, holly, Lord God Almighty"—disclosed that the notebook was the work of a young girl rather than a middle-aged rabbi.[70] Betsy Lowenstein was confirmed in San Francisco in the 1860s. Her confirmation notebook was filled not with her own theological observations but those of Rabbi Samuel Adler of Congregation Emanu-El in New York, whose catechism, *Instruction in the Israelitisch Religion,* she wrote out word for word in her royal blue embossed copybook.[71] Publishing catechetical lectures as textbooks that children could read for themselves circumscribed the need for rote inscription and recognized that children benefited from a printed text. The mass-market publication of catechisms thus represented a progression in American Jewish pedagogy, an acknowledgment that children should be supplied with appropriate resources to support their learning, even if that pedagogy nevertheless continued to think of the child as little more than a blank slate that needed to be filled with memorized catechetical knowledge.

Reforming Religion

The Reform movement came to dominate American Jewish life during the second half of the nineteenth century, and as Reform synagogues embraced the Sunday school as a model for Jewish education, Reform rabbis and educators became prolific authors of catechisms. American Reform authors brought an evolving set of new answers to the catechetical question "What is religion?" that confirmed their indebtedness to their European predecessors while also demonstrating their immersion in contemporary trends in American popular culture.

The first Reform catechisms authored in America were written by German-trained rabbis schooled in the universalist philosophies of Abraham Geiger. Geiger, Reform Judaism's "founding father," had radically proposed that Judaism was not merely a particular instantiation of the universal phenomenon of religion; it was religion sui generis, religion in its very essence.[72] The particular duty of Judaism, Geiger maintained, was its so-called prophetic mission to cultivate the spread of monotheism among the nations, thus heralding the messianic age. "What Geiger sought was not merely a defense of Judaism in the eyes of the Christian world," Susannah Heschel has argued, "but a presentation of Judaism as *the* universal religion."[73] American Jewish catechisms influenced by Geiger characteristically defined Judaism as both a species within the genus religion and the embodiment of the genus itself.

Among the first Reform catechisms published in the United States was Elias Eppstein's *Confirmant's Guide to the Mosaic Religion*, written for use in the religious school of Temple Beth El in Detroit, which Eppstein served as rabbi. Born in Alsace and educated in Germany, Eppstein arrived in the United States in 1854 and became a systematic reformer of the congregations that he served.[74] Under his leadership Beth El abandoned its full-day Hebrew and German school and opened a weekend school for religious instruction.[75] Eppstein's catechism was based upon a series of seven lectures, reimagined in the form of questions and answers, that he had given to the school's confirmation class.[76] Although there were plenty of catechisms to choose from, Eppstein complained in the introduction to his short volume, they were either written in German or were direct translations from German.[77] His own text, Eppstein assured, was composed in English and suffered no such stylistic deficiencies. It would equip the children who read it with a "glow of pride," as they learned that Israel was the "basis of all civilized religions."[78] Published in 1868, *Confirmant's Guide* explored many of the themes that would become foundational to the Reform movement's Pittsburgh Platform when it was compiled seventeen years later.

Following the German format, Eppstein began his catechism with the question, "What is religion?" His answer largely mirrored Isaac Leeser's, explaining that "religion is the knowledge of God and the mode of worshipping Him—by the contemplation of his power, wisdom and goodness, and by a faithful obedience to his law."[79] Religion is "most necessary," Eppstein insisted, "for belief in God is the highest and most holy treasure that man can possess." As in Leeser's catechism, Eppstein's definition of religion was rooted in the experience of the autonomous individual and in the individual experience of the divine. Unlike Isaac Leeser, however, Eppstein, as a reformer, was committed to the concept of Judaism's prophetic mission to spread universal monotheism, and his catechism was therefore attentive to theologies beyond the boundaries of Judaism. He described other religions as a primitive stage within the evolution of human religious history, explaining that before God's revelation to Abraham, the "majority of mankind were so plunged in superstition and ignorance that they attributed to powers of nature the qualities belonging to the great God." It was the particular mission of Israel, he concluded, to "dissipate superstitions" by teaching the world that only God, and not nature, was the true object of worship. Eppstein's catechism promoted the concept of Israel's mission extensively, dedicating an entire chapter to explaining how the Jewish people would ultimately correct the so-called erroneous religions of the world. "We are justified in entertaining the hope that the knowledge of God, in some future time, will become so inculcated among the whole human race, that all of them will acknowledge one God," he concluded. Until that time the duty of Israel was to be a living example of the "highest degree of morality."

Eppstein's confidence that the particular religious identity of Judaism resided in its ethical commitment to monotheism, and that its duty was to spread that commitment among the nations, was characteristic of the Reform theology nurtured in Germany. As Isaac Mayer Wise, the architect of the Reform movement in America, explained in an address to the Free Religious Association in 1869, when all cultures accepted the monotheism taught in the Hebrew Bible, Judaism would "establish its claim as the universal religion. As the mother of all religions it has nurtured the religious idea. . . . Thousands will be glad to hear the honest truth."[80] The principal lesson of Wise's 1872 catechism, *Judaism: Its Doctrines and Duties*, was that Judaism was superior to all other religions.[81] Like Eppstein's *Confirmant's Guide*, Wise's catechism emphasized Geiger's mission theory, describing religion as a universal human phenomenon yet maintaining that true religion was vested in Judaism alone. Wise defined religion as "the inborn desire God plants in man to know Him, and His will, in order to worship Him."[82] Israel's religion was "the true religion," Wise explained, because its "doctrines are taken from the Revelations of God in His works and words."[83] Wise maintained a commitment to the divine revelation of the Hebrew Bible, and his catechism insisted that Judaism constituted a universal religion both because its scriptures constituted divine revelation and because it was fully aligned with human reason. "There is a religion without mysteries or miracles, rational and self-evident," he explained. "This religion is Judaism, therefore it is the future religion of all mankind."[84]

Eppstein and Wise published their catechisms in 1868 and 1872, respectively. Reform authors who wrote catechisms in the last years of the nineteenth century, however, had to contend with an increasingly complicated set of parameters for defining not only Judaism but religion beyond the borders of Judaism as well. If the task for Jewish authors of catechisms at midcentury was to define Judaism as a religion in relation to conceptions of rational individualism and religious universality, the task that confronted their coreligionists at the end of the century was to accomplish the same task within a landscape in which the conceptual foundations that underlay the idea of religion were shifting dramatically. Buoyed by the findings of Charles Darwin and his colleagues, secularist movements speculated that religion was irrelevant in the context of modernity, a false science proved erroneous by the findings of evolutionary geology. At the same time, in European and American universities the new field of religious studies promoted the comparative analysis of religious traditions and hypothesized that the origins of religion lay in beliefs and practices that were fundamental to human culture. Initially, American Jews seem to have greeted comparative studies of religion with suspicion, yet by the last decades of the century rabbis and lay-people across the country had developed an interest in its findings.[85] By 1888 Rabbi Isaac Moses of Chicago could declare that among American Jews, "everyone is interested in the question of where religion comes from."[86] Independent Jewish study circles formed to read and discuss the latest findings in the comparative study of religions, using popular texts published both in Europe and America, even those with implicitly Christian overtones.[87] The ideas promoted by comparative studies of religion were particularly attractive to rabbis and communal leaders who feared for the survival of Judaism in a modern world dominated by religious apathy.[88] "The men of this new science teach us, irrefutably," wrote Rabbi Max Lilienthal in the *Israelite*, "that the human heart was always and in all possible forms, longing and yearning for the infinite Father and creator."[89]

Leeser's catechism, written in 1838, made no mention of religions other than Judaism.[90] Catechisms authored at the end of the century, however, devoted significantly more time and attention to the religious worlds beyond the borders of Judaism. In *Guide for Instruction in Judaism*, the catechism he wrote in 1898, Reform rabbi Kaufmann Kohler explained to students that the ultimate source of religion was not revelation or reason but the human impulse for spirituality.[91] "The true source of all religion," he insisted, "is the human heart. . . . All the patriarchs and prophets of old, like all the good men among the heathen, derived their religion from this source."[92] Religion, Kohler proposed, was not a privilege conveyed to select groups by means of revelation. It was innate to the experience of being human. "Men of all times felt the need of religion," he explained. "They craved to know that God was near." Kohler was abidingly interested in the idea of religion as a human phenomenon. He instituted the comparative study of religion as part of the academic curriculum for trainee rabbis when he became president of Hebrew Union College in 1903, and in 1923 he authored a study analyzing the evolution of conceptions of heaven and hell in comparative religious traditions.[93] "Let religion be presented in its true fascinating garb," he argued in an 1888 sermon, "not as the religion of a sect or a Church, to be at war with others or the target of an infidel, but as the great ideal power of life."[94] The operative understanding of religion in Kohler's catechism eschewed the binary of reason and revelation that had so preoccupied his predecessors. He defined the religious experience as a universal spiritual quest. Religion, Kohler's *Guide for Instruction in Judaism* explained, is the human experience of fearing or "longing" to know God.[95] It was the human religious impulse that made religion universal, not any particular definition of religion based in philosophic rationalism.

As a reformer, Kohler also remained committed to Judaism's prophetic mission. While he sought to articulate the universal dimensions of religion based in human spirituality, his catechism was equally committed to a historical hierarchy of religions that positioned Judaism decidedly at its apex. Kohler actively sought to incorporate the theologies of other religious traditions into a Jewish framework, explaining that "God sent prophets or inspired teachers of morality to other people beside Israel, such as Balaam in the time of Moses, or Buddah in India, Confucius in China, Zoroaster in Persia, Socrates in Greece and the like." Yet it was only to Israel, he clarified, that prophets were given to "reveal God in man, and thus to establish the true *religion of humanity*." "The Jewish religion," Kohler concluded, "as far as it contains the essential truths and laws of morality is intended to be the religion of the whole human family."[96]

"Some Are Excellent, the Majority Are about Mediocre"

The disparate definitions of religion taught in American Jewish catechisms mirrored the diversity of ideas about religion in American Judaism more broadly during the second half of the nineteenth century. By publishing catechisms for use in Sunday schools, authors could add their own contributions to a vibrant conversation about how religion should be defined, and they could stake their own claim for a Jewish theology they believed to be responsive to contemporary concerns. The diverse ideas presented in American Jewish catechisms divided opinions among American Jews throughout the period. As an editorial in the *American Hebrew* concluded in 1881, there had been "numberless" Jewish catechisms printed in America: "Some are excellent, the majority are about mediocre."[97]

Catechisms facilitated ongoing conversations about the nature of religion among nineteenth-century rabbis and educators, as for the purposes of Jewish education they actively engaged in deliberating the parameters of defining religion and defining Judaism in religious terms. In the context of the Sunday school, an arena that most contemporary observers agreed was dominated by women, the healthy appetite for catechisms afforded authors, most of whom were male, an economically viable genre for publishing their own expositions of modern Jewish theology. Catechisms provided writers with opportunities to make a claim for the importance of philosophical content knowledge that was broadly coded as male within the American Jewish educational curriculum. By adopting the German-style catechism, with its customary opening inquiry "What is religion?," American rabbis and educators made the question of how to define Judaism as a religion not only a theoretical philosophical exercise but central to the knowledge that an American Jewish child was expected to learn in Sunday school.

Catechisms remained the most popular textbooks used in American Jewish Sunday schools until the beginning of the twentieth century. They endured notwithstanding a growing awareness in American public education, as well as in Jewish circles, of the limitations of rote memorization as a pedagogy. The continued popularity of catechisms owed in part to the expedience of the genre for schools that sought to teach a breadth of content knowledge in a limited time frame. Perhaps even more decisive in ensuring the continued popularity of catechisms, however, was the common practice of reciting catechetical questions and answers during confirmation, a ceremony adopted by Jewish Sunday schools during the nineteenth century as an alternative to the bar mitzvah to mark Jewish coming of age. Confirmations offered an array of material, aesthetic, and ritual opportunities to celebrate Judaism's distinctively religious qualities. They emphasized that Judaism was an affective child-centered religion, as well as a philosophical and rational one.

3

How Do You Solve a Problem Like Shavuot?

Clara Lowenberg Moses remembered taking the catechism that she learned in her Sunday school in Natchez, Mississippi, very seriously. As her confirmation class made its way through Isaac Mayer Wise's *Judaism: Its Doctrines and Duties*, Clara examined her conduct, thought about her motives, and "tried to be very good and patient" with her stepmother and younger siblings. For Clara confirmation was the high point of her Jewish education, and she recollected with pride that by the time she was confirmed, she had learned enough Hebrew to translate the book of Genesis and had memorized "beautiful old Hebrew songs" like "Yigdal" and "Ein Keloheinu."[1] Catechisms may have been overly philosophical didactic texts, but they came alive at a Sunday school's annual confirmation ceremony. For Irma Lindheim of New York, confirmation was "the tremendous event of my youth." She recalled, "I felt almost suffocated with wonder and joy at the moment when, before the open ark, my rabbi placed his hands on my head and blessed me. To myself I vowed that my life would be forever dedicated to my people."[2]

Confirmation ceremonies were typically held in late spring or early summer during the holiday of Shavuot. The graduating class of the Sunday school dressed in fine clothes, ceremonially paraded before an elaborately decorated synagogue full of visitors, recited theological answers to questions posed in their catechism, and confirmed their commitment to Judaism. American Jewish newspapers reported on the decorations and festivities in various cities, and magazines published for American Jewish children lauded the holiness of the day. Confirmation, the *Sabbath School Visitor*, a Jewish children's magazine, informed its young readers in 1874, was a "solemn and sacred event in a child's life," when they would be called to show their dedication to Judaism.[3] Confirmation was a ritual that proclaimed loudly and proudly that American Judaism was an aesthetic religion. During their confirmation ceremonies, children performed Jewish religion for a public audience, replete with decorous ritual and highfalutin declarations about Jewish theology. As historian Kathleen Wilson has argued, "Performance enacts what a community imagines to be the most important to its survival, establishing a commerce in images, representations and meanings."[4] For nineteenth-century American Jews, confirmation ceremonies offered a public ritual to perform becoming an adult Jew through initiation into a distinctive set of theologies and a refined tradition of communal worship.

The first Jewish confirmation ceremonies were organized in Germany under the auspices of the nascent Reform movement.[5] Initially held in the home or the school, and reserved exclusively for boys to mark their graduation from Jewish education, confirmation was later moved into the synagogue and extended to include girls.[6] Confirmation, a ceremony popular within Christian religious education, seemed to the reformers to be an attractive ritual to mark the transition of a Jewish child to Jewish adult, one that would be more affective and engaging than the old bar mitzvah. Whereas the bar mitzvah imagined the transition of male Jewish children to Jewish adulthood as occurring through the acceptance of legal obligations, symbolized by reading the Torah and leading public prayers in the synagogue, the operative understanding of Judaism in the German confirmation ceremony was as religion rather than as law.[7] European reformers offered scathing indictments of the bar mitzvah, a ritual they judged "Oriental" not only for its focus on halacha but also for its exclusion of girls.[8] "The position of the female sex, according to existing Judaism, has so much that is unnatural and unfavorable for our times," Abraham Geiger argued in 1837, "that an immediate and sufficient alteration of several existing customs, the reason and meaning of which have already been repudiated by our time, is urgently needed."[9]

American Jews had long marked the end of the school year with public exams that tested children on their knowledge, but in August 1846 Isaac Leeser reported in the *Occident and American Jewish Advocate* that during Shavuot two confirmation ceremonies had been celebrated for the first time on the western side of the Atlantic.[10] On the island of St. Thomas, nine children (three boys and six girls) were confirmed by Morris Nathan. They were examined on their catechisms and "promised obedience to the law of God" by placing their hands ceremonially on the Torah scroll. In New York Max Lilienthal held a confirmation ceremony at the Anshe Chesed synagogue for the children of three Orthodox congregations that he served as rabbi. For six months, twice per week, he had drilled the confirmation class of boys and girls in catechism and the Jewish calendar, and on the day of the ceremony his students showcased the fruits of their learning to fifteen hundred people who had gathered to see what this interesting new ritual was all about. Confirmation, Lilienthal explained during his sermon, was fully in accordance with the strictest rules of Orthodoxy. It was a Reform innovation, but it did not represent an embrace of Reform Judaism.[11] Confirmation did not have to replace the bar mitzvah, he assured; the two coming-of-age ceremonies could happily coexist. Confirmation could be introduced as a supplemental group ceremony for boys and girls, a pleasing addition to the Shavuot festivities that had become quite popular among Jews in Europe and would "appeal to every Jew to rally with heart and soul round the standard of our holy religion."[12]

Isaac Leeser was not convinced by Lilienthal's assurances. As editor of the *Occident,* he not only reported on the latest happenings from New York but also shared his hesitancy to affirm a ritual so closely associated with the European Reform movement.[13] Yet by 1853 even Leeser had to acknowledge that a ceremony in which children proclaimed their religious commitments to Judaism could be profoundly moving, and he confessed that he was forced to wipe away a tear upon watching the confirmation of seven children from local Congregation Rodeph Shalom in Philadelphia.[14] Leeser was uneasy about liturgical innovation, but he was realistic about the limitations of Jewish education in nineteenth-century America. He recognized that the Jewish knowledge that children were required to demonstrate during confirmation was more realistic for the average graduate of a weekday congregational Hebrew school or weekend Sunday school than the demands made by the more traditional bar mitzvah, for which boys were expected to master sufficient Hebrew to lead public prayers and chant from the Torah. In New York the Hebrew reading skills of bar mitzvah boys were so lacking that they could barely muster one *aliyah* (segment) of their assigned Torah readings; when a boy could chant his whole portion, the contemporary press considered the feat newsworthy.[15] In place of fumbling Hebrew, confirmation offered loud and proud statements of Jewish commitment, engaging rituals, and inspiring speeches, with girls invited to the bimah alongside boys.

By midcentury the Reform movement had begun to dominate the American Jewish landscape, and with no qualms about liturgical innovation, Reform synagogues enthusiastically embraced the celebration of confirmation at Shavuot. For the reformers confirmation offered a coming-of-age ceremony that affirmed their cardinal belief that Judaism was a religion that boasted theological truths rather than a legal tradition that demanded ritual observance, and confirmation ceremonies became ubiquitous in American Reform Sunday schools. At the age of twelve or thirteen, boys and girls would confirm their commitment to Judaism to mark the completion of their Sunday school studies, accompanied by pageantry, songs, prayers, and poetry, and audiences of hundreds thronged to see the show. The rabbi took center stage in the proceedings, signifying that under his careful tutelage in catechism a new generation of children had been called to confirm their allegiance to Judaism. During the nineteenth century American Jews devised increasingly lavish and decorous pageantries to mark confirmation on Shavuot as they recognized that a ritual centered on celebrating childhood religiosity could entice an increasingly secular American Jewish population into the synagogue to witness the proceedings. Confirmation performed Judaism as an American religion not only for the purposes of Jewish education but for the benefit of American Jewry writ large.

Teaching Torah in Modernity

Shavuot offered fortuitous timing for a ceremony that celebrated the culmination of a Jewish child's religious education. Typically falling in late spring or early summer, Shavuot coincided with the end of the public school year. Beginning in the 1850s, a ceremony to celebrate youth and childhood during this period became popular within American Protestantism, too. Commemorated with special church services at the beginning of June, Children's Day highlighted the children of a local church and raised funds for Christian religious education at home and abroad.[16] All this seemed to affirm that the beginning of summer marked the proper time to celebrate children and their educational achievements, and Shavuot offered an expedient opportunity on the Jewish calendar for Jews to hold a ceremony of their own. By the 1860s

Jewish communities across the United States had begun celebrating Shavuot as a child-centered holiday focused on confirmations.

Confirmation offered a structured ceremony for a holiday that had always been relatively light on halachic mandates and rituals.[17] Described
in the book of Exodus as one of three holidays in which pilgrimage
to Jerusalem was mandated for diaspora Jews, in the Second Temple
period Shavuot was celebrated as an agricultural festival, marking the
time when the first fruits, the bikkurim, were brought as offerings to the
temple. After the destruction of the Second Temple in 70 CE, the holiday
became primarily associated with the anniversary of the giving of the
Torah on Mount Sinai, yet no specific laws attached to Shavuot inform
celebration of the Torah as a commemorative event. Rather, the holiday
has historically been associated with several minhagim (nonbinding
customs), such as all-night study, consumption of dairy foods, and the
reading of the book of Ruth.

With the advent of modernity, the prominence of the Torah within
Jewish life was elevated by new movements within European Judaism. It was extolled by reformers and cultural Zionists alike as Judaism's premier religious literature. For the reformers the Bible took clear
precedence over the Talmud, a text that the reformers deemed overly
parochial, dominated by esoteric methods of study, and incapable of
facilitating dialogue between Jews and Christians.[18] In Europe contemporary Zionist thinkers shared the reformers' elevation of the biblical
text over the Talmud, albeit while rejecting the Reform premise that the
value of the Torah lay primarily in its religious messages. For Zionists
the Torah was a national text, the foundational document informing the
national consciousness of the Jewish people.[19] Jews in the United States
participated in these movements to anchor modern Jewish life in the
Torah and also drew upon specifically American cultural assumptions
about the Bible as a source of exemplary religious literature. Isaac Leeser's 1853 translation of the Tanakh (Hebrew Bible) into English made a
Jewish Bible available to American Jews with little knowledge of Hebrew
and offered an important alternative to translations of the Old Testament by Christians. Leeser's translation was immediately integrated into
Rebecca Gratz's Hebrew Sunday School in Philadelphia, where moral
lessons drawn from Bible stories were central to the curriculum. Gratz's
focus on the Bible was consistent with traditional Jewish attitudes to

education that regarded the Bible as the preserve of women and younger children—the Talmud and rabbinic literature were reserved for older boys and men. Her fondness for drawing out biblical moral lessons dovetailed equally closely with the conventions of nineteenth-century Protestant women's spirituality, which emphasized that women should teach Bible stories to their children at home.[20] At the Hebrew Sunday School in Philadelphia, students began each weekly session by listening to Gratz narrate the weekly Torah portion, and they read the works of Grace Aguilar, a British Jewish devotional author who lionized the Bible as the cardinal source for women's spirituality, as well as for the education of children.[21]

As the American Jewish Sunday school spread beyond Philadelphia, the Bible remained foundational to its curriculum. At the Sunday school at Congregation Ahawath Chesed in New York, founded in 1864, the curriculum for first-year students was devoted to biblical history and Hebrew, and Bible history remained on the curriculum each year.[22] At Temple Beth El in Detroit the Sunday school taught catechism and biblical history as its two primary subjects. But it "branched out," the superintendent of the school proudly reported to the congregation in 1886, "by giving the youngest pupils easy verses selected from scripture and tries to interest them in the stories of the Bible."[23] Sadie Baer grew up in an Orthodox family in Louisville, Kentucky, but she attended the Saturday afternoon Sabbath school at Louisville's Reform Adath Israel Temple when it opened a class for nonmembers in 1910. She recalled that "biblical history" was the only topic that was taught. "But all of our teachers were wonderful, dedicated people," she remembered. "I really appreciated them so very much because I learned Bible history and learned it well."[24]

Instruction in biblical history remained essential to the curriculum taught in most Jewish Sunday schools throughout the nineteenth century. Yet during this period American Jews were also becoming increasingly cognizant of the challenges posed by new scholarship to claims of the Bible's historical reliability. Under the scrutiny of critical historical research conducted at universities and seminaries, the Torah had been revealed to be a complicated text, authored at different periods in the national life of the people of Israel and subject to their various ideological and religious winds of change. Reform Jews, for whom the Bible was the cornerstone of modern Jewish religion, had particular cause to fear the fruits of the so-called higher criticism. Its piecemeal approach to reconstructing the narrative composition of the biblical text seemed to systematically undermine Reform Jews' conception that the Bible, rather than the Talmud, was the primary source of Jewish religious truth. Isaac Mayer Wise refused to allow the teaching of historical critical methodologies at the Hebrew Union College, and as rising tides of antisemitism emerged in the last decades of the nineteenth century, rabbis wrestled with whether the scholarly study of the biblical ur-text would be "good for the Jews."[25] Solomon Schechter, president of the Jewish Theological Seminary from 1902 to 1915, infamously described higher criticism as "Higher Anti-Semitism," observing that many of its Christian proponents were happy to use its methods to denigrate the Old Testament in particular and Judaism in general.[26]

Beginning in the last decades of the nineteenth century, however, second-generation American Reform Jews began to cautiously embrace historical critical approaches to the Bible, reasoning that they attested to the evolution of Jewish religion over time, thus affirming Reform Jews' belief in the ever-unfolding nature of divine revelation in Jewish history.[27] When Kaufmann Kohler succeeded Wise as head of the Hebrew Union College in 1903, he introduced biblical criticism to the curriculum for training new rabbis, convinced that it offered a methodological tool that was useful for the project of defining Judaism as a "progressive religion," evolving throughout its history into pristine monotheism.[28] "It is foolish and wrong to evade the discussion of vexatious problems of the day," he declared in his inaugural address as president. "You fail to train men of power for the ministry if you ignore or simply condemn the Higher Biblical Criticism and Comparative Religion as detrimental to the faith or to reverence for the Bible."[29] America's rabbis, Kohler recognized, needed to have authority to speak to pressing contemporary concerns, and by the closing decades of the century historical biblical research had garnered popular interest among the laity as American Jews read about its findings in newspapers and journals, heard from its exponents at popular lectures, and debated its teachings in study circles and reading groups.[30]

In the context of a growing American Jewish willingness to accept that the Torah was not revealed in a singular event but was the product of a long historical composition by human hands, confirmation ceremonies served not only as an opportune moment on the Jewish ritual calendar for American Jews to celebrate their children but also offered an attractive logic for continuing to celebrate Shavuot. "The Mattan [giving of] Torah is no longer considered in our Jewish households as a Mattanah [gift]," chided San Francisco journalist Isidore Nathan Choynski under his pen name Maftir in the *American Israelite* in 1885. "Were it not for the confirmations, Mr Shabuoth would be looked upon as a toothless penniless grandfather."[31] For many American Jews, celebrating the revelation of the Torah on Sinai as a singular event seemed incongruous when its composition over time had been exposed by historical scrutiny. Designating Shavuot as the time to celebrate confirmation not only created a Jewish ritual for celebrating educational achievements in early summer but also helped American Jews to reimagine a holiday primarily associated with divine revelation. "During the time of the second temple this festival came to be the memorial day of the Revelation on Sinai," wrote a young Miriam Greenbaum in the notebook she kept during her confirmation classes in Baltimore during the 1890s. "But in modern days it has become the festival of confirmation."[32] Shavuot confirmation ceremonies focused on children to provide a ritual apparatus for continuing to celebrate a biblically rooted holiday that glossed over growing American Jewish discomfort with the origins of the Bible itself. "It is a legitimate matter for speculation," wrote Reform rabbi Max Heller in a 1908 letter to the *American Israelite*, "what would have become of the Feast of Weeks [Shavuot] in the Reform synagog [*sic*] had the festival not been reinforced so effectively by the ceremony of confirmation."[33] Abating the challenge of celebrating the revelation of the Torah by emphasizing that Shavuot fell in the season marked for celebrating youth and childhood, confirmation disassociated Shavuot from its more traditional theological precedents. Yet a rite of passage that called upon young people to affirm their commitments to the distinctive principles of Judaism implicitly maintained the Torah at its center, even while it moved away from celebrating its historical revelation.

Cross-Denominational Appeal

In some communities confirmation was a simple affair, with children called up to the bimah, or tevah, for a short ceremony in which they were examined on their catechism, followed by a speech confirming their commitments to Judaism.[34] Other confirmation ceremonies included full Torah and Haftorah (Prophets) readings by the confirmation class alongside professions of faith and other celebratory rituals. At the Eutaw Place Temple in Baltimore, the confirmation ceremony included an entry procession, floral offering, recitation of personal mottos, removal of Torah scrolls and reading of the Torah and Haftorah with accompanying blessings, a confession of faith made by one confirmand on behalf of the class, and closing hymns and prayers. Similar ceremonies were held by the neighboring Temple Oheb Shalom, by the Madison Avenue Temple, and at the Har Sinai Verein.[35] Isaac Mayer Wise believed that confirmation offered a fitting replacement for the old bar mitzvah, but he wrote regularly in his newspaper, the *American Israelite,* that confirmation should broadly replicate its predecessor, adding to the ceremony rather than subtracting. "We are led by the rule that wherever the old forms are good enough we want no new ones," he explained. "The class conducts the whole service, with all ceremonies, prayers and readings. They recite the prayers, take out two scrolls of the law, observing all concomitant ceremonies, speak in chorus the benedictions, and have thus performed the Bar Mitzvah service in full."[36] Whereas a single bar mitzvah boy generally took the responsibility for leading the prayer service and reading the Torah and Haftorah portions, however, at confirmation responsibility for leading the components of the service was shared by members of the confirmation class. Thus many decades before Judith Kaplan was feted as the first American bat mitzvah, in the nineteenth century girls took on the public role of reading the Torah before their congregations during confirmation.

Under Wise's leadership, the Central Conference of American Rabbis (CCAR) began in 1891 to attempt to standardize a liturgy for confirmation that could be used by Reform congregations across the country. The popularity of the ceremony, Rabbi David Philipson told the conference, had become an "established fact" in American Reform communities, where it was lauded for its "efficacy and beauty."[37] It appropriately

conveyed to young people that Judaism was a religion requiring a pro-
fession of faith and belief. When the first edition of the CCAR's *Union
Prayer Book* was published in 1892, it included, as appendixes, orders
of service for confirmation and marriage, and a Haggadah (the ritual
text of the Passover seder). The ritual committee neglected, however, to
submit the appendixes of the *Union Prayer Book* for prepublication ap-
proval by the conference, and its first editions were ultimately recalled,
at considerable cost, because of numerous objections to its form and
content from factions of the Reform rabbinate.[38] The effort to publish a
uniform confirmation liturgy was not abandoned, but the CCAR ultimately decided that the proper location for such a liturgy was not in the
public prayer book but in a *Minister's Handbook*, a volume that the conference ultimately published in 1912.[39] The *Minister's Handbook* offered
two options for confirmation rather than a single standard liturgy; both
included, in various arrangements, a flower service, examination of the
students' catechism, Torah readings, personal essays or mottos offered
by the confirmands, and a declaration of faith.[40] The liturgies affirmed
Wise's conviction that the confirmation service should broadly mirror
the order of the bar mitzvah, with a Torah reading by the confirmands
central to the ritual.

The popularity of confirmation in nineteenth-century American Judaism extended beyond the Reform movement to congregations that
maintained fidelity to traditional Judaism. Though not without a hint of
self-aggrandizement, Isaac Mayer Wise could remark in 1875 that "the
reform movement in this country, making of the Shabuoth confirmation
day, reinstated it again, and made of it a holiday in the strictest sense of
the term."[41] When the *Jewish Exponent* published an editorial defending the adoption of confirmation on Shavuot by traditional Jews in May
1887, it argued that the ceremony did not symbolize the introduction of
"foreign and incongruous matter" but was a tool to aid "the growth of
that which is most essential and permanent." The piece concluded, "At
thirteen, the Jewish youth was wont to take upon himself the Yoke of
the Law. What else is confirmation but the broadening of this idea to
include both sexes, and placing it at an age more in accordance with our
present conditions? We have nothing in common with those who scoff
at this simple rite."[42] Critics of the confirmation ceremony among traditionalists, however, scorned the adoption of confirmation as nothing

more than a selective appropriation of an essentially Reform innovation. Four months later the *Jewish Exponent* featured a story lampooning this penchant for cross-denominational blending of Jewish ritual; it centered a conversation between two rabbis in which one inquired after the denominational proclivities of a third. "Brother," came the reply, "Rev. Dr Blank is a gentleman well-liked by his constituency. As to his religious tendencies and scholarly attainments, it is best expressed thus: On *Rosh Hashanah* and *Yom Kippur* he is a strict orthodox, on *Shabuoth* he is a radical Reformer, and all the year round he is an ignoramus."[43]

In traditional communities as well as in some Reform congregations, individual bar mitzvahs were celebrated despite the concomitant introduction of a group confirmation. In Cleveland, Ohio, in 1890, Reform Temple Tifereth Israel celebrated five bar mitzvahs and hosted a group confirmation ceremony for the Sunday school's graduating class.[44] William Nathan, born in 1894, was brought up in an Orthodox home in Houston, yet his parents decided to send him to the Sunday school at a local Reform synagogue, Beth Israel, when they saw what they considered to be the antiquated teaching methods at the local cheder. At Congregation Beth Israel he was first bar mitzvah and later confirmed, an experience he found so moving that he went on to teach in the religious school and serve on its board.[45] In Reform congregations the continuation of the bar mitzvah was largely driven by parents who maintained a sentimental attachment to the familiar coming-of-age ceremony. In New York, Reform Congregation Emanu-El's sisterhood, founded in 1887, established three religious schools serving a total of one thousand students a year, most of them children of recent arrivals from eastern Europe. The schools offered classes in Hebrew to prepare boys whose parents wanted them to be bar mitzvah, even though confirmation at twelve or thirteen had been instituted by the congregation. This frequently put the parents at odds with synagogue leaders who maintained an ideological opposition to the bar mitzvah, a ritual they judged to be outdated and "Oriental," seeming to signify that Judaism was out of step with the cultural mores of modern America.[46] At Congregation Emanu-El the board of trustees had recommended in 1876 that individual bar mitzvahs should be abolished because they had been "superseded by the public confirmation on Shabuoth."[47] The parents clearly did not agree. The antagonism between parents who maintained sentimental attachments to the bar mitzvah and proponents of confirmation was symptomatic of deeper tensions between clergy and congregants over control of the American synagogue.[48] It pitted nostalgia for tradition against a program of liturgical reform that saw rejection of the past as integral to adapting Jewish life to modernity. Proponents of confirmation in more traditional communities, on the other hand, could claim to be maintaining the precedent set by Max Lilienthal, who had introduced confirmation to New York's Orthodox Jews in 1846 as an additional, rather than replacement, ceremony. Lilienthal had assured his congregants that confirmation added to, rather than subtracted from, the traditional coming-of-age ritual. It offered a supplemental ceremony that could celebrate the whole senior class of the religious school, girls as well as boys. Traditional congregations began to confirm children on Shavuot not because they wanted to replace the bar mitzvah but because confirmation had popular appeal. It offered a fashionable ritual for synagogues to show off the brightest and the best of their young people.

The Flower Children of the 1860s

Across the American Jewish denominational spectrum, confirmation functioned as Jewish ritual theater. Its celebrations were decadent, its pageantry elaborate, and its decorations often ostentatious. It was common for the contemporary American Jewish press to review and compare the ceremonies held by different synagogues, creating competition to put on the best show. Such elaborate celebrations of confirmation day in Reform and traditional communities alike mirrored a broader trend of elevating holidays in post–Civil War America. Beginning in the 1860s, the red letter days of American Protestantism were celebrated with luxury as America's middle classes enjoyed the fruits of increasing material prosperity.[49] The growing market for consumer culture in the second half of the nineteenth century provided a fertile domain for eclecticism and play.[50] Gilded Age celebrations of Easter Sunday became decadent, fueled by an embrace of religious ritual and a taste for elaborate decoration, with Easter parades of high bonnets, high fashion, and ostentatious floral displays that signified the theological themes of new life and abundance.[51] Christmas was transformed into a holiday associated with gift giving and a time for grand family fetes. Children's

Day brought festive celebrations, flowers, picnics, and souvenir cards depicting cherubic chubby-cheeked youngsters. From the purchase and exchange of Valentine gifts to the designation of Mother's Day as a holiday for children to shower mothers and grandmothers with flowers and trinkets, these commercial versions of the major holidays of American public Protestantism forged a calendar in which celebration—and salvation—were enabled through material objects. Jews participated in these moves toward the material and the aesthetic and attached value to religious spending as consumer culture became wrapped up in the business of American citizenship in general and religious citizenship in particular.[52] Opportunities for leisure pursuits proliferated in the last decades of the nineteenth century with the increasing accessibility of museums, parks, concerts, and theaters. Synagogues and churches alike used elaborate celebrations of holidays to sell the relevance of religion in a world that made multiple claims on the free time and the disposable income of middle-class Americans. Confirmation ceremonies made a bid for Jewish equivalence with bourgeois Christian America too, as Jews invented a pageantry of rituals and a set of distinctive aesthetic cultures to designate Shavuot as a day of grand religious festivity.

The objects of the celebration were, of course, the children being confirmed. Childhood became a widely celebrated object of sentimental and religious attachment in the Victorian era, as Americans sought to masquerade their growing unease with institutional religion.[53] Whereas the dominant discourse of the early republic had conceptualized the child in terms bequeathed by Calvinism, as a creature of original sin, sentimental Victorian conceptions of childhood described children as innocent and pliable, ripe for religious education and introduction into the church.[54] Protestant popular literature encouraged mothers to study the individual characters of their children and nurture their growth and development using the Bible as their guide.[55] The women who founded the American Jewish Sunday school movement were indebted to models established by their Christian contemporaries, and sentimental Victorian ideals of childhood left a lasting imprint.[56] In the late nineteenth century, the transformation of Shavuot into a festival focused on coming of age offered a distinctively Jewish opportunity to celebrate youth and childhood at a time when public fears about Jewish continuity seemed to be escalating. Shavuot traditionally commemorated the giving and receiving of the ancient covenant on Sinai, and when confirmands offered their professions of faith to Judaism and the Jewish community, they performed the ceremonial act of accepting the covenant, not as a set of laws to be obeyed but as a promise to remain within the Jewish fold. In place of the agricultural bikkurim, the confirmands symbolized the new first fruits of the Jewish people, offered up before the assembled congregation.

The roles played by confirmands in their confirmation ceremonies were highly performative. Dressed in fine matching attire, they marched ceremonially through the synagogue's sanctuary carrying flowers that they deposited at the foot of the bimah/tevah or around the Torah in the ark. When called upon to give speeches, confirmands waxed eloquent about their profound commitments to Judaism and promised to fulfill the trust placed in them by parents and teachers. Following a formulaic model, confirmation speeches were deferent, typically beginning by apologizing for being so bold as to speak before the elders of the community and thanking parents for being so benevolent as to attend the ceremony, then proceeding to grandiloquent declarations of dedication to the Jewish people and to the Torah as their moral and spiritual guide. "Beloved parents! For my sake you have left your home, on my account you have left behind your children, in order to be present today when I of my own free will join the great community of Israel," began young Maurice Frankel during his confirmation speech at Kehilath Anshe Ma'ariv Synagogue in Chicago. "You have not striven for me all in vain, your efforts have not been rendered by me utterly futile, for the germ of virtue sewn by you has sunk its roots deeply into my soul, the fear of God which you have taught me to be the highest principle of man and which has so powerfully determined your lives shall be to me a light never to be extinguished."[57]

Music was an important aesthetic tool in the arsenal of nineteenth-century rabbis, and it played a central role in the creation of performative spectacles for confirmation as well.[58] When the American Jewish press reviewed confirmation ceremonies, writers typically drew attention to the performance of synagogue choirs and discussed how music had enhanced the ritual celebration of the confirmands. Synagogues with financial means often employed professional singers, while in other communities choirs populated by children from the Sunday school offered a more affordable means of musical enhancement. Using Sunday school choirs also preserved the Jewish identity of the proceedings.[59] At Congregation Ahawath Chesed in New York in 1867, the school committee asked the congregation's board members to "give their full attention" to encouraging Sunday school students to enroll in music and singing classes organized by the community's cantor so as to "eliminate the inconvenience of seeing alien, non-Jewish singers performing during our services as surely and as fast as possible."[60] Young American Jews who sang in synagogue choirs contributed to the public rituals of their communities and participated in a structured attempt to socialize children into adult modes of participation in the synagogue. By encouraging children to join synagogue choirs, synagogues hoped to defray the cost of hiring singers and to secure the commitment of the young confirmands to congregational life.

By far the most popular aesthetic trend within the performative spectacles created to celebrate nineteenth-century confirmation, however, was floral culture. Flowers were used to decorate sanctuaries, were carried or worn by the students as adornments, and were given by relatives and friends as confirmation gifts. "The Shabuoth festival is the most beautiful of all festivals," remarked the *American Israelite's* Boston correspondent in 1883. It contained none of the "onerous" ritual obligations of other Jewish holidays. "No shofar, no fasting, no succah, lulaf or esrog, no mazoh, maror or cheroses—but flowers, lovely flowers, sweet flowers."[61] Each year at confirmation season, the American Jewish press offered descriptions of the flowers adorning different synagogues that descended into lengthy raptures on their abundance and exoticism. "Never had a more impressive ceremony been witnessed in New Orleans," wrote the *American Israelite* of the Tuoro Synagogue's 1890 confirmation service. "In front of the Ark was a pyramid of ferns, and surrounding it were beautiful and dainty flowers. Large wreaths and flowers were scattered around the platform, and sweet floral emblems lent additional enchantment to the heaven-like scene."[62] In Baltimore, meanwhile, the *American Israelite* reported that the Har Sinai Congregation had been transformed by floral arches that held aloft banners emblazoned with the slogans "Seek the truth" and "Confirmation." The front of the altar was completely hidden by palms and potted plants, and "festoons of green and flowers" were strung along the sides of the synagogue and fanned out from the sanctuary's central chandelier.[63] Synagogues spent lavishly on their Shavuot decorations in honor of confirmation. Temple Beth El in Detroit typically paid five dollars to a local florist when the congregation required flowers for a holiday service or a funeral, but each Shavuot it allotted four times that amount to have the floral company decorate the sanctuary with flowers and blooms.[64] In Pittsburgh in 1899 the Rodef Shalom Congregation spent twenty dollars on flowers to decorate the temple for confirmation day and also made a special request of ten dollars to hire extra singers for the choir.[65]

The use of flowers as decoration for Shavuot was not a nineteenth-century innovation. Sources dating to at least the fifteenth century speak of Jews' adorning synagogues with flowers and greenery during the holiday, based on a midrash (story) that upon the granting of the Torah, Mount Sinai was miraculously carpeted with greens and sweet-smelling blooms.[66] The use of flowers to celebrate Shavuot was also an enduring symbol of the bikkurim, the first fruits offered in celebration of the festival in the days of the temple in Jerusalem. While anchored in traditional precedents, however, the excessive lengths undertaken by American Jews to carpet their sanctuaries with blooms in honor of Shavuot and confirmation day reflected the contemporary cultural capital of flowers and floral culture in the nineteenth century. The use of flowers and plants in wallpaper designs, as decoration on women's clothing and accessories, and in the fashion for women and girls to hold or wear flowers when posing for photographic portraits spoke to the enormous appeal of floral culture in the Victorian era.[67] The commercial flower industry was born in the late nineteenth century and was marketed to America's most affluent. As post–Civil War industrialization led to the creation of a newly expansive demographic class that possessed the means and the resources to purchase luxury goods, so a newly burgeoning horticultural industry promised to fill interior spaces with plants. In domestic settings elaborate displays of hot house flowers offered direct evidence of wealth and status, with elaborate bouquets gracing tabletops, mantelpieces, and sideboards, and ferns and trailing ivy hung artistically from wall hooks and draped across shelves and bookcases. A new romanticized, even spiritualized, domesticity was directed at female consumers to convince them their homes would not be complete without a garden, promoted in contemporary women's magazines as a a Victorian femi-

Figure 3.1. The interior of Kahal Kadosh Beth Elohim, Charleston, South Carolina, Shavuot, 1910. Courtesy of Special Collections, College of Charleston Libraries.

nine ideal.[68] Floral culture became a popular leisure-time activity for wealthy American women and a sure sign of their personal affluence. Americans who wanted to proclaim their investiture as part of the moneyed leisure class could, quite literally, say it with flowers. The use of excessive floral decoration in American Jewish confirmation ceremonies also directly mirrored a turn toward ornamented ritual and beautification within American Protestantism.[69] Whereas at the beginning of the nineteenth century flowers were rare as a form of ecclesiastical decoration, beginning in the 1860s the embrace of ecclesiastical ritual among American Protestants prompted an increasing interest in church floral culture for ornamental as well as symbolic purposes, especially at Easter time.[70] Floral handbooks and specialist magazines such as the *Ladies' Floral Cabinet* fostered the art of church flower arranging, offering practical instruction on arrangements and advice about appropriate blooms for the season.[71] These prescriptive guides to best practices for using flowers as ecclesiastical beautification overwhelmingly made floral culture an area of feminine expertise and deemed it a special contribution of women to the life of the church.[72]

American Jews similarly thought of floral culture as a pursuit associated with the women of the community. As historian Laura Arnold Leibman has shown, flowers loomed large in the material, cultural, and educational worlds of middle-class American Jewish women in the nineteenth century. Women used flowers to practice sketching and painting, and as models for learning botany, and they drew upon the resonances of various floral varieties within Victorian literature for romantic and sentimental purposes.[73] The ornamental use of flowers in nineteenth-century American synagogues was thus indelibly infused with the feminine and signified the increasing presence of women in late nineteenth-century synagogue life. Yet when flowers were incorporated as accessories and decorations within the specific context of Shavuot confirmation ceremonies, there was little that directly denoted their gendered associations. Shavuot confirmation class pictures, for example, frequently show both boys and girls holding bouquets and wreaths. Dress demarcated the primary distinction between the sexes, with boys attired in suits and girls in starched white dresses. Flowers, however, functioned as a gender-neutral accessory.

While floral culture might have been a women's art form and a symbol of feminized domesticity, as a form of symbolic currency it was extended, during Shavuot, to both boys and girls. Flowers were associated with women specifically, but they were also associated with sentimentality in general and the sentimentality of childhood in particular. Floral culture was an evocative art form, one that testified to the beauty of nature and to the careful stewardship of a seedling into a proud bloom. It was a pursuit that could not be divorced from the efforts of women—it was women's hands, after all, that were described in most prescriptive and popular literature as tending to the seedling from its infancy—but its range of signifiers extended beyond gender alone. Flowers represented growth, new life, and the cultivation of natural beauty. Christian churches incorporated extensive floral culture in celebrations of Easter, using teeming bouquets, vines, and wreaths to symbolize the seasonal theological message of new life and resurrection.[74] American Jews eschewed the Christological associations with ritual floral culture at springtime, but like their

Figure 3.2. Eoff Street Temple, Wheeling, West Virginia, confirmation photo, c. 1909. Seated on the far right is a young Jacob Rader Marcus. Courtesy of the Jacob Rader Marcus Center of the American Jewish Archives, Cincinnati, Ohio, at americanjewisharchives.org.

Christian neighbors they embraced flowers as representations of vitality and abundance. When boys and girls celebrated their confirmations in synagogues decorated lavishly with fresh blooms, and posed for celebratory pictures holding bouquets and wreaths, floral culture symbolized the vivacity of the young people who had come of age.

Individual varieties of flowers offered an even more extensive repertoire of sentimental language that could be manipulated for aesthetic and ritual purposes, as in Victorian popular culture various blooms were associated with different emotional and affective dispositions. While only a few of the meanings that were popularly attached to flowers are still well known today—red roses as a symbol of love, for example—in the late nineteenth century the different meanings attached to individual varieties of flowers functioned as a widely identifiable symbolic language.[75] American Jews were cognizant of the symbolisms popularly attached to different varieties of flowers and used different blooms judiciously in Shavuot decorations to create spectacles that sought to amplify the themes of the holiday and elevate qualities associated with childhood. Synagogues often used a wide range of flowers to signify a pantheon of human virtues embodied by the confirmation class. In Kansas City, Missouri, for example, all the boys and girls in the 1890 confirmation class carried a wreath made of one of fourteen varieties of flowers to symbolically highlight fourteen different virtues that the class had pledged to intertwine in their own lives.[76] By including humble wildflowers alongside tropical imports and seasonal blooms, extensive varieties of flowers evoked a range of sentimental associations, and fostered extravagance and luxury as congregations competed to stage evocative and compelling celebrations filled with symbolic resonance. A particularly popular motif to evoke through flowers was that of the purity and innocence of the confirmands, a quality associated with white flowers in general and white lilies in particular. On Shavuot in 1883 the *American Israelite* reported that in Baltimore's Hanover Street Temple the many white lilies "unconsciously awakened the comparison in one's mind between the beautiful white flowers and the innocent children who came to give witness before God and man of their attainments in the teachings of our religion." In Nashville in 1882 white lilies were used to complement an arrangement of decorative white doves.[77] Flowers that had not yet bloomed offered a metaphor for the child on the cusp of flowering into adulthood, and white buds emphasized the purity of the young people about to take their place within the community. At Congregation Keneseth Israel in Philadelphia, confirmation began with the class marching to the bimah carrying white buds that they deposited in the ark surrounding the Torah scrolls.[78] "As we enter God's sanctuary today with these white buds in our hands," the children of Baltimore's Temple Oheb Shalom would recite at the beginning of their confirmation celebrations, "we would have them testify that purity is the purpose and dignity of human life."[79]

Flowers, indeed, were not just decorative ornaments for synagogue sanctuaries or accessories for confirmation photographs but took center stage within the ritual proceedings of the day. The flower service, or flower ceremony, was a popular element of Shavuot confirmation celebrations and in some service leaflets even was used synonymously with confirmation itself. The elementary content of the flower service was the procession of the confirmands through the sanctuary carrying bouquets or wreaths that were ceremonially deposited either on the bimah or at the foot of the ark. "In ancient Israel the first fruits were given as an offering unto the Lord," explained the 1912 CCAR *Minister's Handbook*. "Therefore the confirmants bring flowers to the altar."[80] In *Hymns, Psalms and Prayers*, a supplement to his *Minhag America* prayer book, Isaac Mayer Wise instructed that the flower ceremony should take place as the choir sings a short English-language hymn. The confirmands, he explained, should ascend the bimah, deposit their flowers at the steps leading to the ark, and bow before it.[81] One child then remained alone on the bimah to recite a prayer on behalf of the class: "Graciously accept, O Lord, this feeble token of our childlike devotion," the child would request before comparing the flowers offered by the class to the bikkurim offered at the temple in Jerusalem. "May Thy name be glorified by the holy feelings of our juvenile hearts," the child would recite, "which, like these flowers, we offer up to Thee."[82]

As American Jews invented a pageantry of ritual and aesthetic traditions to accompany the celebration of confirmation, they inevitably drew upon materials and themes that were popular among their Christian neighbors. Confirmation was a ritual adopted and adapted into modern European Judaism from Christianity, and as American Jews developed their own versions of the rite during the nineteenth century, they incorporated stylistic elements from local church ceremonies that celebrated children and childhood.[83] The ceremonial parade of the children through the synagogue carrying floral offerings to beautify the bimah and the Torah echoed the processionals of Christian church services, in which crosses and candles routinely made their way through the congregation before taking their ornamental mantle at the front of the sanctuary. The procession of the confirmation class was, as in Christian contexts, typically set to music as the children made their way through the sanctuary. A popular hymn for the occasion was offered by Joseph Krauskopf, rabbi of Reform Congregation Keneseth Israel in Philadelphia, in a service manual published in 1892.[84] "The Floral Offering" opened by comparing the confirmands to blooming flowers and celebrated youth and childhood.[85] As the hymn progressed, however, it turned away from the familiar themes of flowers, youth, and faith and toward the overtly Christian themes of sin and repentance:

'Tis easier far if we begin,
To fear the Lord betimes
For sinners who grow old in sin
Are hardened by their crimes

It saves us from a thousand snares
To mind religion young;
Grace shall preserve our following years,
And make our virtue strong.

To thee, Almighty God, to Thee
Our Hearts we now resign:
'Twill please us to look back and see
That our whole lives were Thine.[86]

Aside from the almost incidental references to youth, a flower, and "mind[ing] religion young," the hymn included few of the major themes associated with Shavuot in particular or Judaism in general. Krauskopf in fact adopted the text verbatim from the Episcopal Church's 1836 Book of Common Prayer. In churches the hymn was used to celebrate Children's Day and was sung by the children of the parish as they presented flowers to the local bishop.[87] In the context of Jewish confirmation, an adaptation of a ritual borrowed from Christian religious education, it is perhaps unsurprising that Krauskopf would borrow a text from the Protestant canon of liturgical texts. The musical inventories of nineteenth-century synagogues drew upon a common canon of lyrics and melodies shared across American religious movements.[88] Such intercultural borrowing was not an effort to Christianize Judaism per se but an attempt to engage Jews in the synagogue by appealing to the sights and sounds of contemporary American religion.

Opulence and Extravagance

The transformation of confirmation into a theatrical spectacle and a show to celebrate childhood placed the focus of the ceremony squarely on material display. Grand speeches, paid choirs, elaborate floral decorations, and stylized rituals emphasized that confirmation was a performance designed to impress the crowds that gathered to witness the proceedings and not only a ceremony to mark Jewish coming of age. Contemporary critics of confirmation derided its opulence and the fixation on the aesthetic, and questioned whether the children themselves had learned anything from their studies. In notebooks kept during their Sunday school confirmation classes, nineteenth-century confirmands often recorded pages of dictation, but few of their own words or sentiments made it onto the page. Editorial criticisms of confirmation, which by the 1880s had begun to accompany the annual newspaper reviews of a synagogue's ceremony and decorations, frequently observed that the children were the objects rather than the subjects of the spectacle and that they had little understanding of the content of their catechisms or the symbolic valence of their ritual performance. As Isidore Nathan Choynski quipped, "The promises to obey and observe roll as smoothly from the lips of the over-dressed little folks as though they were born actors or preachers, but we all know that in a week from now they will not remember a word of their machine confessions, and we might as well own up that this confirmation business is but a fleeting show."[89]

When confirmands recalled the events of their confirmation in diaries and memoirs, they infrequently remembered the particulars of the ceremony or the commitments that they declared to the congregation. They recounted with considerable detail, however, the gifts that they received and the parties that had been thrown in their honor. Emily Seasongood of Cincinnati was confirmed in 1864, but she was hardly a model Sunday school student. She found the Chumash (Bible) classes too challenging to understand, so she persuaded her father to use his influence as president of the board of the Lodge Street Synagogue to have it removed from the curriculum. When she wrote about her confirmation as an adult, she recalled reciting a poem but more extensively remembered the tables of food laid on for her open-house celebration and the silver filigree bouquet holder and ring that she received from her parents.[90]

Gifts quickly became part of the requisite material culture of nineteenth-century confirmation and inevitably exposed the gradations of wealth among members of a confirmation class. Synagogues labored to popularize various initiatives that attempted to ensure that the day would be celebratory for poor children as well as for their classmates whose parents enjoyed the financial means to purchase gifts and throw lavish celebrations. Beginning in 1903, Rabbi Leo M. Franklin of Temple Beth El in Detroit encouraged the parents of confirmands to host a joint party at the temple to celebrate their children rather than pitting rich parents against poor by holding individual "at home's."[91] William Nathan recalled that his mother organized a fund among the ladies of their Orthodox synagogue in Houston, Texas, to help girls who could not afford new clothes and flowers for confirmation, while at the Hebrew Benevolent Orphan Asylum of Northern New Jersey, money that wards of the institution received from paid employment was saved and presented as confirmation presents, sometimes totaling several hundred dollars.[92]

The expense of confirmation gift giving did not stop at the confirmands but extended to the officiating rabbi as well. While women volunteers typically taught the younger grades in Jewish Sunday schools, in congregational contexts the rabbi taught the confirmation class and was customarily feted during the ceremony with thanks and gifts. In 1866 Gustav Cohen, cantor of Anshe Chesed in Cleveland, confirmed twelve girls and ten boys; their parents thanked him with the gift of "an elegant silver tea service, consisting of eight beautiful pieces, of the latest and most elegant pattern, suitably inscribed."[93] At the Touro Synagogue in New Orleans, the *American Israelite* reported that the confirmation class gave the officiating rabbi for the 1887 confirmation ceremony "a costly set of silver of a peculiar style, such as we used centuries ago."[94] As thanks for confirmation services performed in 1880, at the height of the gold rush, Aron J. Messing, rabbi of the Conservative Congregation Beth Israel in San Francisco, received "a very costly locket." The rabbi was unable to speak upon receipt of the gift, it was reported in the *American Israelite*, for "the locket is of massive gold, with pieces of gold quartz from different mines, and beautifully engraved." In the same year Henry Vidaver, rabbi of Congregation Sherith Israel, also in San Francisco, received "a massive diamond ring." Though the *American Israelite* opined that it was "rather in bad taste" to gift a diamond to a rabbi, "inasmuch as the Rabbi sports diamond studs, the class thought it would please him." As a final note, the reporter added, "Dr Vidaver had the ring stored away, but the rebbetzin, bless her soul, she is fond of diamonds, and will eucher the doctor out of it, you may be sure."[95] It was especially newsworthy when, in 1889, Rabbi Bonnheim of Wheeling,

West Virginia, refused a gift for conducting a service of confirmation. "The confirmation, said he, has become [of] late a burden to parents and friends on account of the pomp and show and unnecessary expense usually connected with the ceremony . . . *extravagance of every kind must be excluded.*"[96]

As parents attempted to outrival each other with the lavish sums they spent on gifts for confirmand and officiant, and congregations devised increasingly spectacular rituals and decorations, by the turn of the century even rabbis who endorsed the ceremony had begun to regretfully observe that its opulence and extravagance detracted from the religious import of the day. Women were common targets for the animus of critics, as mothers were blamed for confirmation's overly materialistic fixations. Women provided the unheralded labor of the American Jewish confirmation industry, particularly in the domestic sphere of shopping and gift giving, and it was women who were blamed when critics determined that confirmation's commercial attachments had become too extravagant and excessive. In June 1887, the *Jewish Exponent* ran a series of acerbic columns satirizing a fictional confirmand named Carrie and her mother, Mrs. Reizenstein.[97] Mrs. Reizenstein, the column explained, "represents the Jewish female element of our society," proceeding to satirize a laundry list of Mrs. Reizenstein's halachic violations and religious insincerity, deriding her fixation with the aesthetic spectacle of confirmation and failure to attend to the actual substance of Carrie's Jewish religious education. The fictional Mrs. Reizenstein was initially reluctant, she shared in the first column, to allow Carrie to be confirmed on account of what she called the "trouble" but relented at the rabbi's insistence that having confirmed twenty children the previous Shavuot, he wished to increase the total this year to a more impressive twenty-five—even though this meant including two children that "were not really fit for it." Mrs. Reizenstein complained that her daughter had been forced to give up Saturday piano and dancing lessons for a whole two weeks to attend the confirmation classes led by the rabbi, the caustically named "Dr. Bugleblauer." But Mrs. Reizenstein was consoled by the promise that Carrie would wear her own favorite diamond pin for the celebration. No confirmation would be complete without an elaborate party, and Mrs. Reizenstein's only regret for Carrie's was that she could not obtain a sufficient quantity of oysters.[98]

The derision leveled at Mrs. Reizenstein was explicitly a gendered one, satirizing the "female element of society" as a violator of halachic norms who conducts commerce on the Sabbath, eats shellfish (which are not kosher), and fixates on the aesthetic and the material. Jewish confirmation ceremonies emphasized aspects of Jewish religion that were popularly assumed to be associated with women—the aesthetic, the affective, and the sentimental—and when it seemed to become clear that the recitation of memorized catechisms and performance of stylized floral ceremonies did little to assure the religious commitments of children into adulthood, women bore the brunt of the animus. In 1903 Henrietta Szold offered a caustic appraisal of Reform confirmation ceremonies that claimed to emancipate the coming of age of Jewish girls but that celebrated a minimal Jewish education consisting of "superficial knowledge" with a ceremony that was roundly derided as a feminine indulgence.[99] Even liberal Jews had begun to express skepticism of the overly consumerist nature of the ceremony by the turn of the century. Confirmation was "a crude and angular bit of ritual," wrote Reform rabbi Max Heller in the *American Israelite* in 1903, "full of awkward self-consciousness, of experimental groping, grandiloquent declaiming, garish ostentation."[100]

Ritualizing Jewish Religion

Despite vocal concerns about the opulence and extravagance of confirmation, however, there was no serious move to broadly consider abolishing it or reinstating the bar mitzvah in most congregational Sunday schools during the late nineteenth and early twentieth centuries. Fears about Jewish continuity stoked support for a ritual that asked the next generation to confirm their attachments to Judaism's distinctive religious principles and demonstrated the equality of Judaism with Christianity so profoundly that Jews could celebrate the coming of age for children in essentially Christian ritual terms. Indeed, accounts of confirmation ceremonies printed in the nineteenth-century American Jewish press customarily highlighted the positive appraisals offered by visiting Christians. The 1889 ceremonies at Congregation B'nai B'rith in Los Angeles were considered so magnificent, for example, that "not only Israelites but visiting Gentiles were impressed with them."[101] In Wheeling, West Virginia, in 1889, the *American Israelite* reported that "many of our best Christian citizens, who were present on the occasion, assert that it was one of the most impressive ceremonies they ever witnessed in any church," and in Nashville, Tennessee, a Christian visitor came to the rabbi after the 1882 confirmation service on Shavuot, to ask, "Why do not all our denominations unite in such a mode of worship as this of tonight? It seems to me the best and only universal way of express-ing the religious feeling of civilized society."[102] When the contemporary non-Jewish press published reports from Christians who visited syna-gogues, reporters typically highlighted what Christians found wanting in Jewish ritual practice.[103] American Jews seeking middle-class respect-ability were sensitive to the perception of the public performance of their religion to outsiders, and confirmation offered an opportunity to emphasize the ritual splendor and middle-class aesthetics of American Jewish religion to their Christian neighbors.

Confirmation ceremonies offered extravagant material display, the-atrical rituals, and sentimental celebration of childhood to state loudly and proudly that Judaism was a religion not only theologically but also aesthetically. These ceremonies invoked themes traditionally associated with Shavuot at springtime while also drawing upon a repertoire of sym-bolisms from nineteenth-century American popular culture to create a new child-centered holiday celebration. Just as American Christians embraced elaborate ritual and consumer goods during the Victorian era to underscore the continued relevance of religion in modernity, so too did nineteenth-century American Jews seek to celebrate Jewish religion through an embrace of the material, through pageantry, ritual, and the sentimental celebration of childhood. The nineteenth-century confirma-tion ceremony was not only a rite of passage to Jewish adulthood. It also functioned as a mode of cultural performance, grounded in the material and visual vernaculars of contemporary consumer culture.[104] Confirma-tion ritually and performatively proclaimed the essential lesson of the American Jewish Sunday school: that Judaism was first and foremost a religious tradition. In spectacular theatrical form, it celebrated Jewish coming of age as the ritual acceptance of its distinctive religious message.

4

Expanding the Educational Marketplace

The embrace of consumer culture in American Jewish Sunday schools was not limited to celebrations of Shavuot and confirmation. During the last decades of the nineteenth century, attempts to enliven Sunday school education created a marketplace of Jewish educational objects and a consumer economy for teaching and learning about Judaism. Some of these innovations were brought to Jewish Sunday schools by women who had trained at normal schools and sought to bring new pedagogical best practices from public education into Jewish learning. Others were attempts to replicate popular models from the marketplace of Christian religious education. Magazines, teaching aids, and illustrative objects were marketed to Sunday school superintendents as products that would enhance the understanding and engagement of their students and compensate for the deficiencies of their volunteer teachers. They were marketed to children too, promising to provide entertainment alongside education and an initiation into a nationwide network of Jewish youth. Alongside the theological lessons taught in their catechisms, nineteenth-century American Jewish children were presented with a marketplace of Jewish educational resources that taught that American Jewish religion also required consumer participation. Their teachers, meanwhile, learned that if Jewish religious education was to be successful, it would require a marketplace of signature products to bring its lessons to life.

The expansion of a marketplace of technologies for Jewish learning marked a sharp departure from the first days of the Hebrew Sunday School in Philadelphia, held in makeshift quarters with materials adapted from Christian religious schools. It represented a growing sense that successful religious education would depend on professionalized material resources and not solely on volunteer teachers who were enthusiastic about Jewish religious learning. The expansion of the American Jewish educational marketplace in the years following the Civil War paralleled broader American trends toward spending, the acquisition of consumer goods, and the emergence of a consumer market focused on children. While Americans at the beginning of the nineteenth century took a generally dim view of excessive leisure for children, beginning in the 1870s an expansive array of toys and accoutrements for child-rearing were marketed as essential for the modern American child. In 1875 Macy's opened its first toy department, and popular advertising began to depict Christmas as a season for giving gifts to children around a lavishly decorated tree.[1] American Jews sought to replicate the consumer goods developed for use by American Christian children and borrowed Christian models that seemed applicable to Jewish life. In fashioning a consumer market for Jewish learning in America, Jews sought to emphasize that Judaism was a material religion as well as a theological one.

Home from Home

When Esther Weinstein, a third grader from Goshen, Indiana, wrote to the *Sabbath Visitor* magazine in February 1891, she wanted to be sure that its readers learned all about her hometown. Goshen was the "prettiest little town in all of Indiana," she wrote, with more than six thousand inhabitants, broad shady streets, beautiful houses, and four nice brick schoolhouses. The town was home to twenty-five Jewish families and had built a "very nice" synagogue. Esther attended her local public school, and she went to Sabbath school twice a week, where she learned Hebrew, Bible history, and catechism. "I do think it is very nice to know something about our holy religion," she wrote in conclusion. "If you print this letter, I will try to write more in the future."[2]

Between 1871 and 1910 at least nine magazines were launched for Jewish children in America. They fused the domestic and the pedagogical to teach lessons in Jewish religious citizenship using a medium ostensibly styled as light entertainment. Jews participated in a nationwide trend for serialized print media that boomed in the United States in the middle of the nineteenth century. New printing technologies increased the volume of pages that could be printed at once, revolutionizing the printing business, and developments in transportation made periodicals widely accessible.[3] An American Jewish publishing industry with national reach emerged at midcentury with the founding of a series of monthly periodicals, beginning with Isaac Leeser's *Occident and American Jew-*

ish Advocate in 1843 and Isaac Mayer Wise's *Israelite* in 1854. Publishing houses like the Bloch Publishing Company (founded 1855) and the Jewish Publication Society (founded 1888) published books, magazines, and other ephemera for national distribution.[4] The authors and publishers of literature for American Jews sought to provide edifying Jewish content and forge bonds between fractured Jewish communities through the common culture of print.[5]

In the 1820s the Christian Sunday school movement began to sponsor magazines for children that incorporated Christian themes and shared didactic content. By the 1870s children's periodical literature had cultivated its own independent industry, with magazines like the *Youth's Companion* and *Juvenile Miscellany* becoming national institutions.[6] Enterprising Jewish educators and publishers saw the potential of periodicals for Jewish educational literature.[7] The *Youth's Companion* and *Juvenile Miscellany* rarely featured content about Jews and Judaism, and their columns were saturated with Christian theological themes and images. In magazines published specifically for Jewish children, stories about Jewish characters could socialize American Jewish children into a cultural world where Jews were the heroes and heroines of every tale. Stories from religious literature could serve a more explicitly didactic purpose, paraphrasing biblical and rabbinic legends in prose comprehensible to children. Monthly editions could highlight the Jewish calendar with content that celebrated Hanukkah rather than Christmas in December, Passover rather than Easter in springtime.

The Jewish children's magazine industry emerged alongside the Jewish Sunday school movement. The first periodical for American Jewish children, called *Young Israel,* was founded in 1871 by the New York Jewish Orphan Asylum. It was a subscription-based periodical that was advertised both for individual purchase and bulk order by Sunday school superintendents and teachers. Approximately half of its content was devoted to fiction, the remaining half included articles on Jewish holidays, news about Jewish life around the world, and reprints of rabbinic lectures.[8] It was followed by the *Hebrew Sabbath School Companion*, published in Cincinnati from 1872 to 1873; *Sabbath Visitor (later Hebrew Sabbath School Visitor* and then the *Visitor)*, published from 1874 to 1899; *Jewish Youth*, published by Sam Steinberg of Indianapolis beginning in 1894; *Sabbath School Companion*, published in Charleston,

South Carolina, for one year, 1895–96; *Helpful Thoughts*, published in New York from 1897 to 1905 (titled *Jewish Home* from 1903); *Hebrew Watchword and Instructor*, published in Philadelphia from 1896 to 1898; *Young Israel*, published in Detroit from 1907 to 1911; and *Young Judean*, a magazine published by National Young Judea in New York beginning in 1910.[9]

For children in towns without a synagogue, or whose parents decided not to affiliate with the organized Jewish community, the didactic content of children's periodicals offered Jewish education independent of a bricks-and-mortar classroom. Rose Brown, born in Colorado in 1888, did not attend her local Jewish Sunday school. Jewish holidays were infrequently observed in her family, though she always enjoyed the Christmas tree and Christmas presents that appeared in her home in December. Her Jewish education came from *Helpful Thoughts*, and Brown's favorite column was "Know Your Bible," which encouraged readers to submit answers to questions about biblical history to earn rewards. "To this day," she recalled in 1970, "I can turn exactly to any event or saying without too much study. This was a great asset in the early days in that I won quite a few prizes."[10] Periodicals offered a leisure-time Jewish education for children growing up in an otherwise Christian world. Stories and articles serialized in monthly or weekly installments encouraged annual subscriptions and kept young readers waiting eagerly for the latest edition of their favorite periodical to arrive in their mailboxes. In a letter printed in the March 1874 edition of the *Sabbath Visitor* magazine, a young Louis Helbrun wrote that he gained all his religious instruction from the periodical and offered copies to his non-Jewish friends when they made attempts at proselytizing him with Christian publications.[11]

The letters page, fronted by "Cousin Sadie," was a regular feature of the *Sabbath Visitor*. Opening each column with a few words about the season, Sadie promised that she always wanted to hear from her young cousins and encouraged them to share news from their local Sunday schools. The letters page of the magazine *Young Israel*, founded in 1907 by the Union of American Hebrew Congregations (UAHC), similarly encouraged children to use their free time write to "Cousin Judah," who promised that he was "always glad to find new relatives." Describing the children who would read the magazines as one large family of cousins, the *Sabbath School Visitor* and *Young Israel* painted an imaginative portrait of American Judaism as a familial enterprise and of Sunday school education as an experience that the entire family participated in. Both magazines featured "News of the Religious Schools" columns that perpetuated this creative fiction, publishing short descriptions and anecdotes from schools listed by city that emphasized their similarities and common missions. Superintendents of local Sunday schools fiercely resisted regulation by parent bodies like the UAHC, and in almost all cases American Jewish Sunday school education was a localized endeavor. In children's periodicals editors sought to paint an imaginary network of American Jews united in a common educational pursuit, even if the resources for the task might be unevenly distributed.[12] Nine-year-old Jennie Beitman, who wrote to Cousin Sadie from Washington, Indiana, in July 1886, reported that her town had just eight Jewish families, while in the same issue a letter from Ida Solomon in Columbus, Georgia, boasted of a thriving community with forty Jewish families, a synagogue, and a Sabbath school that hosted grand annual confirmation ceremonies.[13] In their letters children enthusiastically shared information about their home towns, favorite school subjects, Jewish communities, and Sunday schools, painting a portrait of Jewish communal life across America shaped by the special interests of its youngest members.

In the pages of their periodicals, American Jewish children would find biblical narratives paraphrased for child readers, introductory explanations of Jewish holidays, and tales from Jewish history. Editors sought to provide children with a basic knowledge of Jewish theology and calendar and socialize them into a world of Jews past and present. Woven throughout were didactic messages about the importance of good deportment and conduct and models of ethical behavior that readers were encouraged to emulate. American Jewish children's periodicals emphasized that learning to be a Jew required cultivating good character and exemplary morals as well as developing an understanding of Jewish theology, calendar, and rituals. The good Jewish child described in Jewish youth periodicals dovetailed with the paradigm of the model child imagined in contemporary Christian children's magazines: orderly, attentive, studious, and virtuous. Serialized stories wove tales about good Jewish children who attended Sunday school and were rewarded with treats and unanticipated fortune, while bad children neglected their religious duties and were punished by unexpected sickness and failing grades. In Europe contemporary magazines and periodicals published for Jewish children were an extension of Jewish youth movements. They typically foregrounded Jewish ideological education, inculcating children in the rudimentary principles of Bundism, Zionism, and Hebrew language and literature. All this was conspicuously absent from the periodical literature produced by their American coreligionists. In its stead was a healthy dose of moral education that emphasized that in America, Judaism was a religion of ethics and theology rather than the ideology of a national people.

Educators and editors who produced periodical literature for American Jewish children adroitly manipulated a literary genre that was associated with leisure-time reading as well as with formal pedagogical settings to encourage their young readers toward civilized conduct at home as well as Jewish erudition in the classroom. The *Sabbath Visitor*, a four-page illustrated periodical, expertly weaved between the worlds of school and home to remind children that learning to be a good American Jew meant memorizing Sunday school lessons, improving their manners, and perfecting their conduct. The "Visitor," a pseudonym for the magazine's first editor in chief, Max Lilienthal, appeared frequently in the magazine's stories and didactic tales, an omnipresent teacher for both the fictional children within the magazine as well as the actual child reader.[14] In the imaginary worlds of the stories, the eponymous Visitor appeared at Sunday school as well as to children in their homes, nimbly describing the work of religious education as a joint domestic and communal project, one that the Visitor served as an aide. As Lilienthal wrote in his opening column: "Welcome, thrice welcome, my dear good children! How pleased I am to find you all regularly attending your Sabbath school! How glad I am to see you all so orderly, so attentive, so anxious to learn. . . . Good children ought to be rewarded. And therefore I have resolved to visit you every Sabbath morning, and bring you a nice paper full of instruction and amusement. We shall talk together about our sacred Jewish religion."[15] The paradigmatic child who would receive a call from the *Visitor* was always hungry for religious and ethical instruction, not only in school but also at home.[16] Stories in two of the *Sabbath Visitor's* regular columns, "Little Uncle Sam" and "Little Nellie's Catechism," regularly depicted their protagonists learning good conduct by misbehaving and being reprimanded for their errors, raising money for orphan asylums, exhibiting shows of charitable behavior to classmates, or helping parents with chores. "Education," as the *Visitor* explained in the July 1874 edition, "does not commence with the alphabet. It begins with a mother's look; with a father's nod of approbation or a sign of reproof; with a sister's gentle pressure of the hand, or a brother's noble act of forbearance."[17] During his visits to homes and classrooms, the *Visitor* promoted moral virtues through simple and accessible paraphrases of biblical texts, rabbinic legends, and tales from Jewish history, as well as original stories and poems.

Jewish children's magazines were marketed to individual readers in search of edifying and entertaining content, as well as to superintendents and teachers in search of material to incorporate into their Sunday school lessons. The *Sabbath School Companion*, published monthly from 1895 to 1896 "in the interest of the Sabbath School and Bible class" by Barnett Elzas, rabbi of Beth Elohim in Charleston, South Carolina, provided eight pages of stories, poems, and ethical reflections directed at children, as well as reflections on Judaism and Jewish education for teachers, all arranged in a changing set of "departments." Adopting the parlance of public school organization, the division of periodicals such as the *Sabbath School Companion* into departments blurred the boundaries between leisure and learning. Didactically organized periodical literature provided ready-made instructional material for Jewish Sunday school classrooms and was promoted as a helpful resource for the school's volunteer teachers. The materials were also prescribed for students with few connections to Judaism outside the Sunday school. At Congregation B'nai Israel in Galveston, Texas, the superintendent of the Sunday school noted in 1903 that 82 of the school's 167 pupils came from families who were not members of the synagogue. To increase the Jewish knowledge of these less-affiliated students, he reported, copies of a Jewish magazine had been circulated through the school during the year. "Through its good reading matter and influence in the household," the school board noted, it was sure to achieve its mission.[18]

When the Union of American Hebrew Congregations launched a children's magazine, *Young Israel,* in 1907, it hoped to entice Sunday schools to become regular subscribers. From the UAHC's inception it had endeavored to sponsor the production of new literature for American Jewish Sunday schools, but its attempts to promote new textbooks had garnered only limited success. In 1884 the UAHC incorporated the Hebrew Sabbath School Union of America (HSSUA) as its education committee, and launched a new initiative to fund textbook production by charging UAHC affiliated congregational Sunday schools five cents per enrolled student per month to join the organization, with the promise that the school would receive textbooks published by the UAHC. By 1894 few congregations had joined the scheme, and the HSSUA had sponsored only three books and two pamphlets.[19] "As far as we can see," wrote Rabbi Barnett Elzas in the *Sabbath School Companion*, "the only thing that would accrue to a school [by] joining the union is that it would morally obligate itself to purchase a number of textbooks of doubtful value, at a tolerably big price."[20] With little congregational investment, the HSSUA was disbanded in 1905 and replaced with the Department of Synagog [*sic*] and School Extension with a mission to "organize throughout the United States, Congregations and religious schools, primarily in communities where there are no Jewish congregations or religious schools."[21] The department started *Young Israel* two years later.[22] *Young Israel* was an ambitious weekly thirty-two-page magazine, offered at just a dollar per year to subscribers.[23] In his opening column, editor in chief George Alexander Kohut promised his readers that the magazine would teach them "to become good Jews and Jewesses." Of course, it would also include stories, poems, and jingles "to delight boys and girls of all ages," as well as weekly "Sabbath School News" columns, and a "Letter Box," in which "all letters that bring a bright, cheery message" could be assured of publication., But the mission of the magazine was to instruct, not just to entertain, to "tell Jewish children all over the country what they ought to know about the things that are beautiful and uplifting in the Jewish faith and in Jewish character, and to make them feel that it is an honor and a glory to be part of a people who have wrought so much good for all mankind." Readers might acquire all sorts of new knowledge in their public schools during the week, Kohut explained. But they should read *Young Israel* and go to Sunday school to learn religion. "In the daily school," he concluded, "we learn useful things; in the religious school, we are to obtain the Light by which to be guided in using them."[24] Alongside jokes, stories, puzzles, and games, the magazine included departments that offered lesson plans for Sunday school teachers synchronized to the Jewish calendar, summaries of key events in Jewish history, primers of classical Jewish texts, reviews of new Sunday school textbooks, and an explicitly didactic "hints to teachers" feature. By 1911, however, it had garnered only twenty-five hundred subscribers.[25]

The financial health of American Jewish children's periodicals was always precarious, and running advertisements inevitably became unavoidable as the revenue was needed to keep publications afloat. When the *Sabbath Visitor* began publishing in 1874, advertisements were restricted to other publications published by the magazine's parent company, Bloch Publishing. By June 1881, however, the *Sabbath Visitor*'s young readers would find that their puzzles were printed alongside a half-page ad for Dr. Clark Johnson's Indian Blood Syrup, and on the letters page they would read that a Mrs. M. Frazell of Seymour, Indiana, had been "attacked with severe pains in my stomach . . . but then I tried Dr. Clark Johnson's Indian Blood Syrup, which immediately relieved me."[26] Jarringly juxtaposed with juvenile stories, letters, and joke columns, the advertising in nineteenth-century periodicals for American Jewish children routinely promoted domestic and commercial goods that seemed to have little relevance to the lives of children.[27] 's The September 1872 edition of *Young Israel, published by the* New York Hebrew Orphan Asylum, included a half-page of advertising for women's undergarments, as well as pages advertising the Hamburg America Line (a steamship company), real estate brokers, and attorneys at law.[28] Thirty-five years later, the first edition of the UAHC's *Young Israel* in November 1907 included Hanukkah readings, stories, and poems printed alongside four full pages of advertising targeted to readers' parents. Children reading the magazine would learn not only about the life of Judah Maccabee but also that the Union Central Life Insurance Company in Cincinnati could boast $58 million in assets, that Weber offered a combined pianola and piano for sale, that the Mosler safe company offered the largest and most complete safeworks in the world, and that Belding Spool's silk thread was the "first requisite of good work."[29] Advertising in children's periodicals offered aspirational images of domestic affluence. Promotions for safety-deposit boxes implied that the reader should own sufficient material wealth to necessitate secure storage, while the Weber pianola-piano advertisement offered to accept payment in installments so the upwardly mobile American Jew could acquire a domestic trophy prized in genteel circles at the turn of the century.[30] While advertising in the nationally distributed *Young Israel* of 1907 focused on domestic and consumer goods available for purchase in various locations, periodicals that targeted local markets offered regional images of the American Jewish good life. The *Sabbath School Companion,* published in Charleston, South Carolina, turned over its entire front page to consumer advertising. Children, parents and teachers reading the March 1896 edition would learn where in Charleston to find the best steam laundry for summer suits, how to get wedding invitations engraved, and that "Ben Rice of 504 Meeting Street respectfully informs the Jewish public that matzoths, kosher sausage, beef, tongues etc for the coming Passover were available at the lowest market price." Directed principally at the adult consumer of children's magazine literature—parents, teachers, and Sabbath school superintendents—advertising in the periodicals marketed for Sunday school education nevertheless embroiled Jewish children in a world of commerce. While they were learning to be good Americans and model students through the magazine's didactic literature, children were also inducted into capitalist consumption as a mode of Jewish American citizenship, a world full of companies with Jewish names and taglines directed at a Jewish consumer market.[31] Photographs and sketches illustrating goods for sale showed even the youngest student what a properly ordered American Jewish home should look like, creating economies of aspiration for children as well as for their parents and teachers.

While advertising served the implicit mission of civilizing Jewish children to become genteel consumers of domestic and commercial goods, it was first and foremost a raw necessity to ensure the economic viability of Jewish children's periodicals in a market that proved to be particularly precarious.[32] Subscribers always seemed few and far between, and editors complained that they could not succeed in their work without the financial support of the community at large, and especially bulk subscriptions by sabbath school superintendents. Of the nine magazines begun between 1871 and 1910, only four were able to remain in print for more than five years. The market for individual subscribers was relatively small, limited to families with sufficient disposable income to purchase magazines for their children—as well as sufficient interest in purchasing didactic Jewish children's literature rather than more popular alternatives such as the *Youth's Companion.*[33] In 1900 editor Julia

Richman noted that the editorial team of *Helpful Thoughts* was pleased with its progress and its influence but that the publisher was dissatisfied with the financial returns and the reluctance of most Sunday school authorities to commit to a subscription. Forecasting the likelihood that "in a few years *Helpful Thoughts* may go the way of all Jewish juvenile periodicals," she noted that the failure to support the Jewish children's magazine publishing industry through subscriptions was a "sad commentary upon the mistaken and short-sighted policy of Jewish Sunday school boards."[34]

Prizes and Paraphernalia

The publisher to which Julia Richman referred in her—sadly prescient—prediction of the demise of *Helpful Thoughts* was Bloch. Founded in Cincinnati in 1855 by Edward Bloch, brother-in-law of Isaac Mayer Wise, the company was indelibly linked to the moderate wing of American Reform Judaism, publishing numerous works by Wise, including his newspaper, the *American Israelite*, as well as liturgies and hymnals.[35] The birth of the Sunday school movement in 1838 opened a new market for Jewish educational publishing in the United States, and Bloch dominated with some of the first age-appropriate texts designed for American Jewish children.[36] Beginning with adaptations of European volumes, Bloch went on to publish Sunday school textbooks written in America as well as two periodicals: the weekly *Sabbath Visitor* and the monthly *Helpful Thoughts*. As historian Jonathan Sarna has observed, the company was utilitarian in its approach to Jewish publishing; reputedly Charles Bloch "considered favorably any manuscript which in his judgment would yield him a profit."[37] By the 1870s Bloch had moved into publishing miscellaneous educational Hebraica, including catechisms and confirmation certificates.

Bloch's preprinted confirmation certificates were embossed with gold decorations and seals and featured an inset illustration of a group of children in elaborate dresses and starched suits receiving a confirmation blessing before an elaborate ark, or hekhal. The certificate had space for the student's name and the signatures of the president, secretary, and rabbi of the congregation, as well as for the student to inscribe the personal motto they pledged during the ceremony. The line for the date included preprinted first numerals of the year according to both the Hebrew and Gregorian calendars, symbolizing fidelity to both the Jewish calendrical tradition as well as American cultural norms. The confirmation certificates published by Bloch mirrored the trend for decorous illustrated certificates printed for Christian confirmations, and they directly copied the style of the preprinted short ketubahs (marriage certificates) that Bloch published for use in American Jewish wedding ceremonies.[38] New printing technologies developed in the second half of the nineteenth century made it possible to produce images with intense color, and imagery became ubiquitous in consumer packaging as well as popular literature.[39] Bloch took full advantage of these innovations to market Jewish life-cycle products that commemorated special occasions with decorative keepsakes, albeit ones that deferred more to the conventions of contemporary visual culture than to any halachic requirements around coming of age or marriage.

Bloch's decorative confirmation certificates were part of a broad spectrum of material incentives and rewards that became part of the commercial landscape of Jewish Sunday school education in the nineteenth century. Prizes for good performance and regular attendance were popular and associated religious learning with material returns. American Jews followed a well-established practice within Protestant religious education, where books, religious ephemera, treats, and reward tickets redeemable for tracts and Bibles were commonly awarded to students to encourage attendance and reward good behavior and diligent scholarship. *Eddy's Tickets*, a tract published by the General Protestant Episcopal Sunday School Union in 1864, encouraged parents to adopt the Sunday school ticket method at home to incentivize good behavior and to reward children with new Bibles when they had collected fifty tickets.[40] Sunday school prizes and tickets immersed children in economic principles deemed virtuous by promoters of Sunday schools and publishers of Sunday school literature, linking consumerism with piety and teaching children that good religious behavior brought material rewards.[41]

Jewish children were susceptible to the trinkets proffered by the Christian Sunday schools, and Jewish teachers quickly surmised that children would be lured into local churches if the Jewish schools did not offer comparable material incentives. Rebecca Allen, superinten-

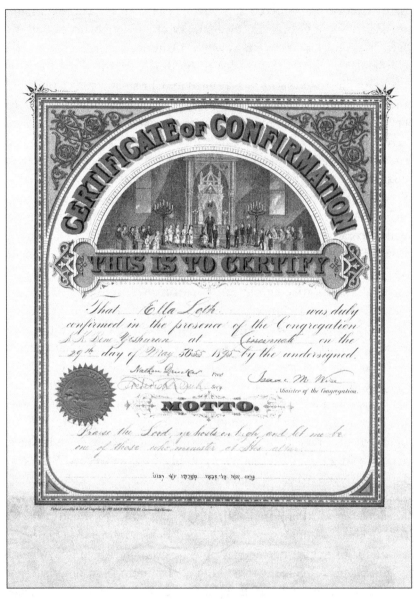

Figure 4.1. Decorative confirmation certificate published by the Bloch Publishing Company and used in the confirmation of Ella Loth in Cincinnati, Ohio, 1895. Courtesy of the Jacob Rader Marcus Center of the American Jewish Archives, Cincinnati, Ohio, at americanjewisharchives.org.

dent of the Hebrew Sunday School in Philadelphia, observed in 1898 that "prize giving is the great feature of the closing day. The influence exerted in countering the Christian missions is incalculable. No other method could accomplish it."[42] Jewish children who saw their Christian peers rewarded with prizes for attending Sunday school would come to resent their Jewish heritage, educators feared, if Jewish children were not offered similar rewards. "The Jewish child of the small town can not comprehend why she is not permitted to dress up each Sunday in all of her pretty furbelows that her neighbor does and trip off to Sunday school, returning with a pretty picture card that means so much to the childish heart," explained Josephine Grauman Marks, a Jewish Sunday school teacher in Georgetown, Kentucky.[43]

At the Hebrew Sunday School founded by Gratz in Philadelphia, students were initially rewarded for academic achievement and good conduct with prizes that were primarily didactic. At the school's annual examination in the spring, Rosa Mordecai recalled, "the first prize was always a Bible; or rather, a Bible and two books were given to each class. These books were most carefully selected by Miss Gratz herself, and handed by her to each child with a kind, encouraging word, often with a written line on the flyleaf."[44] During the school year good conduct and academic prowess were rewarded with colored tickets that could be exchanged for books or items made by the teachers, such as the Ten Commandments inscribed on silk or a hand-illustrated psalm.[45] Later on, new printing technologies helped to enlarge the supply of didactic gifts that could be awarded to children. In 1866 Isaac Leeser announced in the *Occident and American Jewish Advocate* that the Ten Commandments and "The Creed" (likely Maimonides' Thirteen Principles) had been stereotyped and printed on cards that could be sent "to any part of the world" for fifty cents and forty-eight cents, respectively.[46]

As the Jewish Sunday school spread beyond Philadelphia, prizes and trinkets became more frivolous. At Kahal Kadosh Beth Elohim in Charleston, South Carolina, in 1878, thirty children received books, games, and toys to celebrate the end of the Sunday school year. According to a local correspondent for *American Israelite*, it was "a rare treat to see the faces of the children as they arose to receive the reward of their labors."[47] At Rodef Shalom Congregation in Pittsburgh, the board awarded the school committee forty dollars to purchase candy to celebrate examination day in 1884.[48] At the Jewish Sunday school of Lafayette, Louisiana, in May 1891, Clara O. Bloom was awarded a gold lead pencil for achieving the highest standards of scholarship and conduct in the school, and by July 1897 the top graduates of Philadelphia's Hebrew Sunday School were being rewarded with cash prizes as well as homemade didactic treats.[49]

The toys, cash rewards, and expensive souvenirs awarded to Sunday school students were often donated by members of the local community, especially in the case of free schools and mission schools founded in the 1880s to serve the children of new Jewish immigrants. At a meeting to develop a constitution for the Hebrew Free School in St. Louis in 1880, it was decided that the curriculum should be "confined to instruction in the rudiments of the Hebrew language and the religious faith and customs of the Jews," and it was suggested that prizes might encourage children to attend, as many of them lived far from the site proposed for instruction. Immediately, one of the officers offered ten dollars in gold as a prize for the best scholar in attendance and deportment, a proposal that was greeted with enthusiastic applause.[50] Philanthropic donations to a Sunday school prize fund both supplied handsome rewards for its students and established Sunday school education as a community endeavor in which local philanthropists were celebrated as promoters of religious learning. Solomon L. Cohen donated $100 for prizes to be awarded to the students of the Sunday school at Congregation Shearith Israel in New York in 1876 and was thanked in the *Jewish Messenger* with the hope that "he and all others will continue to show such a lively interest in, and support of the Sunday school connected with the Congregation."[51]

Medals were a common prize for graduates and high achieving scholars in American Jewish Sunday schools and mirrored the awards given in the public schools for academic performance.[52] "For the promotion of learning among the pupils of its religious school," recorded the board of Congregation Beth Israel in Houston in April 1904, two gold medals were to be commissioned each year, one for the pupil making the greatest advances in the study of the Hebrew language, the other for the pupil making the greatest advances in the study of Bible.[53] In Charleston, South Carolina, Herbert A. Moses was awarded a merit medal when he celebrated his confirmation in 1891. At Beth Elohim prizes were awarded

Figure 4.2. Confirmation medal awarded to Herbert A. Moses,
Kahal Kadosh Beth Elohim, Charleston, South Carolina, 1891.
Courtesy of Special Collections, College of Charleston Libraries.

as part of the confirmation ceremony, after the children had recited their
mottos and before the closing hymn. These were elaborate military-
style medals cast in bronze and gold with a decorative star tinged in two
shades of blue. The medals reified the achievements of the grade's top
scholars, suggesting that achievements in the Sunday school were on par
with those of the armed forces as well as the public schools.

Gifts and prizes were also a popular feature of Sunday school Hanukkah celebrations. As Christmas became increasingly celebrated with the
giving of gifts to children in the years following the Civil War, American
Jewish leaders emphasized the importance of offering Jewish children
comparable experiences in specifically Jewish contexts. They encour-

aged women who volunteered in American Jewish Sunday schools to organize grand Hanukkah celebrations featuring entertainments and treats, ceremonial candle lighting, and gifts for their students.[54] At Temple Israel in Boston in 1876, each child enrolled in the religious school received a toy to celebrate Hanukkah and was treated to an elaborate party, while at the Willson Avenue Temple in Cleveland in 1899, female volunteers organized an entertainment for nearly one thousand children that featured "beautiful marches, unique drills, pantomimes, dialogues, songs," and of course, the kindling of the Hanukkah lights.[55]

While gifts and prizes were understandably popular among Sunday school students, however, educators worried that material incentives to promote Jewish education constituted little more than outright bribery for the cause of religious learning. Prizes "weakened the moral nature of children by purchasing their attention," Sunday school teacher Mathilda Lemlein told the Jewish Chautauqua Society in 1899, while a correspondent for the *Jewish Messenger* complained the Sunday school "defeats the very purpose of a religious school by multitudinous prizes and certificates . . . it arouses the vanity of children and feeds their pride by 'exhibitions' and public displays."[56] Richman, the editor of *Helpful Thoughts*, was forthright in denouncing prizes, systematically outlining her opposition to material rewards with an address presented at the second annual meeting of the Jewish Chautauqua Society that she titled "What Are Proper Incentives in Religious School Work?" Prizes, she argued, secure only temporary enthusiasm. Children should be encouraged to develop intrinsic motivation to succeed in their Sunday school studies— the desire to please their teacher, the desire to learn, and the desire to be virtuous. "In the religious school especially, children should be taught to cultivate character," she insisted. "Prizes do more harm than good."[57]

Object Lessons

Both Mathilda Lemlein and Julia Richman found the summer assembly of the Jewish Chautauqua Society (JCS) to be receptive to their pleas for pedagogy over prizes. Founded in 1893 by Rabbi Henry Berkowitz, a member of the first graduating class of rabbis ordained by the Hebrew Union College, the JCS was modeled on the Chautauqua assemblies that were begun in upstate New York in 1874 by the

Chautauqua Institution and which initially refused entry to Jews and Catholics. From 1897 the JCS staged an annual summer assembly with lectures, seminars, model lessons, and "cultured" entertainments.[58] Targeted toward the American Jewish affluent classes, the movement's summer assemblies were held in Atlantic city from 1897 to 1907 to capitalize on the large numbers of Jewish vacationers already gathered there and to remedy what Berkowitz described as the "the Jewish summer problem"—card playing, idleness, and neglect of all Jewish religious obligation in place of oblique observance of the Christian Sabbath.[59] A major focus of the summer assemblies was the Teachers' Institute, which offered model lessons and pedagogical training for volunteer Jewish Sunday school teachers.[60] The Teachers' Institute was undoubtedly one of the major successes of the JCS, providing teachers with practical instruction in classroom management, school organization, and insights from secular pedagogy, as well as offering books and pedagogical aids for purchase.[61]

Berkowitz was committed to the cause of Jewish education in America and to improving the American Jewish Sunday school. At the Teachers' Institutes, he brought together rabbis and scholars who lectured on topics connected to classical Jewish literature and Jewish theology, and teachers who taught model lessons and classes on religious school pedagogy. The 1897 Teachers' Institute at the first JCS summer assembly represented, in Berkowitz's estimation, the "first time that practical methods were adopted to demonstrate how modern methods and principles of pedagogy might be applied in the work of our schools of religion."[62] Essential to the institutes were women, including Julia Richman, Mathilda Lemlein, and Ella Jacobs, who served as Sunday school teachers and worked as public school educators. While rabbis and scholars at the Chautauqua summer assemblies offered lectures on classical Jewish literature and theology, Richman, Lemlein, and Jacobs taught that trying to imbue students with expert content knowledge was futile if teachers did not also think about how students learned, how to manage a classroom, and how to plan lessons that would stimulate children's imaginations. The gender division between the pragmatic and the theoretical implicitly underscored the idea that while the great ideas to be taught in Sunday school would be generated by men, it would be women's work to develop the pedagogical expertise to bring them to life.

The practical methods that Richman, Lemlein, and Jacobs promoted at the Teachers' Institutes of the JCS summer assemblies sought to align Jewish education with best practices for classroom pedagogy promoted in secular school settings. During model lessons and pedagogical lectures, Richman, Lemlein, and Jacobs emphasized the importance of engaging students in Sunday school lessons using objects that illustrated their key themes and in surroundings that illuminated their messages. The women argued against the common practice of holding Sunday school in the basement of a synagogue, emphasizing the importance of "bright and cheerful surroundings" if the children were to learn productively and enjoy their time at Sunday school.[63] Sunday schools should always be conducted in ventilated rooms, Richman insisted, and they should be filled with comfortable furniture.[64] Richman's recommendation that school environments should prioritize comfort and decoration was tailored to affluent German American Jewish communities with resources for spacious architecture. It was hardly feasible for institutions run on shoestring budgets in cramped quarters. Nevertheless, in focusing on both the content that was taught and the environment of the Sunday school, the women who offered lessons on pedagogy at the Chautauqua summer assemblies stressed that the aesthetic experience of the classroom had a direct bearing on what was learned within it. Contemporary conventions of gender assumed that women were especially attuned to aesthetics and that women bore primary responsibility for creating interior environments that could uplift, educate, and entertain.[65] In framing the aesthetics of the Sunday school classroom as a pedagogical consideration, Jewish women educators paired capabilities assumed by their gender with the expertise they had acquired as graduates of normal schools.

The emphasis that Richman and her colleagues placed on the importance of considering the physical environment of Sunday school education also extended to more explicitly curricular concerns. Contemporary child-rearing manuals and teacher training literature emphasized that children learned best from visual stimuli, recommending that primary grade teachers should make liberal use of art and images, while more advanced classes should have their lectures illuminated by maps, charts, and illustrations. Economic investment in the decoration of classrooms, Lemlein told volunteer Sunday school educators who gathered for the second JCS summer assembly in 1898, was necessary for educational success. A teacher must purchase pictures for her classroom walls, she insisted, and use her own money to acquire decorations appropriate to the season.[66] Jacobs highlighted the use of decorations in the model lessons she conducted at the JCS, explaining that physical props not only created aesthetically engaging learning environments but could also highlight the American resonances of Jewish religious life. She gave an immersive model lesson at the first JCS Teachers' Institute focused on the Passover seder, illustrated by comparing seder themes with American ideals of democracy and freedom. Attendees entered a mock classroom at Atlantic City's Congregation Beth Israel that she had decorated with pictures of Moses, "Israelites as Slaves in Egypt," "The Sacrifice of the Passover," and portraits of George Washington and Abraham Lincoln festooned with garlands of red, white, and blue. Participants later sat down at a table laid with a festive seder plate and ceremonially sampled matzoh, wine, eggs, and bitter herbs. In a discussion that followed the mock lesson, participants lauded the "bright and cheerful schoolroom" and the "inculcation of the American spirit." A second model lesson given by Jacobs the following day focused on Thanksgiving, with the decoration in the room switching to grains, fruits, and autumn colors. "Great interest was manifested in these practical object lessons," the record of the summer assembly noted, "which are a departure from the old-style methods of teaching in Sabbath schools."[67] Volunteer teachers attending the JCS's summer Teachers' Institutes would learn from Jacobs that the key to being a successful educator was to have the right material goods to bring their lessons to life.

Jacobs was an experienced educator. She was superintendent of the primary department of Congregation Rodeph Shalom's religious school, a public school principal in Philadelphia, and served on the board of the Jewish Publication Society.[68] She was a member of the organizing committee of the Teachers' Institute for the first Chautauqua summer assembly, and by the second annual meeting she had become its principal. Jacobs was a staunch advocate of object lessons, a pedagogical initiative that advocated that children should learn new ideas and concepts by investigating physical objects.[69] Derived from the sensory educational theories of Johann Pestalozzi, object teaching was widely promoted in US teacher education beginning in the 1860s.[70] At the second summer assembly of the Jewish Chautauqua Society, Jacobs extolled the benefits of object lessons and encouraged Sunday schools to invest in pedagogical aids, particularly maps. "Children should see the models of things about which they study," she insisted, deploring the "dullness of instruction in our Jewish schools due to the absence of such helps."[71] Christian religious education, she pointed out, had long incorporated object lessons into Sunday school pedagogy. At the summer meetings of the main branch of the Chautauqua Society, Bible teaching using illustrative objects was promoted, and illustrator Charles Beard offered popular "chalk talks" and hieroglyphic Bibles that illuminated scriptural passages with pictures and puzzles.[72] At the Jewish Chautauqua Society, Jacobs sought to replicate the efforts of her Christian counterparts, encouraging Jewish educators to invest in material aids, object lessons, and props. She organized an "exhibit of appliances" at the 1899 summer assembly, showcasing materials, courtesy of various educational publishing houses, with opportunities for delegates to purchase their wares, for which the JCS would receive a commission.[73] Acknowledging that the best examples of such aids were produced by Christian religious educators and publicized in the Christian *Sunday School Times*, she recommended the magazine to Jewish educators as well.[74] "It became a function of the society," Henry Berkowitz later recalled, "to provide Jewish ceremonial objects, maps, records, teachers' books, Sabbath school libraries, pictures, lantern slides, and all available helps for teachers. It was the first and for many years the only Jewish organization to serve the schools in this practical way."[75] Not to mention that selling such items for purchase also enabled the society to turn a small profit. Jacobs would later advocate for the JCS to sponsor a traveling library of books, charts, maps, ceremonial objects, and models for use by religious schools without the resources to develop a permanent inventory of their own.[76]

The Jewish Chautauqua Society never quite approximated the success of its Protestant counterpart. Yet it was instrumental in the field of Jewish teacher education, especially in promoting an expansive range of resources for use in American Jewish Sunday schools.[77] Its success owed in no small part to the expertise of women who bridged the world of public education and Jewish schooling and who advocated for American Jewish Sunday schools to adopt material pedagogies that would bring their instruction up to date with the latest developments in public education as well as in Christian religious schools. By promoting pedagogical aids and visual stimuli, educators like Mathilda Lemlein, Julia Richman, and Ella Jacobs laid the groundwork for an approach to Jewish education that emphasized educational technologies, a pedagogy of things that prescribed classroom aids, decorations, and illustrative material objects as requirements for religious learning. If religious sentiments were to be nurtured in the young, they insisted, the lessons of the Sunday school had to be brought to life with aids and technologies that could attach color, texture, and images to ideas.

The Magic Lantern

Abraham Cronbach remembered the precise moment that he first felt a connection to the divine. It began with a walk to the Indianapolis YMCA with his piano tutor, who had been engaged to provide music to accompany a stereopticon show. His tutor was blind, which made his services indispensable—only a player with no need of sight could play in the darkness needed for the illuminated slides. Cronbach stayed to watch the presentation, a talk illustrated by photographs projected by the stereopticon, with songs sung by the audience and accompanied by his tutor on the piano. As the audience sang the Christian hymn "Rock of Ages," the stereopticon projected an image of an ocean, followed by one of a ship, a storm, then a shipwreck, followed by images of "hapless voyagers floundering in the billows," before a large rock appeared on the screen, upon which finally appeared "a white-robed female form, symbolic of the human soul." Cronbach was astounded. Years later he would learn that "Rock of Ages" was intimately connected with his own Jewish tradition, learning from a Jewish song book that "Rock of Ages," or "Maoz Tzur," was a hymn popularly associated with Hanukkah.[78] "But that Sunday afternoon, at the Indianapolis YMCA, all that lay in the future," he recalled. "There, I adopted the metaphor rock of ages," and into my youthful mind the conviction entered that, in the Rock of Ages, the tempest tossed human soul must seek anchorage."[79] For young Abraham Cronbach, the stereopticon slideshow that he attended at the Indianapolis YMCA was an intensely dramatic experience. In darkness, as the audience sang a poignant hymn, the images that flashed before his eyes forged a sequential narrative.[80] Anxiously awaiting each new slide to see what had become of the tempest-tossed ship and its fate-ful passengers, it is perhaps unsurprising that the experience seemed to become intensely spiritual. As if by magic the stereopticon resolved the tragic shipwreck with an image of a rock to cling to, mirroring the lyrics that the audience had sung together. The stereopticon projector was a dynamic technology. By magnifying and projecting images, particularly when accompanied by evocative music and compelling interpretation, it seemed to bring the pictures to life.

Developed in Europe in the seventeenth century, the first "magic lanterns" used oil lamps and gas jets to project hand-painted images onto a screen.[81] By the second half of the nineteenth century, electricity had made the magic lantern a less dangerous technology, and the mass production of projectors and glass slides made it a relatively affordable luxury, too. Beginning in the 1850s, American newspapers regularly featured advertisements from manufacturers and photographers who promised to enliven lectures, Sunday school classes, sermons, and talks with projected slides at competitive prices.[82] The American Jewish press was no exception. The Jakobi and Hart firm of Boston regularly adver-tised in the *American Hebrew* newspaper that its twelve-dollar stereop-ticon machine offered quality and affordability, and a set of twenty-five picture slides could be yours for just ten one-cent stamps.[83] Stereopti-con exhibitions became a popular entertainment among American Jews, used for at-home gatherings as well as public functions. Some shows were didactic and informative, others were curated purely for amuse-ment. To celebrate the end of the school year, the Sunday school of Con-gregation Sherith Israel in San Francisco rented Golden Gate Hall in 1899 and presented the children with souvenirs, prizes, and a lecture on Palestine illustrated with stereopticon slides.[84] In 1890 New Year's Eve was celebrated at the Philadelphia Jewish Foster Home and Orphan Asylum with an exhibition of pictures of local parks photographed by the institution's professor of gymnastics.[85] A more raucous time was had at the nearby school of Anshe Emeth Memorial Temple in 1882, where the children were treated to a magic lantern show to celebrate Hanuk-kah along with generous quantities of cake and candy, and a "long fit of laughter at the funny pictures shown on the screen."[86]

The stereopticon was enticing to teachers and superintendents who wanted to invigorate instruction in American Jewish Sunday schools.

It was a fashionable technology, one that could facilitate communal experiences that were entertaining as well as informative.[87] Ella Jacobs featured stereopticon projectors and slides in her exhibit of religious school aids at the Jewish Chautauqua summer assemblies, recommending that slideshows offered effective visual illustrations to illuminate religious instruction.[88] Jeanette Miriam Goldberg, a public school teacher and Sabbath school superintendent from Texas, became field secretary of the National Council of Jewish Women in 1904, and in that role she made it her special mission to promote the use of stereopticon slides in American Jewish Sunday schools.[89] Goldberg commissioned a series of slides on the history of Israel, as well as an exhibit illustrating Jewish ceremonial customs, that she promoted to Sabbath schools across the country. "She believes that the most effective way of teaching the child is through the eye," reported the *American Israelite* in 1905. "No instruction can teach the story and sentiment attached to it with the same force as an illustrated form."[90] Congregation B'nai Israel in Galveston, Texas, embraced Goldberg's recommendations and introduced stereopticon slides into its Sabbath school Bible class beginning in 1905. According to the school superintendent, Rabbi Henry Cohen, it had "been very helpful to the scholars and greatly enthused them in their work."[91]

For Sunday school superintendents like Cohen who wanted to incorporate stereopticon exhibitions in their Bible classes, slides featuring photographs of the Holy Land were easily available as packaged sets. The Holy Land was a popular topic for stereopticon slideshows, as in the nineteenth-century Palestine became a site of fascination for Americans who wanted to visit the land of the Bible. Package tours of the "exotic orient" offered Western-style comforts for American tourists, and accounts from travelers described with fear and fascination the various ways that the East seemed to lag behind the modern West. Developments in flash photographic technologies made images of biblical sites readily available to homebound enthusiasts, and the mass-market availability of the stereopticon projector enabled them to be shared with large groups on a screen. Stereopticon shows offered a photographic tour of the Holy Land that was both intimate and cinematic, projected sometimes as large as life size, with dissolving technologies used to add animation to slides and transitions. Slides of Holy Land scenes were commonly advertised to religious educators as a technology that could bring new life to ancient texts.[92] "We are confident that our series of lantern slides of the Holy Land," boasted a promotion by the New York manufacturer T. H. McAllister, "will supercede [sic] all other views of that country, and will commend themselves to those contemplating Illustrated Lectures as an aid to Biblical Instruction; enabling them to bring that great Centre of our Religious History to the attention of audiences just as tourists see it to-day."[93] Temple Israel in Boston acquired more than two hundred lantern slides for use in its Sunday school, including a set of slides of the Holy Land manufactured by T. H. McAllister.[94] The McAllister Holy Land set featured photographs by William H. Rau, who had visited Petra, Sinai, and Palestine with archaeologist Edward L. Wilson in 1882 with the goal of photographing biblical sites. Flash photography was in its infancy at the time, and Rau's ambitious plans to ascend Mount Sinai and photograph the "alleged spot" where Moses received the tablets of the law and confronted the burning bush produced few results.[95] But the trip did yield photographs of a range of holy sites, portraits of Jews and Arabs living in Palestine, street scenes, and landscape panoramas.[96]

The slides produced by the McAllister company implied that contemporary Palestine had changed little from ancient times. Photographs of Jews praying at the Western Wall, crowds at the Jaffa Gate, and bustling market stalls painted a portrait of communal life that ostensibly paralleled the biblical era. Landscapes and panoramas offered beautiful sweeping scenes that emphasized the sites of biblical narratives and the map of biblical Israel.

Alongside stunning vistas, Rau made sure to capture local residents in his landscape shots. Guides to Holy Land tours and travel diaries marveled that local dress seemed to be unchanged from biblical times, evocatively describing the contemporary Middle East as the cradle of biblical religion. Photographs of biblical sites, carefully ornamented by locals who seemed to attest to the texture of ancient life, offered compelling illustrations for Sunday school classes, as packaged stereopticon slide sets claimed to take the viewer inside the world of the Bible. In reality the images were carefully staged to elide evidence of modernity and emphasize continuity between the current residents of Palestine and their ancient ancestors. Ignoring modern building construction, advances in technology, and locals who wore Western-style attire, pho-

Figure 4.3. *Bird's Eye View of Samaria*, 1882. Photograph by William H. Rau, photographic print from lantern slide produced by T. H. McAllister, New York, 1903. Courtesy of Temple Israel of Boston Archives.

tographs of the Holy Land reproduced in stereopticon slideshows creatively imagined a world where time had stood still. If inhabitants of the land were included in the photographic record, they were featured as exotic primitive curios.[97]

Temple Israel also acquired a series of images photographed by Elijah Meyers and manufactured by the American Colony in Jerusalem. The American Colony was a utopian Christian sect founded in 1881, and Meyers, a Jewish convert to Christianity, was one of its early devotees. Meyers's photographs of the Jewish residents of Palestine emphasized subjects that seemed to conform to the sect's ideological interpretation of Jews as the stubborn "People of the Book," heirs to an authentic re-

Figure 4.4. *Jews of Jerusalem at Abraham's Vineyard*, photograph by Elijah Meyers, American Colony Studio, c. 1898. Photographic print from lantern slide produced by Walter L. Isaacs, Inc., New York. Courtesy of Temple Israel of Boston Archives.

ligious lineage who clung to a religious law that had long since been superseded.[98]

The supersessionist theology that Meyers adopted toward his Jewish subjects would have been distasteful to the American Jews who bought his images as stereopticon slides. In the context of American Jewish Sunday schools, however, images of Jews praying at holy sites, reading the scriptures, and celebrating the Jewish calendar in the land of Israel offered a romanticized portrait of Jewish religious life. In the late nineteenth century American Jews publicly lamented the corrosive impact of assimilation on American Jewish vitality. Rosa Sonneschein, editor of the *American Jewess,* observed in 1895 that aversion to religion had become a trend among American Jews, who showed little interest in the synagogue or public prayer.[99] Meyers's stereopticon slides offered paradigmatic images of faithful religious Jews reading their holy books and praying at their holy sites. The images offered a compelling portrait of a world in which Judaism seemed to permeate the atmosphere.

Stereopticon slideshows featuring paintings of Jewish religious activities were also used by American Jewish Sunday schools to provide visual illustrations of religious devotion. For its Sunday school, Rodef Shalom Congregation in Pittsburgh purchased a set of stereopticon slides featuring paintings of Jewish ceremonial life by German Jewish artist Moritz Daniel Oppenheim. Like the Holy Land photographs, Oppenheim's paintings were highly idealized. Here, though, the subjects of the sentiment came from Oppenheim's memories of his youth in early nineteenth-century Germany rather than images of contemporary Palestine. Oppenheim's paintings were unabashedly sentimental and nostalgic. Loving families and earnest religious rituals took center stage; none of the difficulties of Jewish life in Germany made their way onto the canvas. Reproduced and included in a series of mass-produced albums in the early part of the nineteenth-century, Oppenheim's paintings of Jewish ceremonial life became immensely popular in America, included as illustrations in books as well as slides for stereopticon shows.[100] In December 1881 Abram Samuel Isaacs, professor of Hebrew and German language and literature at New York University, gave a talk to a large audience he titled "Pictures of the Jewish Past," featuring stereopticon slides of Oppenheim's paintings. His remarks were "often interrupted by applause," a correspondent, Julian Werner, noted in the *American Israel-*

ite, adding that "a lecture of this kind would be listened to with profit by our religious schools."[101] The superintendent of Rodef Shalom's school evidently agreed.

Paradoxically, the stereopticon slides used in American Jewish Sunday schools like Temple Israel's and Rodef Shalom's extolled the values and virtues of traditional religion in the context of institutions that, for the most part, maintained an ambiguous relationship with actual practitioners of traditional Judaism within their own communities. When viewed through the distancing prism of the stereopticon, however, images of traditional religious observance offered assimilated American Jews a nostalgic glimpse of a world in which family-centered Jewish devotion seemed to permeate the atmosphere. When *the American Jewess* reviewed Henry Berkowitz's book, *Sabbath Sentiment*, in September 1898, it praised his inclusion of Moritz Oppenheim's paintings in the volume as having the power to "inculcate the aspiration to realize the highest ideal of worship."[102] Amid fears that assimilation threatened the survival of Judaism in America, stereopticon slides featuring photographs of Palestine and paintings of modern Europe offered an idealized portrait of Jewish religious life. They were incorporated in Sunday schools like Temple Israel's and Rodef Shalom's as visual illustrations of Jewish religious devotion that teachers hoped their students would embrace, albeit while leaving most actual halachic observances behind.[103]

Elaborate Tableaux

When the first Hebrew Sunday School opened its doors in 1838, it occupied a makeshift space and used borrowed textbooks to put together basic lessons in Jewish religion. Rosa Mordecai fondly remembered the simplicity of its inaugural classes, recalling that at the conclusion of annual examinations children were rewarded with an orange and a pretzel. By the end of the century, Gratz's Sunday school boasted four large campuses, each with many hundreds of children enrolled. End-of-year oranges and pretzels, Mordecai observed with regret, had long been superseded by "theatrical productions and elaborate tableaux."[104] Other educators shared Mordecai's misgivings about the commercialization of American Jewish Sunday school education, fearing that prizes offered false incentives and that the stereopticon slideshows and visual aids were a distraction that entertained rather than edified.[105] In Baltimore it took prolonged discussions at Temple Oheb Shalom before it was decided to introduce one blackboard and one map of Palestine in the Sunday school classrooms, while at the neighboring Chizuk Amuno Congregation, catechism was not complemented by more interactive pedagogies until the 1920s.[106]

The expansion of the Jewish educational marketplace in the late nineteenth century set a new course for Jewish education in America, one that linked educational success to financial investment. The Sunday school fostered pedagogical innovation and change as American Jewish educators sought solutions to pedagogical problems in the marketplace, advising volunteer teachers to spend their own money on decorating their classrooms and encouraging Sunday schools to invest in devices and props that could animate and illuminate as well as instruct. Educators innovated with contemporary technologies, such as the periodical and the stereopticon, that were fashionable in American culture more broadly and that signaled entertainment as well as education. Tactile, colorful, and engaging to the senses, these new materials were incorporated into Jewish education to make the Sunday school more engaging. In the process the American Jewish Sunday school during the nineteenth century taught that Judaism was a modern religion not only because it boasted a proud theological tradition that could be summarized in catechisms but also because it commanded a material marketplace of objects that could bring lessons in Jewish religion to life.

5

Religious Education as Americanization

In 1880, on the eve of the mass migration of Jews from eastern Europe to the United States, the public face of American Jewish communal life was largely shaped by the Reform movement. Traditionalist communities had dominated the nascent American Jewish community at the beginning of the nineteenth century, yet by 1880 Orthodox synagogues represented only a handful of the roughly 275 synagogues that served the country's Jews.[1] The expectation that Reform Judaism would serve as the umbrella ideology for American Judaism, an ambition cherished by the movement's chief architect, Isaac Mayer Wise, was enshrined in the names given to its major initiatives and institutions, Hebrew Union College, the Central Conference of American Rabbis, the *Union Prayer Book*, and the Union of American Hebrew Congregations. The arrival of more than two million Jewish immigrants from eastern Europe and Russia between 1880 and 1924, however, transformed the American Jewish landscape and expanded the religious and ideological spectrum of American Judaism exponentially. The new arrivals included Jews committed to traditional Judaism, defined by observance of halacha. They also included Jews who reimagined Judaism in nonhalachic and ideological terms, from Bundism to Yiddishism, and various forms of Jewish nationalism. The ideological diversity of the new immigrants led to the proliferation of new Jewish educational institutions, including cheders offering elementary instruction in Jewish subjects, Talmud Torahs for older students, and schools focused on Yiddish culture and Jewish socialism, as well as a plethora of private tutors who offered training in Hebrew, the siddur *(prayer book)*, and other Jewish texts, mostly for boys preparing for their bar mitzvah.

For most immigrant families, enrolling children in a Jewish school was a low priority. A survey conducted by the Union of American Hebrew Congregations in 1889 estimated that only 29 percent of American Jewish children were enrolled in some kind of Jewish educational institution.[2] When Julius Greenstone compiled data on attendance at Jewish educational institutions in Baltimore for 1908–1909, he estimated that in a population of more than 50,000 Jews, only 2,845 children were enrolled in a Jewish school.[3] Just as Rebecca Gratz had discerned when reflecting upon the pragmatic concerns of Western European Jewish immigrants in 1838, four decades later the children of the new arrivals from the East faced considerable barriers to accessing institutions for Jewish learning. Many helped to financially support their families by engaging in paid employment, piecework, or the care of younger siblings, leaving little time or financial capacity to enroll in a Jewish school. In congregational Sunday schools enrollment was typically restricted to the children of members, and new immigrant families were either loathe to join synagogues with unfamiliar ritual practices or could not afford the expense of a seat. Enrollment had a gendered component as well. Male children might study with a private tutor at least until their bar mitzvah, yet Orthodox parents were often reluctant to sacrifice time and resources on Jewish education for girls. A survey conducted by the newly founded New York Kehillah in 1911 estimated that 70,000 of the 80,000 Jewish girls in New York received no Jewish education outside the home.[4]

During the 1880s and 1890s American Jews pioneered a series of new initiatives to expand the reach of American Jewish Sunday schools. Critical to the implementation of these efforts were women who assumed more conscious roles as public activists for Jewish religious education at the end of the century, as organizations like the National Council of Jewish Women and congregational sisterhoods of personal service promoted women's involvement in educational policy making and founded schools to encourage a new generation of immigrants to attend to the religious education of their daughters, as well as that of their sons. These women's organizations provided critical support to new American Jews and labored to mitigate the influence of the Christian groups that preyed upon immigrants with offers of charity and classes in Jewish religion, thinly disguising their proselytizing intent. Yet the Jewish free schools run by affluent German Jews were imbued with their own missionary ideologies, as they too sought to realign the Jewish practices of their charges to conform to what they understood to be a more appropriately American religious model for Jewish life. Rather than offering Jewish educational training based on lessons in halacha, or in the languages and national cultures of the Jewish people, the free schools and Jewish mission schools set up by women to serve new immigrants endeavored to impress upon their students the lesson that being Jewish in America was a religious commitment, defined by knowledge of the Bible, moral and ethical conduct, and harmonizing Jewish attachments with commitments to American cultural norms.

Women as Activists

In 1887 Gustav Gottheil, rabbi of Congregation Emanu-El in Manhattan, founded a Sisterhood of Personal Service to organize the women of his congregation toward social welfare causes. It marked the beginning of American Jewish women's participation in a range of initiatives to forge roles as public activists. Inspired by Protestant models and motivated in no small part by the need to thwart the Christian missionaries who targeted indigent Jews, the sisterhoods and women's auxiliaries that followed Emanu-El opened settlement houses and founded religious schools for new immigrant children while also raising funds to support educational work within their own congregations. For decades American Christian women had advocated for child welfare initiatives and promoted local and national school reform. American Jewish women got started later than their Christian counterparts, but buoyed by the necessity of providing for the needs of the new Jewish immigrants arriving on American shores in increasing numbers, by the last decade of the century Jewish women were engaged in advancing a broad range of political and charitable causes, particularly educational ones.[5]

The adoption of activist roles in Jewish welfare and education marked a new departure for American Jewish women in the last decade of the nineteenth century. While benevolent societies had organized affluent women's participation in charitable projects during the first half of the nineteenth century, following the Civil War men had largely taken over leadership of charitable organizations. Even public projects that might have been presumed to have been attuned to sensibilities associated with women in nineteenth-century America came under male leadership. In 1889, when a committee was appointed to oversee the decoration for Shavuot at Congregation B'nai Jeshurun in Newark, New Jersey, four men were elected to undertake the task. At Temple Beth El in Detroit the religious school's annual picnic was organized by men until the 1890s.[6]

When invited to participate in social welfare activities, however, women proved themselves more than capable of exceling at the tasks at hand. In 1891 Rabbi Louis Grossman organized the Women's Club of Temple Beth El in Detroit to provide continuing education for the women of the congregation and to organize women's philanthropy. By the early 1900s the club had taken over the annual picnic, established free libraries for the factories of Detroit, and organized penny lunches for the children of two city public schools. "Fifty years ago, such a gathering of women representing so many callings and vocations of life would have been looked on as a strange body of feminine creatures, hardly women, for to be employed in labor usually performed by men was not considered womanly," remarked the club's first president, Mrs. Bernard Ginsberg, at its inaugural meeting. "It was womanly to spin, to knit, to weave, to cook, to bake, to churn. Who ever heard of a woman going into an office? Who ever heard of a married woman doing aught but look after her husband and children?"[7] Women who joined sisterhoods and synagogue auxiliaries understood that they were doing something radical by extending the boundaries of their domestic sphere to include the needs of American Jewry at large, even while the work itself may have reified contemporary presuppositions of gender that assumed that educational and charitable work was naturally the domain of women. Their efforts transformed American Jewish women's philanthropy from the benevolent society models of the midnineteenth-century into what its members described as scientific models of charity.[8] When she joined the board of trustees of the sisterhood at Reform Congregation Emanu-El in New York, Rebekah Kohut recalled that she learned not to give aid indiscriminately but to aim for a "proper, scientific, constructive administration of relief."[9] In her first report as chair of the Bureau of Associated Charities, a federated structure to organize women's philanthropy in Chicago in 1897, Hannah Greenebaum Solomon wrote, "We can no more run charities on the old lines than a business house can chalk the names of its customers on the barn door."[10]

In the context of Sunday schools, congregational sisterhoods provided for a holistic range of needs that connected educational success to material comforts. Sisterhoods led fundraising campaigns to renovate synagogue basements and vestries to provide more comfortable settings for congregational Sunday schools and to fund the construction of new and more spacious temples with classrooms built into the design. The Miriam Frauen Verein (Women's Organization), founded at Congregation Oheb Shalom in Newark, New Jersey, in 1880, raised money by organizing dances and balls to celebrate Simchat Torah and Purim, as well as by organizing an annual picnic. The women's efforts paid for new robes for the rabbi and cantor, new curtains for the ark, reupholstered seats in the sanctuary, new carpets, and decoration on the sanctuary walls.[11] The Miriam organization also offered sewing classes for girls enrolled in the congregation's Sunday school and led a story hour in the vestry rooms.[12] In Cincinnati, K.K. B'nai Yeshurun's sisterhood got started later than most, not until 1912. But within a month of its founding, drinking fountains, paper towels, and wastepaper baskets appeared at the congregation's religious school. Within three months the women had started a regular children's service, organized refreshments for the Sabbath school, and arranged for the school building to be kept open to provide a reading room and social space for children.[13]

Sisterhoods led entertainment efforts too, taking a leading role in organizing plays, pageants, and festivities to celebrate Jewish holidays and raise funds for congregational education. The Sabbath School Festival at San Francisco's Congregation Emanu-El in 1895 was held at the California Theatre and presented a comic operetta in three acts, with more than one hundred children in the company.[14] The school's Hanukkah festival in 1908 took place at the local California club and offered a program of dancing, singing, and recitals, as well as a Hanukkah play.[15] Hanukkah festivals, which became popular in American Reform synagogues beginning in the 1870s, were typically organized by women.[16] "Whereas, education is one of the most valuable legacies that we can bestow on our children, those interested in the dissemination of knowledge deserve the highest commendation at the hands of the public and the gratitude of all who have at heart the welfare of the rising generation," resolved the religious school board of neighboring San Francisco Congregation Sherith Israel, in 1896, thanking Mrs. N. Schlessinger and Miss Josephine Leszynsky for organizing a performance by the children of the religious school that "advance[d] their minds and brought to the surface their intelligence and brightness."[17]

Figure 5.1. Children at a pageant held at the Sunday school of Temple Beth Israel, Portland, Oregon, February 1898. Courtesy of Jacobs Family Photographs Collection, Oregon Historical Society, Portland.

The educational activities of sisterhoods were not limited to the children enrolled within their own congregations' Sunday schools. They also extended to efforts to found satellite branches of their Sunday schools in immigrant neighborhoods. Satellite, or free, schools offered a religious curriculum that followed the Sunday school model, alongside practical assistance, English lessons, and vocational training for the children of the new arrivals. The women of Congregation Emanu-El in New York founded a branch of their Sabbath school to serve new immigrant children in 1880 that was funded by contributions from the children who belonged to the temple. The teachers in the school quickly realized that the immigrant children needed assistance with basic needs as much as Jewish education, and the school began to offer baths as well as meals of hot coffee and bread and butter, alongside its religious curriculum. Within a year it had two hundred girls on its register.[18] Superintendent Minnie D. Louis was adamant that the school would teach Jewish religion according to the American Jewish Sunday school

model rather than the subjects central to the cheders (weekday afternoon Hebrew schools) and yeshivas of eastern Europe. "Hebrew will not
be taught," she insisted, "but portions of the Bible will be read and com-
mented upon, pleasant anecdotes told, and the children made to take
an interest in their own welfare."[19] The school also conducted classes
in personal and environmental cleanliness. As historian Jenna Weismann Joselit observed, the curriculum for domestic affairs deployed in
Sunday schools for recent immigrants was corrective in nature, aiming
to reform the students' domestic skills.[20] In Cincinnati the women of
the United Jewish Charities organized classes in practical hygiene and
domestic science for the girls of immigrant families and offered seminars in parenting for the mothers of children who were enrolled in their
kindergartens. In private the wealthier women despaired of the parents
and hoped that the younger generations would be more receptive to
corrective instruction. "For the older mothers there is little hope of redemption; our faith must be placed in the children," observed Emma
Guiterman, who conducted visits to immigrant families in Chicago's
second and fifth districts in 1898.[21]

Kindergartens were a new addition to the American Jewish institutional landscape, and were enthusiastically promoted by Jewish sisterhoods and free schools during the 1880s and 1890s. Developed by
Friedrich Froebel in Germany with an emphasis on learning through
play, kindergarten was enthusiastically embraced across the United
States beginning in the 1870s; by 1885 there were 565 kindergartens in
America, with more than twenty-nine thousand students enrolled.[22] The
creation of Jewish kindergartens was a necessary intervention to block
Christian evangelists who had set up free kindergartens that explicitly
targeted the Jewish poor. Yet the wealthier women in Jewish sisterhoods
also recognized that early childhood offered an expedient opportunity to
Americanize the new arrivals, as well as to introduce them to a particular religious form of Judaism.[23] The trustees of the Temple Free Kindergarten in Louisville, Kentucky, founded in 1891, marveled at the end of
their first year in operation at the progress that their young charges had
made in decorum and obedience and the "harmonious cooperation" that
they had learned from group activities and singing lessons.[24] "The Kindergarten has firmly established itself not *only* as the garden where little
ones grow and are nurtured in a daily atmosphere of justice, purity, and

love, but as the standard for all that is truest and best in the life of mankind," reported Grace A. Fry, director of the Plum Street Kindergarten to the United Jewish Charities of Cincinnati in 1898.[25] "There is no better method of proving the never-ending beauties of nature and the controlling hand of Almighty God," opined a correspondent to the *Jewish Exponent* announcing the creation of a kindergarten class for the school of Baltimore's Eden Street Synagogue. By attending a Jewish kindergarten, the child "will develop an intelligent faith in God as nothing else can."[26]

The National Council of Jewish Women

Congregational sisterhoods focused their efforts largely on concerns within their local communities, but the National Council of Jewish Women (NCJW) sought to organize women's activism and philanthropy on a national level. Founded in 1893 by a group of women aggrieved at the erasure of female voices from the Denominational Congress at the World's Columbian Exposition in Chicago, the NCJW sought to advocate for women's participation in Jewish communal affairs and to organize women's charitable work around common projects.[27] The women of the NCJW carved out an activist approach to Jewish women's involvement in charitable projects that responded to distinctly Jewish concerns. The NCJW maintained a station at Ellis Island to assist new Jewish immigrants and provided social services to Jewish families to counter Christian missionary organizations that tried to evangelize the Jewish poor.[28] The leaders of the NCJW understood their work as proceeding from specifically religious concerns, and they sought to preserve Judaism in America by forestalling the evangelization of the new arrivals.[29] Education would prove to be a critical component of the NCJW's mission. When Hannah Solomon, president of the NCJW, addressed its first national convention in 1896, she told delegates that the most important arena for their philanthropic work was Sunday school education. Whether organizing Sunday schools, raising money for educational causes, or teaching in classrooms, NCJW members were "leading and guarding the men and women of the future," Solomon explained. "Therein lies our greatest power."[30]

The NCJW charged its members with working to improve Jewish education in their regional communities and to ensure that women were included in determining educational policy at a local level. Its leaders recognized that although women were disproportionately represented as Sunday school teachers, women had been excluded from administrative decision making as the congregational Sunday school had come under the control of rabbis and congregational education boards. Some congregations proved to be amenable to proposals for women's representation, theorizing, along with the NCJW leadership, that women brought a natural aptitude for spirituality and education to the work. Suggesting that a women's auxiliary be added to the school board of Congregation Bene Israel in Cincinnati, Rabbi David Philipson explained to the congregation's board that women "naturally take a special interest in the religious training of our children." They brought to the work not only dedication but also particular aptitude, in Philipson's opinion, for such tasks as beautifying the congregation's schoolrooms and organizing entertainments.[31] The vice president for Colorado had to regretfully report to her NCJW colleagues at the organization's first national meeting, however, that attempts to engage their local synagogue had been acrimonious and that consequently the Colorado chapter "had no connection with the Sabbath Schools of the Temple."[32] Relationships between NCJW chapters and their local congregations could be adversarial when rabbis perceived that council women were interfering in synagogue affairs. Emil Hirsch, rabbi of Chicago Sinai Congregation, was ambivalent toward the NCJW, despite the fact that two of its founders, Hannah Solomon and Sadie American, were members of his congregation. In 1895 he wrote in the *Reform Advocate*, the newspaper that he served as editor, that women's meddling in the Sabbath school could make its already challenging conditions considerably worse.[33]

The NCJW was cognizant, however, that congregational Sunday schools could serve only a fraction of the American Jewish community's growing educational needs. As new Jewish immigrants flooded into American cities in the last decades of the nineteenth century, NCJW women were active in establishing Jewish mission schools, settlement houses, orphan asylums, and free schools that offered evening and weekend classes in vocational skills, alongside a religious curriculum that followed the Sunday school model.[34] In San Francisco Rabbi Jacob Voorsanger invited a local community member, Hattie Hecht Sloss, to found an NCJW chapter for local women in 1900. Together with the sisterhood from local Congregation Emanu-El, the San Francisco NCJW established a settlement house, Sunday school classes for the children of Russian immigrants, a kindergarten, and a gymnasium, as well as a Mothers' Club. The women of the San Francisco NCJW chapter also deployed "home teachers" to visit Jewish immigrant families in their homes and advise them on American methods of child-rearing.[35] In Pittsburgh the NCJW mission school organized instruction in vocational skills and classes in Jewish religion for the children of the new arrivals. By 1916 more than a thousand children were attending eighteen Sabbath schools organized by women from the Pittsburgh chapter.[36] The NCJW mission schools placed a special emphasis on schools for girls, observing that many of the educational frameworks created by Orthodox immigrants were restricted to classical Jewish education for boys. The NCJW delegates from Baltimore reported at the organization's first national council in 1896 that female students were clamoring to attend the community's one mission school, and they would therefore focus their efforts on founding more. In Buffalo, New York, meanwhile, the work of the NCJW had the enthusiastic backing of not only the congregational Sabbath school's board but also that of the local superintendent of public school education, who had been enlisted to provide the chapter with the names of all Jewish students enrolled in his district so that they could be encouraged to enroll in the NCJW's Sunday morning classes.

One of the largest NCJW mission schools was organized in Cleveland. It enrolled nearly thirteen hundred Jewish children. Cleveland's NCJW chapter was organized in 1894 as an amalgamation of three existing women's organizations—the Ladies' Benevolent Society, the Ladies' Sewing Society, and the Personal Service Society. The founding president was Rabbi Moses M. J. Gries rather than one of the women involved in these organizations. Nineteenth-century Jewish women's organizations were often organized under male leadership—it was assumed that women were incapable of leading themselves.[37] Women quickly proved their capabilities, however, and took over the presidency in 1896. Among the Cleveland chapter's pioneer ventures was the Friendly Club, organized for working girls; it offered classes in vocational skills, including sewing, cooking, dressmaking, and stenography. In 1897 the chapter opened a night school, followed by a kindergarten in 1898 and Martha's House, a home for working girls, in 1909. The chapter expanded its activities exponentially following the gift of a substantial residential property in 1899. A library organized in the house was opened to the public, and baths were available for the charge of a couple of cents, which included the provision of soap and a towel and an attendant who would assist with bathing children. On Sunday evenings entertainments and lectures offered at the home included a children's theater, classes in cooking and housekeeping, and classes in hygiene that focused on "sex hygiene, home nursing, and laboratory work to test food values."[38] The greatest expense to the council was its milk deliveries, which it supplied to children and the sick at a cost of more than $1,500 per year. The NCJW supported these efforts with donations from its members as well as fundraising initiatives, including a popular strawberry fair that the council organized each summer.

The Cleveland chapter's Religious School was founded with a $500 donation by the trustees of local Temple Tifereth Israel in 1897. The school quickly became popular among Jewish children and could soon boast an average attendance of 350 children at each of its Saturday and Sunday morning sessions, with even higher numbers on days when bad weather kept the children from playing outside. The school's entertainments were especially popular, with Hanukkah parties and an annual picnic always drawing a crowd. By 1903 the council could boast not only that its Sabbath school had 12,440 children enrolled but that all sixteen of its teachers were paid for their efforts, the only Sabbath school in the city to do so. What is more, all instructors were public school teachers who brought training in pedagogy and classroom management to the work of religious education. American women, including American Jewish women, became teachers in record numbers during the nineteenth century. Teaching was one of the few professions open to educated women and was popularly viewed as an extension of women's domestic and nurturing roles.[39]

By 1902 sixteen NCJW sections sponsored eighteen Sunday schools across the United States, with 162 teachers and an average attendance of 2,500 children. The Cleveland chapter was viewed as a model for other regions to aspire to. The Cleveland chapter represented "the banner section of the council," pronounced NCJW field secretary Jeanette Goldberg when she visited the area in 1905. Its chief value, she concluded, lay in the "stimulus" that it gave to local young people through its religious education programs.[40] NCJW women who founded Sunday schools saw their work in religious education as a continuation of the project that began in Philadelphia in 1838. "Could Miss Gratz look down upon these schools now," declared Mrs. Henry (Clara) Hahn in an address recounting the achievements of the NCJW mission schools at its 1896 council, "she would surely feel that no nobler monument could have been consecrated in her memory than is represented by them."[41]

The educational initiatives promoted by NCJW chapters were not limited to children but extended to NCJW members themselves. While NCJW members took for granted that their labors to organize mission schools and to be included on the boards of congregational Sunday schools was work that was expressly appointed to Jewish women, they also recognized that women had little Jewish knowledge of their own to bring to the task. Some contemporary American Jews blamed the circumscribed educational curriculum of the Sunday school for the limited Jewish literacy of the community's women.[42] Yet in reality most American Jewish children, and especially American Jewish girls, did not attend receive any Jewish schooling at all.[43] In January 1895 Sadie American, a founder of the NCJW, "absorbed" ten Jewish ministers as she described how women felt estranged from Jewish life because they were ignorant of Jewish subjects, while in the *American Jewess*, editor Rosa Sonneschein denounced men who had deprived her sex of an education in Hebrew and Judaism.[44] "Blind obedience to prescribed laws," she wrote in 1895, "made of Jewish women religious automats, that move and follow closely the lines directed by man. . . . She has blabbered the Hebrew prayers without understanding a word of them, adhered to commands never explained to her, and followed a routine of harassing precepts transmitted with sublime ignorance from dame to daughter."[45] The NCJW emphasized the importance of continuing Jewish education for council members, theorizing that it would both aid them in their work in Jewish schools and benefit them personally as wives and mothers. "We neither know nor understand Judaism," wrote Sadie American in 1896. "'Tis time we did. We would study its teachings in order to live its principles. I know of no more adequate raison d'etre, no higher purpose."[46]

By 1896 almost half of all NCJW members were involved in one of the society's study circles, an initiative that took the groundbreaking step of using skilled women as leaders.[47] The national leadership of the NCJW prepared a study circle syllabus listing forty-two topics, including Jewish history, prayer, and Jewish philosophy. But the most popular topic by far was the study of the Bible. In NCJW study circles, Sadie American explained, women were advised to study the Bible for themselves and to dismiss their fears that the Bible "was too deep for them, or that it was the property of the few—the theologians."[48] The Cleveland NCJW chapter organized a popular Bible circle for women, which by necessity was held at Temple Tifereth Israel rather than the council's own property to accommodate the large numbers who wished to attend.[49] In Baltimore the NCJW organized four Bible study circles that by 1898 had an average of 68 attendees, a healthy proportion of the chapter's 360 members.[50]

The NCJW's efforts to sponsor Jewish education for women were not unanimously applauded, particularly among rabbis who feared that such female-led initiatives threatened public perceptions of rabbis themselves as the legitimate teachers and spokespeople for Judaism. Kaufmann Kohler extolled the spirituality and religious sentiment that women brought to communal volunteer work when he offered a prayer before the first national convention of the NCJW in 1896, but he was less enthusiastic about women's developing expertise in Jewish religious literature. In 1895 he told the New York branch of the NCJW that its plan to found women's Bible study circles was too focused on intellectual matters. If women were to engage themselves in study, he advised, it should be to develop their prowess as writers with "womanly hearts," writers who possessed "that spirituality that gives us the needed motive power," rather than troubling themselves with scholarly concerns.[51] Five years later Kohler congratulated the NCJW for its achievements in founding study circles to provide continuing education for women but lamented that they had much work still to do to kindle enthusiasm for Judaism among their children and families. Women should not preoccupy themselves with intellectual matters or "try to solve problems that vex the oldest and most skillful theologians," he advised. Women should commit themselves to their proper sphere of influence, their homes and their children, and "rekindle the fire of religion on her own heart [and] elicit the music of prayer from her own children."[52] While Kohler valued the contributions of women to the cause of Jewish education, he was adamant that their efforts should focus on the affective domain. Men brought intellectual skills and dispositions to Jewish religious education, he argued, women brought sentiment and spirituality.[53]

Cultural Progress

The American Jews who engaged in charitable work to benefit their newly arrived coreligionists in the late nineteenth century typically described their work as a program of moral uplift. They sought to bring cultivated values to the culturally deficient and offered themselves as models toward which they hoped the eastern Europeans would aspire. The efforts of these established American Jews could be paternalistic at best and patronizing at worst. At a meeting of the school board of Detroit's Temple Beth El in 1892, the acting president, Louis Felling, proposed that the congregation should start a free school for new Jewish immigrants, complaining that while Christian missionaries would travel far and wide to "religionize and civilize the heathens . . . we stand idly by and see hundreds of Jewish born children roaming about our fair city, as bootblacks, newsboys and loafers."[54] Felling at least communicated his sentiments behind the relatively closed doors of a congregational board meeting. In 1889 the presidents of the Hebrew Educational Society of Newark, New Jersey, issued a public appeal for financial contributions to support a new Hebrew free school for Russian immigrant children. Describing their Russian coreligionists as "anarchists and apostates," the society asked for contributions of two dollars per year, assuring their supporters that the school would "never be a cheder of the olden times" but would inculcate "into [immigrants'] hearts lessons of morality and religion that shall serve as powerful factors in sowing the seeds of usefulness and sound character in these future men and women of our faith."[55] The school, founded two years later as the Plaut Memorial Hebrew Free School, offered instruction on Sunday mornings and weekday afternoons. It followed a traditional curriculum to appease its diverse board as well as the eastern European families they hoped to recruit. Yet the curriculum did little to erase the dismissive attitude toward new immigrants that was proclaimed so publicly by its founders. Saul Schwartz of Newark recalled enrolling in the Plaut Memorial Hebrew Free School when he was five. One week later his father noticed the school's dedication plaque, inscribed with the message that the school had been established to bring "the civilizing influences of democracy to our Eastern European brethren." Saul never attended the school again.[56]

The rhetoric of cultural advancement that pervaded efforts to found schools to serve Jewish immigrant children also extended to the educational materials used in their classrooms. In children's periodicals and magazines written for use in American Jewish Sunday schools, new immigrants were urged to adopt American customs and adapt their halachic practices to American Jewish norms. The children's periodical *Helpful Thoughts* was edited by Julia Richman, a public school educator and Jewish philanthropic worker active in the National Council of Jewish Women. An affluent German Jew, Richman was superintendent of schools for the Lower East Side. She described her educational work in the New York public schools as an intervention in the acculturation of her eastern European coreligionists, a sentiment she also brought to her volunteer work in supplementary Jewish education.[57] The cheder should be exterminated, she told the National Council of Jewish Women in 1896. "It is un-American, unprogressive and unethical in its influence." Mission schools, teaching religion and decorum, she proposed, were much better educational models for Jewish life in America.[58] Richman hoped that *Helpful Thoughts* would provide a fitting resource for the project of Jewish religious education and "proper ethical reading for children of our own faith."[59] The title of the magazine hinted at the moral didacticism within its covers. *Helpful Thoughts* stressed the importance of cultivating American cultural conduct and encouraged its readers to leave behind their immigrant ways. Stories and columns emphasized the benefits of American citizenship and the advantages of liberal assimilated Judaism. In a regular series of columns called "Jewish Life in Palestine," Reform rabbi Martin A. Meyer explained that the halachic practices he saw among Jewish communities in Jerusalem were "characteristics of the oriental Jews." Describing traditional religious practices as a custom of "there," Oriental and bizarre for the readers "here" in America, Martin A. Meyer and *Helpful Thoughts* informed children that traditional halachic observance was a foreign custom—American citizenship required a different mode of Judaism.[60] When George Alexander Kohut replaced Richman as editor in 1903, he embraced the magazine's didactic moralism, changed its title to the *Jewish Home,* and featured stories that emphasized the importance of cultivating genteel American Jewish domestic values. He also introduced jingoistic stories that celebrated the advantages of America over Europe as a homeland for the Jewish people.[61] With editions typically themed around the Jewish calendar, the 1904 December edition offered a retelling of the Hanukkah story that applied the motifs of European anti-Semitism to the Greek villains of the story. The Passover edition of the same year explained that while Jews once were driven from country to country, in America they could celebrate Passover without fear of having to leave their new home again. The Jewish home that Richman and Kohut presented to children modeled Reform modes of American Jewish religion, celebrated America as a Jewish homeland, and attempted to acculturate new immigrants into American life.

Assuming that children were more culturally malleable, more capable of cultural redemption than their immigrant parents, German American Jews made children's religious education central to efforts to acculturate the eastern Europeans to a different mode of Jewish citizenship. As Mrs. Henry (Clara) Hahn of Philadelphia told the first convention of the National Council of Jewish Women in 1896, the Russians were "a people to be cared for and civilized," and education of the young was the means to do it. "Recognizing that only through the children could the elders be reached," she reported, "the Hebrew Sunday School Society of Philadelphia extended its field to meet the emergency."[62] By applying tropes of cultural deficiency and reform to new Jewish immigrants, acculturated American Jews subverted hierarchies perpetuated by Protestants that framed white Christian domesticity as the archetype of a cultured civilization.[63] These Protestant narratives blended ideals of evangelical Christian benevolence with social evolutionary theories, creating hierarchies that assumed that Anglo-American Protestants were culturally, as well as racially, superior to other peoples.[64] While Protestant hierarchies recommended that cultural progress could be attained through the adoption of Christianity, in the hands of German Jews movement up the ladder came through Americanization and the embrace of their own brand of Jewish religion rather than through theological conversion.

The efforts of American Jewish sisterhoods, mission schools, and free schools, as well as local and national chapters of the National Council of Jewish Women, provided important social services, countered the efforts of Christian missionaries, and made Jewish learning accessible to a newly arrived population with few financial resources. Yet they also emphasized that education in Jewish religion required initiation into values that established American Jews considered essential to Americanization. Emphasizing that Jewish religious learning in an American cultural idiom should focus on the cultivation of ethics and morals, belief in God, and Bible stories read in English, these initiatives eschewed much of the core content knowledge that was taught not only in traditional Jewish educational settings but even in congregational Sunday schools, which typically still taught some Hebrew as well as Jewish theology through catechism. Such limited curricula often derived from the women's self-perception of themselves as illiterate in Jewish subjects, a perception that through its study circles, lectures, and other initiatives the National Council of Jewish Women endeavored to change. The limited curricula also reflected the women's condescension toward most of their eastern European coreligionists, however, for whom they determined that the primary educational goal was the acquisition of genteel values rather than Jewish knowledge. The free schools and mission schools founded by women's organizations at the end of the nineteenth century emphasized that Jewish education should focus on learning to be religious in the right ways. They made Jewish education part of the broader project of American cultural citizenship.

6

From Theology to Religion

In 1897 Abraham Flexner, a progressive educational reformer and the son of German Jewish émigrés who had settled in Kentucky, was invited to speak to the Hebrew Sabbath School Union of America, the umbrella organization for Jewish Sunday schools of the American Jewish Reform movement. He told the assembled rabbis that the primary problem that institutes of religious learning would have to overcome—if they were to survive into the twentieth century—was that they were too focused on theology. They determined educational success by the perpetuation of their theologies and dogmas. Such particularistic claims had all been proved null and void, he argued, by scholarship on the origins of religion that had demonstrated that religion was universal rather than sectarian. These scholars had shown that no theological system had a monopoly on religious truth. "The idea of salvation has been spiritualized," he advised. "Instead of fixing the narrowest possible religious adherence, an allegiance which is more and more likely to fail and involve in its ruin all religious affiliation whatever, how much wiser to look after the religious sense, which will endure with or without a more limited religious connection?"[1]

For educators within the Reform movement, Flexner's proposition—that religious education should focus more on the cultivation of an individual child's religious character, or "sense," rather than on the particular theologies of the Jewish people—seemed to have credible logic. Pointing to rising tides of atheism, agnosticism, and religious universalism, movements that seemed in step with the secular and scientific spirit of the age, rabbis in the American Reform movement at the end of the nineteenth century began to argue that the Sunday school should focus on cultivating each child's emotional attachments to religion rather than attempt to convey Jewish knowledge.[2] "According to the traditional method of Religious Schools, the men and women of the Bible are little more than pawns upon the cosmic chessboard, showing how God did this and that by them," Reform rabbi Louis Grossman would explain in a 1919 book. "But this is a theological view. The aim of the Religious School should be not to prove the principles of theology, but to cultivate the religious instincts of children."[3]

Beginning in the late 1880s, calls to refocus Jewish education on the cultivation of religious character abounded among Reform rabbis and educators who described their proposals as scientific. They devised theories of Jewish childhood that they believed aligned with the emerging science of child psychology, built upon so-called scientific models of race and cultural progress. Debates about how to teach biblical narratives that were contested by geology and biblical criticism proved an important springboard for these new ideas, as Reform rabbis wrestled with the question of when a child should be introduced to biblical narratives that had been proven inaccurate. The embrace of contemporary psychological models for pedagogy by turn-of-the-century Reform rabbis transferred the question of how to educate children in religion from the sphere of Victorian middle-class motherhood to the hands of professionals who boasted that they were equipped with a purportedly scientific understanding of how to inculcate religion in the young.

The stakes of the endeavor were high. Reform rabbis recognized that children seemed to show little interest in their Sunday school studies and even less interest in the synagogue as adults. Rabbi David Philipson complained that while Cincinnati's wealthy Jewish families joined his congregation, they prioritized other extracurricular activities for their children, such as dance recitals, music lessons, and French and German classes over the congregational Sunday school. "Would you deprive the child of a full and intelligent knowledge of what this Jewish heritage is?" Philipson admonished the recalcitrant parents of Congregation Bene Israel in 1904. "Your Rabbi, your chairman of the school board, and your teachers are doing all that they can. Will you not assist us at least in so far as to enroll them in the school?"[4] Sabbath school boards regularly exhorted the parents in their congregations to encourage children to take Sunday school seriously. "The members are urgently requested to use every endeavor to induce and persuade their children to attend school regularly," announced the school committee of San Francisco's Congregation Sherith Israel in 1899, "thereby enabling them to gain a thorough knowledge of our holy faith and the history of our people."[5]

The experience offered by Sunday schools themselves was hardly conducive to the cause. Rabbis knew that the common pedagogy of rote memorization of catechism and Bible history did little to entertain children or engage their imaginations. "In most Sabbath Schools," Reform rabbi Kaufmann Kohler admitted to the delegates who assembled at Pittsburgh to compile the movement's eponymous platform in 1885, "Bible history means nothing but cramming of memory with dry chronological facts and dates. Religious Instruction is a parrot-like rehearsing of hardly intelligible paragraphs about Metaphysics and ancient Hebrew rites, and Hebrew is the dim impression made upon the juvenile mind that Jewish history and literature read backward, instead of forward."[6] Calls for reform of the Sunday school curriculum crystalized around opposition to catechisms.[7] Memorization did not necessarily lead to understanding, and in most Sunday schools catechisms were dictated rather than explained. While feats of rote memorization wowed the crowds that gathered to hear the youngsters narrate their catechisms at Shavuot confirmation ceremonies, by the end of the century criticisms of the pedagogical strategy of verbatim recitation increasingly filled the columns of the American Jewish press and sounded from the pulpits of American Jewish synagogues. "Let me be candid," confessed Sabato Morais, hazan of Congregation Mikveh Israel in Philadelphia, in an appeal on behalf of the Hebrew Sunday School, "we want less of the sentences of a printed catechism, and more of oral explanations, and plain and soul penetrating language. We want less studying and more comprehending."[8] As "abstracts of metaphysical thought," advised Reform rabbi David Philipson in an 1890 *Guide for Sabbath School Teachers*, catechisms "are sufficient to tax the powers of fully developed minds. For the child, they lead to nothing but 'weariness of the spirit' and are in most cases unintelligible." Nineteenth-century catechisms commonly bore titles like "manual of religious instruction," implying that students were passive recipients of content being delivered, empty vessels waiting to be filled with knowledge. In his 1839 *Catechism for Younger Children*, the first Jewish catechism written in America, Isaac Leeser proposed that the child, knowing nothing of religion, should memorize the catechism and become obedient.[9] Subsequent catechisms authored on American soil mirrored Leeser's emphasis on rote learning, while the ideal of a learned American Jewish child—one who had a stock of memorized theologies and scriptural quotations at their disposal—was also lauded within the didactic literature serialized in periodicals for American Jewish children. In a story for the *Sabbath Visitor magazine*, Rabbi Max Lilienthal described a young child, Nellie, receiving her first catechism at Sunday school. Nellie was given her text with the instruction, "This book contains verses from the Bible. We shall learn them by heart during the week, and if we would know them we could answer all the questions our teachers would put about our religion."[10] "Little Nellie's Catechism" became a regular column in the *Sabbath Visitor*, and every week Nellie would offer some new feat of memorization of theology or the Bible, often waking up well before sunlight to learn new pages of her catechism.[11] Another regular column, "Little Uncle Sam," portrayed a young boy who regularly bested his Christian neighbors in knowledge of biblical passages. Nellie and Sam offered their young readers embodiments of the masthead of the *Sabbath Visitor*: "Hear counsel and accept instruction, in order that you may become wise."[12]

By the closing decades of the century, however, a growing cadre of rabbis in the American Reform movement had begun to insist that children could no longer be described merely as empty vessels to be filled with knowledge. No educational endeavor could be successful if it did not take into account what the new science of child psychology had to say about the nature of childhood and a child's stages of educational growth. "It is almost a truism to say that teaching is a science," Kaufmann Kohler observed in 1890. "Instruction, which means the piling up of knowledge upon a mind still unprepared, suggests the *old* method of pedagogues. Education, which means the drawing forth of the seeds of truth hidden in the human heart, indicates the *new*."[13] Defining the child and their abilities at various stages of childhood became a central preoccupation for the volunteers, teachers, and rabbis who sought to reform the American Jewish Sunday school at the end of the nineteenth century. In the process, children became the subject, rather than the object, of American Jewish education.

The Priceless American Jewish Child

The proposals for child-centered Jewish Sunday school education promoted by Reform rabbis and educators at the end of the nineteenth century aligned Jewish pedagogical insights with ideas about children that were pervasive within contemporary American popular culture. While the continuing popularity of catechisms still fueled the idea that children were empty vessels to be filled with memorized knowledge, the nineteenth century had seen the simultaneous rise of a venerable cult of childhood in America that was influenced by various strains of Romanticism. Beginning in the decades after the Civil War, romantic idealizations of children were elevated by new social structures that celebrated childhood as a distinct stage of life.[14] With the passage of the first child employment laws in the 1870s came an explicit protection of childhood as a distinct life stage, a period of education and discovery.[15] The ideal of the economically worthless but emotionally priceless child served as the basis for a model of childhood as a prolonged period devoted to play and learning, an idea that fueled parenting manuals, the emerging child welfare movement, and campaigns for progressive educational reform.[16] Advocates of progressive education promoted the child-centered educational theories of Johann Pestalozzi, insisting that children themselves should drive the educational experience. The progressives emphasized object lessons and nature study, taking children into natural habitats to develop their curiosity about the environments in which they lived.[17] A plethora of books offered theories of child development and practical advice about child-rearing, and new teacher-training colleges founded across the country emphasized that educators must be versed in pedagogies appropriate for different ages and stages of childhood as well as the content that they aspired to teach.[18] The one-room schoolhouse with its one-size-fits-all course of study was increasingly becoming a thing of the past. In its place were schools that housed multiple classes organized around graded curricula, with lessons tailored to the needs of the child.[19] Beginning in the 1880s, urban public schools were transformed into bureaucracies, organized into districts, and structured around graded curricula, influenced by paradigms from the business world as well as pedagogic ideas developed in Germany.[20] In the last decades of the nineteenth century, the question of how to educate children, as historian Ann Hulbert surmised, "had grown up. It was going to school, becoming professionalized."[21]

American Jewish educators began to incorporate these child-centered approaches to Jewish Sunday schools in the 1880s, as they strove to reorganize their pedagogical infrastructure to more closely resemble best practices in public education. Separating class instruction into grade levels was an immediate intervention, although spatial constraints would first have to be overcome. In 1880 Rabbi Elias Eppstein of Congregation B'nai Jehudah in Kansas City, Missouri, convinced his board that the temple's basement should be partitioned into classrooms so that each Sabbath school grade could receive instruction separately, rather than meeting in the sanctuary as one large group.[22] In other contexts new synagogues were built with education in mind. The impetus to restructure the Jewish Sunday school around graded levels aligned with a major transformation in Reform synagogue architecture beginning in the 1880s that emphasized the role of the synagogue as a community center as well as a space for public prayer.[23] As Reform congregations constructed new synagogue centers, space for Sunday schools was prioritized with classrooms included in the architectural design. When the Jewish community of Sioux City, Iowa, built a synagogue in 1901, the *Sioux City Journal* admiringly reported that its schoolroom was 25 by 37 feet— almost as large as its main auditorium—with a large rostrum in front and an impressive seating capacity of three hundred.[24]

Attempts to organize Sunday schools around graded instruction were also initiated at a national level. In 1886 the Union of American Hebrew Congregations incorporated the Hebrew Sabbath School Union of America (HSSUA) with the express mission to standardize instruction around graded curricula in Reform Sunday schools. The work of the HSSUA focused largely on attempts to create a uniform system for Bible instruction, the mainstay of the Reform Sunday school curriculum.[25] For primary classes the HSSUA prioritized materials that related biblical narratives to events in the child's own life and in language appropriate for their young age. When Rabbi David Philipson took over as president of the HSSUA in 1894, he spearheaded a series of instructional leaflets for volunteer instructors who had little knowledge of the biblical material.[26] A survey of 114 congregations conducted by the HSSUA in 1889 identified 563 teachers working in Reform Sabbath schools, of whom the majority, 377, were volunteers with no training in Jewish religion or pedagogy.[27] By 1901 the HSSUA had distributed 109,400 leaflets to paid subscribers, across 120 schools.[28] The leaflets used questions to frame the biblical text like an object lesson, a stimulus that could generate thoughtful questions that encouraged the child to think deeply about the world and their place within it. "When you look up at the world," the first leaflet in the series began, "you must wonder, who made it? When you take a flower into your hand do you always think how long it took for that flower to grow, and that God made it to delight us with its sweet odor and beauty?"[29] For the volunteer teachers the leaflets provided not only ready-made questions to pose to the children but also ready-made answers expressed in child-friendly language.[30]

When considering graded curricula for older children, however, the question of how to appropriately teach biblical narratives generated more sustained debate. Bible history textbooks used in American Jewish Sunday schools customarily paraphrased biblical narratives as positivist chronologies of biblical stories, interpreting them as objective historical records, unambiguous accounts of the people of Israel's collective past. As American Reform Jews became increasingly comfortable with historical biblical criticism and scientific theories of evolution, however, educators struggled to reconcile this new knowledge with the positivist approaches to teaching Bible history that dominated their Sunday schools. Rabbi Harry Meyer of Reform Congregation B'nai Jehudah in Kansas City complained to the Central Conference of American Rabbis in 1902 that in Jewish Sunday schools, the Bible was taught as a historical text rather than as a religious one. Protestant Sunday schools had standardized Bible classes through lessons assigned by their international Sunday school board, he explained, which used the Bible as a "storehouse of ethical and religious passages." Jewish Sunday schools, on the other hand, still assumed that the Bible could be taught as a historical record of the Jewish people.[31]

As the nineteenth century drew to a close, Reform rabbis pointed with increasing frequency to the limitations of teaching the Bible as positivistic history. They pointed first and foremost to the accounts of Creation in the book of Genesis as particularly challenging to frame in historical terms. The Creation narratives layered seemingly contradictory chronologies of the same events and recounted the act of creation as a process of divine innovation, a stark contrast to the picture painted by contemporary geology. Reform rabbis saw little value in pitting Judaism against science, a battle that they felt sure that Judaism would lose. The dilemma posed by biblical criticism and evolution to the teaching of the book of Genesis centered primarily on the question of whether—and when—the child could appropriately be taught the Bible's nonscientific account of Creation. Reform rabbis argued that the Torah's account of Creation should be reframed and taught not as a historical text but as a religious one.[32]

"The People of the Book Have Become the Bookless People"

If there was one organization that systematically took on the challenge of finding an intellectual and pedagogical answer to the question of how to teach the story of Creation, it was the Jewish Chautauqua Society (JCS). It was responsible for the dissemination of a particularly controversial approach to the biblical account of Creation, which presupposed that the book of Genesis was a primitive text that was wholly unsuitable for impressionable young minds. At the JCS Teachers' Institute, held at its annual summer assemblies, participants debated not only the content of what should be taught in their respective Sunday schools but also pragmatic issues of teaching Jewish children of different ages and stages. From its inception the primary philosophical and educational problem discussed at the Teachers' Institute was the question of how to teach the Bible. "The Bible is a sealed book to thousands," JCS founder Henry Berkowitz wrote in the prospectus for the first summer assembly. "Yet it is the world's best treasure. It is Israel's greatest gift to humanity. To come to the aid of the general reader, to unseal the pages of scripture, to make Bible reading simple, sensible and stimulating, is the chief need of today."[33] Observing that an increasingly secular American Jewish population, convinced by the insights of historical biblical research as well as by evolutionary science, largely did not believe that the Bible offered anything relevant to modern life, Berkowitz was convinced that the JCS needed to intervene. "The People of the Book have become the bookless people," he lamented in 1896.[34] The Bible had become, to the general reader, a "wilderness of confusion, a jungle of terrors and superstition, a sanctuary of breathless darkness."[35] The JCS, he promised, would rescue the Bible from the death throes of intellectual irrelevance, acknowledge its historical origins with reference to the most contemporary historical research, and reconstruct its significance as great religious literature. The Chautauqua approach to biblical study, Berkowitz explained at the first summer assembly, "presents the results of the best thought without fear and seeks to conserve and deepen a reverence for the sublime teachings of the Bible."[36]

In 1896 Berkowitz published *The Open Bible* for use in reading circles created by the JCS for local communities to study Jewish topics together.[37] Intended for a general audience, *The Open Bible* offered a series of guided introductions to the different books of the Hebrew Bible, accompanied by reading assignments from selected secondary sources. It would become one of the most popular texts published by the society.[38] Though *The Open Bible* was essentially little more than a syllabus of readings, it was immediately controversial. The debate was engendered not by words written by Berkowitz but by a textbook assigned as a reading companion —Claude Montefiore's *Bible for Home Reading*, also published in 1896. Montefiore, a British scholar and advocate of liberal Judaism in England, directed his *Bible for Home Reading* at parents who were reluctant to allow their children to read the Bible, knowing that it did not offer an accurate historical chronology. "They are well aware," Montefiore acknowledged, "that it is widely maintained by the best authorities that Moses did not write the entire Pentateuch, and that it is not the work of one author or of one age, but of many authors and many ages."[39] Montefiore embraced a historical critical approach to the compilation of the Torah, arguing that the religious imagination of the Bible writers evolved during the long redaction period of the Hebrew Bible. The first five books of the Torah, he explained, were an assemblage of ancient fragments that reflected archaic immature phrases of religious thinking. The later books of the Prophets, on the other hand, reflected a more mature religion that was monotheistic and ethical.[40] Reform thinkers in Europe and America who lionized the Bible as the cornerstone of modern Jewish religion had to reckon, often with significant discomfort, with the Bible's canonization of bloody battles as well as ethical and theological ideals. In *The Bible for Home Reading* Montefiore revised and reordered the biblical material to minimize what he presumed to be its chief intellectual inadequacies. Montefiore entirely omitted the books of Joshua and Judges, which he dismissed as "tales of bloodshed and slaughter, unredeemed by moral teaching," and the story of the Creation was presented not at the beginning of the volume but in its very last chapter. *The Bible for Home Reading* began with the story of Abraham and continued with expositions of the biblical texts through the standard order of the Tanakh, ending with the first chapters of the book of Genesis. "I consider these early chapters too full of grave moral and religious difficulties to form a suitable beginning," Montefiore explained. "There were no such six days, nor were there plants upon the earth before there was sun or stars in the heaven." Montefiore argued that the book of Genesis should be studied last, when the child was older, and after they had been impressed by the more refined religious ideas of the Prophets. "I cannot attempt to write any sort of commentary to this famous chapter," he explained in his introduction to the Creation narratives. "The writer seems to have imagined that before 'creation' there had existed from interminable time a chaotic mass of matter and a limitless tumult of waters. This story of creation is a pure work of fantasy."[41] A child raised on *The Bible for Home Reading*, Montefiore predicted, would learn to appreciate that the authors of the Bible refined their religious ideas over time. "He will learn to love the Bible with a love at once emotional and intelligent. The growth of religious ideas will prove as interesting to him as the history of the people among whom these ideas ripened and developed," Montefiore reasoned.[42] *The Bible for Home Reading* celebrated the religious evolution of the biblical writers, even while it dismissed their earliest literary works as dangerous for childhood consumption.

Berkowitz's 1896 endorsement of *The Bible for Home Reading* as a required text in the Jewish studies reading circles of the JCS immediately set the tone for the society's approach to Bible education. Through its patronage of Montefiore, the JCS popularized the idea that the first chapters of the Torah represented "primitive" literature, dangerous for young children who had not yet developed the critical intellectual faculties to appreciate the evolution of Judaism during the redaction period of the Hebrew Bible.[43] They were innocents who needed to be saved from dangerous texts originating in the ancient Near East. The membership of the JCS, particularly among its more traditionalist demographic, did not accept without question the terms of engagement outlined by Montefiore. At the JCS's first summer assembly, Berkowitz's endorsement of *The Bible for Home Reading* was debated at length. Henrietta Szold declared that the primary task of the Sunday school was not to cultivate religious character but to introduce children to Jewish knowledge. The

Bible, she argued, should be taught in its classical, canonized form. It did not need to be reordered to align with theories about the religious evolution of the Bible writers and justified by the vague rationale of protecting the religious sensibilities of children.[44] Reform rabbi William Rosenau was more amenable to the idea that the primary objective of the Sunday school should be defined in terms of religious character cultivation but contended that Montefiore was unduly negative in his assessment of the story of Creation. Rosenau advised that there was "no biblical story so long as it did not treat up the licentious which children could not be told with profit"—any biblical text could be taught as long as educators could bring it to life.[45] The sentiment of the conference, as the proceedings of the first summer assembly recorded, was generally averse to teaching historical criticism in the Jewish Sunday school.[46] *The Open Bible* received a similarly lukewarm reception outside of the Jewish Chautauqua Society. Sabato Morais denounced the volume in the strongest terms, describing it as both dangerous and offensive.[47] Historian Richard Gottheil, on the other hand, called it excellent, explaining that he had "long contended that it is wrong to teach to little tots in our religious schools these attempts at dealing with the most awful problems that are presented to our thought—creation, life, sin and punishment. They are problems which can only be comprehended at a much later period of thought."[48] A debate about *The Open Bible* flared at the first meeting of the National Council of Jewish Women in 1896, and when Berkowitz was invited to speak, he offered a gendered caution to the council, saying that he did not think it wise for the women to engage in "discussion of a theological question" yet nevertheless conceded that he did not recommend the book without hesitation.[49] Berkowitz later recalled that the book's publication "aroused quite a storm of discussion" in American Jewry.[50] Despite the opposition, the controversial text was not withdrawn from the JCS's Jewish studies catalogue. Participants in the JCS reading circles that formed across the country would learn that the Creation story was a religiously immature and dangerous text, one that should not be taught to innocent children in American Jewish Sunday schools.

A Primitive Text for a Primitive Child

A quite different approach to the pedagogical problem of how to teach the biblical story of Creation shared Montefiore's assessment of the Creation story as primitive but argued that it was therefore perfectly suited to the equally primitive American Jewish child. The image of the child as a primitive—or its equally harsh synonym, *savage*—drew from broader contemporary narrative tropes that equated young people with the characteristics that were anthropologically applied to non-Westerners and, more explicitly, to nonwhites.[51] It was an image that was used extensively in missionary discourse and in texts for American Christian Sunday schools to describe the project of making "primitive heathens" into "good little children."[52] It equated children with an early stage of human evolution. "As with the early man, so with the child," explained the *Christian Register* in 1901. "It learns by imitation."[53]

Beginning in the 1890s, the narrative trope of the child as primitive was bolstered by research emerging from the new field of child psychology. In Germany scholars Wilhelm Wundt and Gustav Fechner gathered empirical data to support their theory that the human psyche was a matter of the mind rather than the soul, providing the conditions for the separation of psychology from philosophy.[54] Their work was taken up in the United States by psychologist G. Stanley Hall, who inaugurated the child study movement in psychology with a survey that attempted to assess and tabulate the contents of a child's mind and chart their mental development. Hall's theory of childhood proposed that children went through distinct and observable stages as they grew and could understand increasingly complex information along the way. His interest in child psychology transcended pedagogy and school reform; he theorized that studying children offered a microcosm of the history of the human race. "Child study as I regard it," wrote Hall in the first edition of the *Paidologist*, the journal of the child-study movement, "marks the advance of evolutionary thought into the field of the human soul."[55] The psychology of childhood that Hall popularized was situated within an evolutionary framework he styled as "recapitulation," a purported archaeology of the mind.[56] Hall proposed that the development of an individual, through the stages of childhood, adolescence, and adulthood, was analogous to the historical development of humankind from primitive to civilized forms.[57] The child, simply put, was the "survival" of primitive man. The "child primitive" was studied by psychologists like Hall not only for its own sake but as an entry point to the historical development of human culture more broadly.[58] Hall described the progression of recapitulation as peaking with the emergence of the rational muscular Christian man and advised boys to embrace their inner savage to become physically adept adults.[59]

Recapitulation quickly made an impact in America, appearing in general texts of psychology, studies of pedagogy, and an emerging body of literature on child-rearing. For some American Jews, Hall's embrace of Christianity as the telos of cultural and racial evolution offered sufficient cause to reject recapitulation as a philosophy of childhood.[60] For others, however, Hall's theories, as well as his growing celebrity stature, seemed to be convincing. Rebekah Kohut sought opportunities to audit courses taught by Hall and fondly remembered learning with a scholar she felt was unequaled, not only in intellectual acumen but also in kindness.[61] Hall's theory of recapitulation was reviewed in the American Jewish press, and advocates promoted its findings at the Chautauqua summer assemblies, the Central Conference of American Rabbis, and the meetings of the Hebrew Sabbath School Union of America.[62] For Jews in the American Reform movement, inclined toward the maskilic (European Jewish enlightenment) message of redemptive modernity, casting the child as a primitive savage dovetailed with their own evolutionary approach to Judaism. It mirrored their thesis of the progress of the Jewish people, from the primitive early biblical literature to the scientific reasoning of the reforming Jewish modern.[63] Jewish champions of recapitulation rejected Hall's demarcation of muscular Christianity as the telos of cultural evolution and his stress on the importance of embracing the manly savage. Instead they emphasized that the child, like "primitive man," had an innate belief in religion and shared an appetite for the divine. In the hands of American Jews, Hall's child primitive became an intellectual rather than a physical specimen. The child exemplified pure religion rather than pure physicality, offering a window into a nostalgic time when humanity was attuned to the transcendent and looked at the world with wonder.

When the Hebrew Sabbath School Union of America (HSSUA) published a *Guide for Sabbath School Teachers*, an 1890s collection of essays on Sabbath school pedagogy, they included two essays that argued that because children were primitive in their comprehension of religion, they could appropriately study the Creation story in the book of Genesis. In his contribution Kaufmann Kohler explicitly rejected the approach taken by Montefiore, in which the story of Creation was taught only to older grades. "It does not speak well for the pedagogical wisdom of some of our leaders that they advise Sabbath-school teachers in the lowest grade to omit the chapters on creation and the first men, and to begin the history with Abraham," Kohler maintained. As this was a period in children's lives when they were particularly receptive to fairy tales, myths, and legends, the story of Creation was entirely appropriate. Children were not rational thinkers, he insisted, hence their textbooks did not need to be either. A second essay in the *Guide for Sabbath School Teachers*, Edward Calisch's "How to Teach Biblical History in the Primary Grade," echoed Kohler's contention that the Creation story in Genesis was particularly well suited to younger students. The young child, Calisch maintained, was endowed with credulity, the implicit willingness to believe. To what age could the Creation story be better suited? "The history of a single child's mental and religious development is a microcosmic reproduction of the history of the human race," Calisch explained. "In the childhood of humanity nothing was too stupendous for belief. God and goblins, deities and devils, innumerable and indescribable, held sway within the pantheon of ancient credulity. But as the race grew older and wiser it winnowed the wheat and the breezes of passing centuries blew away the chaff." The child, yet to lose the chaff of belief in fairy tales, Calisch concluded, would be especially receptive to the primitive myth preserved in the biblical account of Creation.[64] Through Kohler and Calisch's contributions, the HSSUA's *Guide for Sabbath School Teachers* provided an alternative rationale to navigate the so-called danger of teaching the story of Creation to children, one that assumed the intellectual equivalence of the contemporary American child and the ancient writers of the Bible. This paternalistic anthropology of childhood painted child spirituality as pure and uncorrupted, even while it derided the child's lack of intellectual sophistication. It married the concept of the child as an empty vessel who needed to be filled with rational knowledge to the sentimental Victorian conception of the child as innately credulous. It endorsed religious emotion too, celebrating the "primitive" religion of the emotive child with recourse to theories described as scientific.

For American Jews who were convinced by Hall's theory of recapitulation, defining the child as primitive was not a disparaging assessment of children and their capabilities but rather opened the door to child-centered pedagogies. Louis Grossman, professor of theology, ethics, and pedagogy at Hebrew Union College from 1898 to 1922, and head of the college's training institute for Hebrew school teachers from 1909 to 1921, was a lifelong proponent of Hall's theory of recapitulation.[65] "The science of education," Grossman maintained, "lays down the law that the soul of the child passes through certain periods of development. These periods mirror the periods that the race has passed."[66] At the first Teachers' Institute at the Chautauqua summer assembly, Grossman offered three addresses on Sunday school pedagogies in which he argued that teachers must understand the nature of the "youthful soul" and the "processes of its mental and moral life" so to effectively undertake the work of teaching it.[67] He insisted that educators should better understand the child's primitive religious nature so that children could be taught using instructional methods more appropriate to their development. Religious schools, he argued, "must establish themselves upon the basis of fact, of scientific, pedagogic fact. They must arrange their curricula in accordance with what child growth demands. Jewishness is not an end product but a process. And the child has all sorts of Judaisms, a childish one, an adolescent one, and a number of intellectual and emotional varieties of it, all on their way to become the adult, balanced faith."[68] The progressivism of Grossman's "all on their way to become the adult, balanced faith" was a testament to his perception of the redemptive possibilities of education for the American Jewish child. This marked an essential difference between the trope of the Jewish child savage and the nonwhites to whom this appellation was also applied. The child primitive, for Grossman, was a psychological, rather than essentially biological, category. The American Jewish primitive child could redeem itself through the cultivation of rational intellect and modern civility, taught according to their primitive nature while they awaited their intellectual coming of age.

Embracing Religious Emotion

The proposition that the new science of psychology could scientifically prove that the child was naturally credulous in matters of religion was attractive to American Jewish communal leaders at the turn of the twentieth century. It seemed to offer an antidote to the disaffection for Jewish life that they observed among their congregants and to the tendency toward secular rationalism among educated American Jews. The question of how to teach the Bible to develop the religious sentiments of children was not merely a pedagogical problem to be solved on behalf of overwhelmed Sunday school volunteers. It was a question that seemed to have stakes for the future of assimilated American Jewry. For American Reform rabbis the research conducted within the new field of child psychology, including its evolutionary branches, offered the tempting prospect of scientifically explaining how to make religion matter to American Jews. "The religion of the child is largely, if not altogether that of primitive man," argued Colorado rabbi Montague Cohen before the 1907 meeting of the Central Conference of American Rabbis (CCAR). "It cannot but be admitted that children possess a remarkable individuality and a capacity for religion which is apparent early in life and which if properly tended and developed, will produce the choicest fruit."[69] While Jewish religious education had been described at the beginning of the nineteenth century as a project especially suited to women, at the turn of the twentieth century the new field of child psychology offered a language for describing children's receptivity to religion as a scientific, male-dominated domain of expertise. If the purpose of Jewish educational training was to facilitate children's innately religious commitments, for many Reform educators it seemed intuitive that the psychology—literally, the study of the *psyche,* or soul—offered a scientific framework for the task that designated it as an intellectual and male endeavor.

Early childhood seemed to be the critical moment of intervention, particularly in light of research that identified adolescence as the time when children were most likely to stray from the Jewish fold. G. Stanley Hall's pioneering 1904 empirical study, *Adolescence: Its Psychology and Its Relations to Physiology, Anthropology, Sociology, Sex, Crime and Religion,* borrowed the vocabulary of the German *Sturm und Drang* literary movement to define the transition from youth to adolescence as a time of storm and stress characterized by a lack of emotional steadiness, unreasonable conduct, and enthusiasm that culminated in the birth of a "new individual."[70] The concept of adolescence immediately struck a chord in the American popular imagination, as it seemingly isolated the precise moment that a virtuous child could transform into an obstinate, even criminal, adult.[71] In February 1905 Rabbi Henry Berkowitz invited Hall to address Congregation Rodeph Shalom in Philadelphia, asking him to speak to the question of why Jewish young adults seemed reluctant to affiliate with the synagogue, at least until they married and had children. Adolescence was to blame, Hall explained. This most impressionable time of life was a volatile period when children were most likely to stray from the path on which their parents had set them. Berkowitz's sermon the following week elucidated the importance of Hall's address for Jewish education, explaining that in childhood, "the whole world was as beautiful to us as the Garden of Eden," whereas in adolescence youth become "disillusioned and rebellious."[72]

The identification of adolescence as the critical moment when children were most likely to depart from the innate religiosity of younger years focused attention on early childhood as a vital inflection point for Jewish education. If children could be encouraged to embrace their innate love for religion during this most influential period, proponents maintained, these sensibilities would stay with them through adolescence and into Jewish adulthood. Some rabbis proposed deferring the age of confirmation, inferring from scholarship on adolescence that childhood did not end until the later teenage years. Delaying confirmation would also, they argued, more closely align the ceremony with graduation from high school, which toward the end of the century was celebrated by increasing numbers of American young people, including American Jews. The topic was keenly debated at the annual meetings of the CCAR beginning in the 1890s, yet the sense of the conference was that children from less affluent families were still unlikely to remain in high school until graduation, having by necessity to seek paid employment. Raising the age of confirmation would likely exclude them from participation.[73] The number of children enrolled in confirmation classes was declining already, rabbis noted, owing to decreasing family sizes among second-generation American Jews. There was little enthusiasm for adding to the problem by extending confirmation into adolescence.[74] Besides, there were affective benefits to confirming children when they were young and celebrating their enthusiasm for religion. "Every sect must have a children's day," argued Rabbi Louis Grossman in 1901. "A religion that does not set apart a day to celebrate its children is a religion that is dead." Even if confirmation did not ultimately lead to long-term commitments by the confirmands, he insisted, confirmation should celebrate childhood and the religious experiences that are particular to a community's children. "We get refreshment from the sight of innocent childhood," he concluded. "We want to be stirred by the things of long ago, when we ourselves were young, and the world was full of sweet scents, and God was not quite so far away."[75]

Grossman framed the value of confirmation in emotive rather than theological terms. It was less important, he maintained, that confirmation celebrate what children learned about Judaism. It was much more significant that it highlighted what it was possible to feel. His argument for the importance of religious emotion aligned with ideas about religion in contemporary American popular culture, as at the turn of the twentieth century scholars who specialized in the growing field of comparative religion publicly argued that emotion stood at the core of religious life.[76] "Religion is the feelings, acts and experiences of individual men in their solitude," suggested American philosopher William James in 1902, "so far as they apprehend themselves to stand in relation to the divine."[77] Emphasizing the individual affective dimensions of religion, most theories of the role of emotion in comparative religion barely concealed their grounding in Protestantism.[78] Yet for nineteenth-century rabbis struggling with declining synagogue attendance and the intellectual challenges of free thought and agnosticism popularized by influential men of the moment such as Robert Ingersoll, academic studies of religion that emphasized emotion offered data to bolster their arguments for the continuing importance of religion in the modern world, even despite their characteristically Protestant emphasis on religion as an individual rather than a collective affair. For American Reform Jews theories that emphasized the importance of religious emotion became popular at the precise moment that the Reform movement was beginning to negotiate its own departure from the emphasis on reason and rationalism that earlier generations of reformers had argued should be central to Jewish communal life. While these efforts may have served to establish Reform Judaism in America, rabbis regretfully acknowledged, they had done little to secure affection for Judaism among American Reform Jews. As the Jewish Sunday school entered the twentieth century, Reform educators embraced Jewish religious emotion as a strategy not only to educate the next generation of Jewish children but also to demonstrate the validity of Judaism as an American religion in a cultural climate that was increasingly secular.

A Short-Lived Embrace

The peculiar ruminations of nineteenth-century Reform educators, dwelling on the dangers of reading the Bible and delighting in the parallels between children and "primitive man," seem jarring in the context of the twenty-first century. The language of "primitive religion," not to mention "primitive childhood," is indelibly associated with the racialized schemas that nineteenth-century Americans applied to ethnic and religious others and that deemed people of color less worthy than their white contemporaries. Acknowledging that American Jews participated in these discourses is critical, however, to acknowledging the racialized ways that Jews navigated and negotiated the world of American religion in the late nineteenth and early twentieth centuries. Schemas that ranked the cultural and racial evolution of ethnic groups were common narrative tropes in contemporary American popular culture, and Jews applied them to others even while they were also the subjects of such classifications themselves.

Reform rabbis and educators who emphasized religious feeling as the primary purpose of Jewish education adopted a nontheological, anthropologically focused, idea of religion that stressed that Judaism offered a universal moral code and a handbook for character cultivation in tune with broader religious discourse at the turn of the century. They rejected the idea that Jewish learning should focus on the content knowledge of the Jewish people in order to stress that religion was primarily about cultivating personal character and affective sensibilities rather than the acquisition of divisive dogmas. As historian Melissa Klapper has observed, religious education for American Jewish girls grew more popular in the first decades of the twentieth century precisely at the moment Jewish families recognized the Sunday school's potential to make Judaism a meaningful part of their daughters' lives and to add spiritual significance to their nascent national identities.[79] By attending Sunday school and learning about the importance of personal spirituality, American Jewish children not only developed ties to their communities but also imagined religious identities that would shape their character as well.

The proposition that Jewish Sunday school education should focus on inculcating religious sentiment rather than on teaching Jewish knowledge was by no means unanimously accepted. Reform rabbis at the turn of the century emphasized an affective and universalist approach to Jewish learning just as the American Jewish educational landscape was becoming increasingly populated by new institutions that emphasized content acquisition as essential to Jewish schooling. Reform Hebrew schools began to emphasize the cultivation of religious sentiment over the acquisition of Jewish languages and literatures at the same time that Heder Metukan–style schools emphasizing Hebrew, and cheders and Talmud Torahs focused on Jewish textual study, were founded by new eastern European immigrants across the country. New Jewish revival organizations like the Menorah Association and *Menorah Journal*, a Jewish organization and publication for college students, began to stress that Judaism represented a national, ethnic, and legal culture and not only a religion in the idiom of American Protestantism. As waves of new immigrants expanded the range of possibilities for enlivening traditional Jewish education, the Reform Sunday school plowed a different furrow, emphasizing the universality of religious emotion rather than the particularity of Judaism as a distinctive people and culture.[80]

Their proposals would not prevail long as a model for Jewish learning in America. The Reform movement would itself undergo a revolution in Jewish education with the arrival of "Benderly boy" Emanuel Gamoran to head the movement's Department of Synagog [sic] and School extension in 1923, and embrace Jewish religious and cultural distinctiveness later in the twentieth century. It is critical, nonetheless, to recognize the ways that rabbis and educators attempted to define Jewish childhood for the purposes of reforming Jewish education at the turn of the twentieth century, even if their proposals were ultimately short-lived. For in the process of attempting to define childhood, children became levers for animating changing conceptions of religion in American Judaism. Throughout the nineteenth century, American Jews, like American Christians, had deflected their doubts and concerns about religion onto children. What amplified that stance at the turn of the twentieth century was the use of scientific theories of childhood to lend credence to the philosophy that real religion could be found in the young. Just as scholars of religion announced that emotion stood at the core of the religious experience, American Jews pointed to Jewish children as evidence that Judaism offered emotive religion in its purest form. The range of ways that American Jews sought to define and imagine Jewish childhood at the turn of the twentieth century thus powerfully illustrates how the Jewish Sunday school's attempt to teach Judaism as a religion was indelibly yoked to changing popular dynamics associated with the concept of religion more broadly. By claiming the Jewish child's innate credulity of religion, American Jews ultimately sought to claim that Judaism was, indeed, archetypal religion itself.

Conclusion

Is Judaism a Religion?

In 1901, members of the committee appointed by the Central Conference of American Rabbis to compile a catechism for Reform Jewish Sunday schools appeared before their colleagues at their annual conference to report on their progress. In the year since their last meeting, there had been much debate about whether a catechism that standardized Judaism into a single set of doctrinal statements was, in fact, a legitimate enterprise. For the committee the matter was simple. Sunday schools should be provided with a catechism that explained the beliefs and doctrines of Judaism because Judaism was a religion. "The difficulties in the definition of Judaism are no cause for dismissing the subject altogether, as some have proposed, for the condition is simply this," they explained. "There are Jews, consequently, there must be something which characterizes them as such. It can't be race, because there have been converts throughout Jewish history. A scientific Judaism must cover all individual facts. We have to define Judaism as a religion."[1]

Today many Jews would argue that the category of religion, with all its Protestant inflections of individualistic belief, seems inauthentic in application to Judaism, a tradition in which peoplehood, ethnicity, culture, language, and law have historically functioned as equally central components of Jewish self and communal identity. Nationwide surveys of Jewish Americans conducted by the Pew Research Center in 2012 and 2020 have emphasized that religion is only one of the ways that contemporary Jews define and practice Judaism and that Jews who eschew religion entirely are a growing demographic within the American Jewish population.[2] The rabbis and educators, teachers and children who attended American Jewish Sunday schools in the nineteenth century would have found these hesitations about religion and Judaism perplexing. For them it was axiomatic not only that Judaism was a religion but also that Judaism represented the most replete incarnation of the very idea of religion itself.

An intersecting set of contexts and causes led the Sunday school and its program of Jewish education as religious education to become the regnant model for Jewish learning in America during the nineteenth century. Rebecca Gratz's adaptation of the Victorian cult of true womanhood made religious education into a benevolent cause for Jewish women, while the translation of the Tanakh into English by Isaac Leeser made the Bible, the principal text of Protestantism, accessible to an American Jewish audience. The existence of free public schooling underscored the logic of a Jewish educational system that was separate and supplementary rather than holistic, emphasizing that Judaism represented a private, leisure-time set of faith commitments that did not interfere with Jews' abilities to participate in American public life. The theological parameters of Jewish faith commitments were explicated in the popular contemporary technology of the catechism, which provided an inexpensive textbook for Sunday schools, as well as a vehicle for rabbis to insert specifically male-gendered theological and philosophical expertise into the Sunday school curriculum. The affluence of upwardly mobile American Jews played an important role too, as Jews embraced consumer culture to create ritual theater in the celebration of confirmation and to promote a marketplace of material aids for Jewish religious pedagogy. As new immigrants arrived in the United States at the close of the century, the Sunday school offered a model for free schools and mission schools to make affordable Jewish education available to the children of the new arrivals while emphasizing that Judaism and Americanization must go hand in hand.

The heyday of the Jewish Sunday school ended as the new century began. A wave of Jewish immigrants arriving on American shores between 1880 and 1924 expanded the spectrum of institutions for Jewish learning, adding new cheders, Talmud Torahs, and day schools to the educational landscape. The Bureau of Jewish Education, led by Samson Benderly, was founded in 1910 to establish order from the chaos of competing Jewish educational institutions in New York City. From there he developed an ambitious program to found bureaus of Jewish education across the country to reform Jewish education in America writ large. With pedagogical investments in Hebrew and Jewish culture rather than in theology, Benderly and his colleagues saw the minimalist religious program of the Sunday schools as a problem to be erased rather than improved.[3] "Paradoxical as it may sound," opined Benderly's colleague Mordecai Kaplan in his magnum opus, *Judaism as a Civilization*, "the spiritual regeneration of the Jewish people demands that religion cease to be its sole preoccupation."[4]

Joined by a cadre of protégés, Benderly and his "boys" worked in communities across the country to support the creation of more intensive multiday supplementary schools that prioritized Jewish cultural immersion and Hebrew language rather than theological and moral instruction. The Benderly group attempted to create a communal model for Jewish education based on a shared sense of peoplehood, a purposefully vague concept that sought to achieve a rapprochement between traditionalists and progressives.[5] The animus of the Benderly group toward the Sunday school was pragmatic as well as ideological. For Benderly and his colleagues to secure the support of the Talmud Torahs that they hoped to integrate into their communal system, they had to convince the schools' leadership that the Benderly group had no intention of transforming them into Sunday schools.[6] Benderly heaped derision on the Sunday school in part to reassure his more traditionalist colleagues that the vision for Jewish education that he had in mind was rooted in Hebrew culture rather than in Protestant models of religious learning.[7]

Benderly could not have anticipated, however, that even traditionally inclined American Jews would ultimately embrace the congregational weekend model of Jewish religious learning promoted by Sunday schools in the midtwentieth-century context of postwar suburbia.[8] The suburban synagogue was an inhospitable environment for the intensive Hebraist nationalist pedagogy to which Benderly aspired; he could not have imagined that, barely two decades after his death, Jews would be living in a sprawl of newly developed suburbs rather than in the dense Jewish enclaves of downtown.[9] The model for Jewish schooling that triumphed in the second half of the twentieth century, much to Benderly's likely chagrin, would remain firmly attached to the idea of Jewish education as religious education conducted under the auspices of synagogues.

Today, despite considerable ambivalence among teachers, parents, and, not least, students themselves, the model pioneered by the nineteenth-century Jewish Sunday school is still very much in evidence.

Non-Orthodox American Jewish parents still overwhelmingly opt for supplementary schooling over Jewish day schools, notwithstanding the rising profile of full-time Jewish educational options.[10] Bar, bat, and b-mitzvahs, just like nineteenth-century confirmations, mark the ambivalent embrace of American Jewish religion by teenagers who are often highly prepared for their special performance but little equipped for making lifetime commitments to Judaism.[11] Sociological studies of the contemporary American Jewish population, meanwhile, have typically evaluated the efficacy of Jewish educational institutions according to the limited metrics of how well their graduates demonstrate knowledge of, and participation in, characteristically religious activities, such as joining a synagogue, lighting Shabbat candles, or fasting on Yom Kippur—despite overwhelming evidence that American Jews profess a broad range of ethnic, cultural, and familial Jewish identifiers.[12]

To note the indelible impact of the nineteenth-century Sunday school upon contemporary American Jewish education is not intended here as a justification for its use of religion as a framework for Jewish life. Although the idea of Judaism as a religion, defined by the exercise of private faith, quickly became the pervasive categorical marker for Jewish difference in America, it left little space for Jews who define their Jewishness in terms beyond the religious rubric. From halachically observant Jews, whose commitments to Jewish law function more broadly as a way of life rather than as a belief system, to ethnic and cultural Jews for whom the theological plays no role in their experience of Jewishness, the idea of religion may have made Judaism look more like American Protestantism, but it did not offer a category that was capacious enough to include all American Jews.[13] Furthermore, as I have observed, in their efforts to Americanize new immigrants, American Jews who defined Judaism as a religion integrated racialized hierarchies of cultural progress that marked the religious other as deficient, even when that other was in fact a Jew.

Rather than validate the pervasiveness of religion as a framework for Jewish life in America, I have sought in this book to emphasize the instability of religion as a descriptor for Judaism. When American Jews chose to define Judaism using the vocabulary of religion, they adopted a concept that was mutable—unstable rather than absolute. The principles that Gratz and the female volunteers who served alongside her in the first American Jewish Sunday school considered inviolable to the performance and practice of religion became, by the end of the century, hotly contested, from the place of the Bible to the idea of the divine. During the nineteenth century American Jews, like other Americans, wrestled with changing ideas about religion, changing ideas about good religion, and the changing roles of objects and ideas that previous generations had considered central to religion as an enterprise. Ideologies of religion as feminine and affective were pitted against ideals of good religion as masculine and rational, as religion was gendered by men and women in search of new ways to define Judaism and Jewishness. By the end of the nineteenth century, however, male rabbis began to claim the language of affective religion for their own, in response to both new scholarship on comparative religion and the daunting reality that most American Jews saw little value in synagogue membership. Rabbis in the American Reform movement embraced the idea of religion as affective to reassert the value of Judaism for a new generation of American Jews for whom claims of rationalism seemed better suited to secular spaces than religious ones.[14]

Changing ideas about Jewish religion fueled lively discussions and pedagogical innovations that attempted to animate the classrooms of Sunday schools during the nineteenth century. Yet in most historiographic literature about this period, the curricula offered in Sunday schools beyond Philadelphia and after Gratz have been dismissed as static and stagnant. It has broadly been assumed that Sunday schools offered little that was educationally valuable, with lessons dominated by feminized, saccharine, sentimental religiosity delivered by good-hearted but otherwise uninformed female volunteers. This critique was sounded first by nineteenth-century rabbis and educators who were aggrieved at the slight to their own educational institutions by the popularity of the Sunday school movement and fearful for their own abilities to make a living as teachers. It was then taken up by twentieth-century educators who sought to secure the rapprochement of Talmud Torahs by dismissing the curriculum offered by Sunday schools. These educators hoped to promote the professionalization of Jewish education over Sunday schools staffed by untrained volunteers. The narrative that the Sunday schools promoted the feminization of Jewish education was later adopted by historians of American Judaism who assumed that the failings of the Sunday school could logically be attributed to the limitations of instruction in sentimental religion and the prevalence of volunteers as teachers in the classroom.[15]

The persistence of the narrative that the nineteenth-century Sunday school offered nothing more than feminized saccharine sentimentality may ultimately reveal more about the willingness of American Jewish historians to uncritically reproduce the discourse of Jewish educators and communal policy makers than it does about the realities of the Sunday schools themselves. The narrative of sentimental religion pedaled by female volunteers has broadly been used as a shorthand, first by educators and then by historians, to explain the Sunday school's failure to both equip children with Jewish knowledge and interest them in engaging with the Jewish community as adults. This shorthand has equated the limitations of the religious curriculum of Sunday schools with the presence of female instructors—women's bodies with qualities assumed to be associated with women's concerns.[16] Sunday schools thus offer a concrete case study of the dynamic noted by historians Lila Corwin-Berman, Ronit Stahl, and Kate Rosenblatt, who observed that in issues related to American Jewish continuity, women and women's bodies have all too frequently been made the scapegoat for so-called American Jewish communal anxieties.[17] As I have shown, the narrative that the failings of the Sunday school can be attributed to the sentimental religion of untrained female volunteers evades the complex realities of gender and power within nineteenth-century American Jewish education that limited women's agency. Sunday schools were an innovation forged by Jewish women, but within a generation leadership within congregational schools had been taken over by men. Women may have volunteered as teachers in the classrooms, but they did not set the curriculum or choose the textbooks and subjects that could be taught.

The narrative that female volunteers brought nothing more than feminized religion to their roles as Sunday school teachers also overlooks the fact that women made critically important and informed contributions to Sunday school pedagogy and organization. At the end of the nineteenth century, women became activists for education and founded mission schools and free schools to ensure that children of new immigrants had access to Jewish educational training as well as other basic needs. Female graduates of normal schools brought training in instruction and classroom management to their work as Sunday school volunteers and promoted tactile and material enhancements to Sunday school instruction, from the stereopticon slide to object lessons. The feminization narrative erases the professional expertise of women as education providers and overlooks the variety of ideas and instructional methods pioneered by Jewish women in and outside the classroom.

Over the course of the nineteenth century, the religious curriculum offered in Jewish Sunday schools reimagined not only Jewish education in America but Judaism and Jewishness itself. Sunday schools taught that Judaism was a religion in order to show children where Judaism fit into their lives as modern Americans, and what they taught mirrored the changing landscape of ideas about religion in America more broadly. Sunday schools described Judaism as a system of ethical training, a vehicle for character cultivation, a heritage steeped in pioneering monotheism, and a vision for human relationships with the divine. These lessons were enacted through the memorization of Jewish catechisms, the ritual performance of confirmation ceremonies, the production of a commercial landscape of Jewish educational consumer goods, and a range of social welfare initiatives designed to bring the children of newly arrived Jewish immigrants into line. The attempt to reconfigure Judaism as a religion was, in many ways, the central project of the Jewish experience with modernity. Sunday schools provided a critical space for nineteenth-century American Jews to wrestle with the evolving dynamics of defining Judaism as a religion and of defining themselves as religious Americans who were also American Jews.

ACKNOWLEDGMENTS

I found the stories of nineteenth-century Jewish Sunday schools in historic Jewish newspapers, textbooks, and other printed literature, but mostly I found them in archival collections preserved by synagogues, communal institutions, and families. What survived was often fragmentary, a clipping here or there, a line or two about education in a treasured memoir. I owe an enormous debt of gratitude to the archivists and librarians who helped me locate these fragments in their collections. My thanks to Amy Roberts at the Beth Ahabah Museum and Archives in Richmond, Virginia; Alisha Babstein at the Oregon Jewish Museum in Portland; Catherine Cangany at the Michigan Jewish Historical Society in Farmington Hills; Susan Porter and Chris Spraker at Temple Israel in Boston; Dale Rosengarten at the College of Charleston; Laura Gottlieb at Temple Beth El in Bloomfield Hills, Michigan; Jill Hershorin at the Jewish Historical Society of MetroWest in Whippany, New Jersey; Martha Berg at Rodef Shalom Congregation in Pittsburgh; Eric Lidiji at the Heinz History Center in Pittsburgh; Anne Mininberg at Central Synagogue in New York City; Melanie Meyers at the American Jewish Historical Society in New York City; Paula B. Freedman in San Francisco; Maggie Hoffman and Joanna Church at the Jewish Museum of Maryland in Baltimore; and Abby Glowgower, curator of Jewish Collections at the Filson Historical Society in Louisville, Kentucky. I made multiple visits to the American Jewish Archives (AJA) in Cincinnati during the course of this research, and I am grateful to have received the Loewenstein-Wiener Fellowship in 2013 and the Joseph and Eva R. Dave Fellowship in 2019, which made my visits possible. My thanks to Kevin Proffit and to Dana Herman for sharing their expert knowledge of the AJA collections and to Julianna Witt, who conducted remote research for me when visiting the archive became impossible because of the COVID-19 pandemic.

I am grateful to mentors and colleagues who have helped to nurture this project over years of research and writing. I received helpful feedback on early drafts from Marc Lee Raphael, Elizabeth McKeown, Ariel Glücklich, Jose Casanova, and, especially, Jonathan Ray. More recently, I have benefited from conversations with Judah Cohen, Karla Goldman, Jenna Weissman Joselit, Melissa Klapper, Mira Sucharov, and the late great Dianne Ashton. Laura Arnold Leibman was a phenomenally supportive mentor and cheerleader, and I am so grateful for her support and encouragement as I wrestled through the writing of this book. Many colleagues read drafts of various chapters and offered feedback that honed my ideas, tightened my prose, and sharpened my analysis. I am grateful to Sharon Avni, Amy DeRogatis, Jodi Eichler-Levine, Sarah Imhoff, Kirsten Fermaglich, Rachel Gordan, Sarah Hurwitz, Ben Jacobs, Jenna Weissman Joselit, Laura Arnold Leibman, Alan Levenson, Arielle Levites, Shari Rabin, and Cara Rock-Singer. Special thanks to Jonathan Krasner for his insightful and generous reading of the full manuscript. The feedback from the reviewers for New York University Press made this into a better book and encouraged me to keep writing it. Jennifer Hammer at NYU Press has been enthusiastic about this book since my first email to her, and I am so grateful for her assistance in bringing this book to life.

In 2018, I joined Michigan State University. I am enormously grateful for the support of my colleagues in the Department of Religious Studies. They have been my cheerleaders and advocates, and I count myself fortunate to have found a wonderful departmental home. I owe particular thanks to Amy DeRogatis, who has never missed an opportunity to encourage me and celebrate my work. I have a second home in MSU's Jewish studies program, and I am grateful for the support of our program director, Yael Aronoff, and for the friendship and the encouragement of my Jewish studies colleagues, particularly Kirsten Fermaglich and Amy Simon. Outside MSU, I am grateful to the small but mighty group of colleagues who study Jewish education and who have encouraged my interest in Sunday schools. My thanks to Ari Kelman, Jonathan Krasner, Sharon Avni, and Ben Jacobs for their long-standing support of this project.

The majority of this manuscript was written during the COVID-19 pandemic. Completing it sometimes felt impossible, with many cycles of child care closures, quarantines, the pivot to online teaching, the shuttering of archives, and the trauma of the pandemic itself. I am grateful to

Nana, Grandad, Uncle Adam, and Auntie Rachel in the UK for reading endless stories to my children on FaceTime, to Johanna in East Lansing for pitching in to help us with tasks big and small, and to Sara, Cameron, Sarah, Anna, and Tozer in Washington, DC, for their endless friendship and support. You are our village.

Ultimately, though, this book got finished because I had a spouse who took care of our two children and did more than his fair share of household labor so that I could hide away and keep writing. All this while also holding down his own job as an elementary school teacher during a time when it has arguably never been more difficult to be in public education. Last but by no means least, I am grateful to my husband, Gavri, for his unfailing support and love. Our children, Nadav and Jonah, did not contribute materially to this book, but they bring joy to our lives each day. Being their parent has brought a whole new perspective to my research on Jewish children and their education, and I am so grateful for them. Even if they are continuing that age-old American Jewish tradition of being decidedly ambivalent about Sunday school.

NOTES

INTRODUCTION

1 Diner, *A Time for Gathering*, 49.

2 Wise also received $550 a year in compensation for his other rabbinical duties. Temkin, *Creating American Reform Judaism*, 47.

3 Wise concluded by assuring his readers that this "snake" of inadequate education would "soon have its head crushed." Wise, *The New American Jew*, 2.

4 A complete history of Rebecca Gratz and her efforts to found the Hebrew Sunday School in Philadelphia is Ashton, *Rebecca Gratz*.

5 On the missionary activities of Christian Sunday schools, see Boylan, *Sunday School*, 22–59.

6 Pyke, *Scriptural Questions*.

7 On Leeser's support for the Sunday school, see Sussman, *Isaac Leeser*, 95–101.

8 Isaac Leeser, "News Items," *Occident and American Jewish Advocate*, April 1, 1852, 47–50. Leeser was the founding editor of the *Occident and American Jewish Advocate*. It was one of many independent projects that he took on alongside his duties at Mikveh Israel.

9 On women's move into public-facing roles in synagogue life during this period, see Goldman, *Beyond the Synagogue Gallery*.

10 Gartner, *Jewish Education in the United States*, 89.

11 On the ideologies of Reform Judaism, see Meyer, *Origins of the Modern Jew*, and *Response to Modernity*.

12 Jacob, *Changing World of Reform Judaism*, 104–23.

13 Bricker and Marcson, *Jewish Education in Chicago*, 6.

14 On the eastern European backgrounds of these schools, see Adler and Polonsky, *Jewish Education in Eastern Europe*; Zalkin, *Modernizing Jewish Education*. On Yiddish and secular schools, see Kadar, *Raising Secular Jews*

15 Krasner, *Benderly Boys*. See also Miriam Heller Stern's reassessment of the Benderly era, and Carol. K. Ingall's important edited collection of essays about the women among Benderly's "boys." Miriam Heller Stern, "'A Dream Not Quite Come True'"; Ingall, *Women Who Reconstructed*.

16 Benderly's reference to "otherwise intelligent men" seemingly ignores the fact that female students attended Sunday schools in (slightly) larger numbers than males. See Krasner, *Benderly Boys*, 10, 28.

17 There have been relatively few surveys of modern Jewish education in America, but all to varying degrees find the Sunday school deficient. Eduardo Rauch, for example, described the adoption of the Sunday school as "an act of surrender, a recognition of priorities within the Jewish community that made Jewish education, and thus traditional Jewish life, a matter of secondary importance," concluding that the schools were "truly ineffective" and a "true spectacle of superficiality." Rauch, *Education of Jews and the American Community*, 304–308. Michael Meyer described early twentieth-century Reform Jewish education as "thin," requiring only one morning a week. But then, "learning the basic tenets of monotheism and morality did not require much more than this." Meyer, *Response to Modernity*, 286. See also Graff, *"And You Shall Teach,"* 27–28; Gartner, *Jewish Education in the United States*, 9; Grinstein, "In the Course of the Nineteenth Century," 27.

18 On this historiography, see Sarna, "American Jewish Education," 12.

19 On the equating of religion and Protestantism in America, see Fessenden, *Culture and Redemption*, 1–12.

20 The Protestant reformers, as sociologist Peter Beyer explains, "underscored their conviction that religious goals, namely salvation, were to be attained or determined uniquely by religious means such as faith and the providence of God. What religion was about was thus precisely those factors: salvation, sin, faith, sacraments, providence, and other such religious determinants." Beyer, *Religions in Global Society*, 8.

21 Masuzawa, *Invention of World Religions*; McCutcheon, *Manufacturing Religion*; Fitzgerald, *Ideology of Religious Studies*; Asad, *Genealogies of Religion*.

22 Neusner, "Defining Judaism," 5. See also Neusner, *Take Judaism, for Example*, xvi.

23 Jonathan Hess has proposed that Mendelssohn's project of depoliticizing, or denationalizing, Judaism to present it in religious terms was not apologetics but a polemic that subverted governing paradigms of late eighteenth-century Protestant theology to negotiate a place for Jews in the modern nation-state by contesting Christian self-representations as dominant. See Hess, *Germans, Jews, and the Claims of Modernity*, 91–135.

24 Stanislawski, *For Whom Do I Toil?*, 5.

25 The term "Oriental" is pejorative. It has been used, and continues to be used, in harmful ways to stigmatize a range of cultural and ethnic groups. I use it here mindful of its limitations and its potential for harm, owing to the fact that the term was so ubiquitous in the discourse of nineteenth century American Jews. It was a label used by Jews both to identify Judaism in general, and to identify certain groups of Jews in particular. It signified a particular kind of Jewish racial and ethnic identity for nineteenth century American Jews as they engaged racialized definitions of Jewishness. Eric Goldstein explores this thoroughly in *The Price of Whiteness*, 11–34. On Reform attempts to reconfigure Judaism in religious terms, see Meyer, *Response to Modernity*. Todd Endelman has emphasized that these definitions of Judaism as a religion were ambiguous, as modern

European Jews also proclaimed secular Jewish identities and thus did not fit neatly into the paradigms of classical liberalism. Endelman, *Broadening Jewish History*, 47–48.

26 This is the central thesis of Leora Batnitzky's *How Judaism Became a Religion*, which traces the adoption of the appellation of religion within the context of modern Jewish thought. On the imposition of the category of religion upon Jews in a US context, and on Jewish difference in America specifically, see Levitt, "Impossible Assimilations, American Liberalism," and "Other Moderns, Other Jews."

27 Grinstein, *Rise of the Jewish Community*.

28 Isaac Leeser, "Sunday Laws in Virginia," *Occident and American Jewish Advocate*, December 1, 1849, 467–70. See also Wolf and Whiteman, *History of the Jews of Philadelphia*, 146–64.

29 Rock, *Haven of Liberty*, 113–36.

30 The paradigmatic rendering of this ontology of American Judaism is Will Herberg's 1955 sociological assessment of American religious diversity as a triple melting pot of Protestants, Catholics, and Jews—a portrait of religion in suburban America defined by its three Bible-based Abrahamic faiths. Herberg, *Protestant, Catholic, Jew*.

31 For examples of this historiographic argument, see Sarna, *American Judaism*, 275; Dash Moore, *To the Golden Cities*, 93–12.

32 Smith, *Relating Religion*, 179. Mapping the cultural construction of the category of religion was one of the central themes explored by Smith, whose work has been enormously influential in the field of religious studies. See also Sheedy, "Making the Familiar Strange"; Smith, *Imagining Religion,* and *Map Is Not Territory*.

33 Jessica Cooperman has illustrated this, for example, in her identification of discourses of religious pluralism that emerged within the context of World War I. See Cooperman, *Making Judaism Safe for America*.

34 On the global context of education as a site for the navigation of multiple Jewish modernities, see, for example, Zalkin, *Modernizing Jewish Education*; E. Adler, *In Her Hands*; Rodrigue, *French Jews, Turkish Jews*; Seidman, *Sarah Schenirer*.

35 The pernicious implications of the assumption that women' bodies bear primary responsibility for American Jewish continuity have become apparent since 2018, when sociologist Steven M. Cohen was forced to resign from Hebrew Union College "amid allegations of sexual assault and harassment that dated back decades." Dreyfus, "Steven M. Cohen, Shunned by Academy." Cohen became influential in contemporary Jewish communal policy making through demographic research in which he claimed that women's commitments to inmarriage and child-rearing were essential to the Jewish future. This study draws on the analysis produced in the wake of these revelations that has encouraged historians to look closely at the implications of arguments that make women responsible for Jewish continuity within historical sources—and the motivations of the scholars who make them. See Berman, Rosenblatt, and Stahl, "Continuity Crisis."

36 Kaplan and Cronson, "Report of Committee on Jewish Education."

37 The (male) author of the report noted with pride that this ratio eclipsed that in the nation's public schools, where men represented only 12.5 percent of teachers. Pollak, "Forty Years," 410.

38 See, for example, Meyer, *Response to Modernity*; Chazan, Chazan, and Jacobs, *Cultures and Contexts*, 95–100; Ackerman, "Americanization of Jewish Education." Ashton, on the other hand, celebrates the feminization of Jewish education as "one of the most successful strategies for strengthening Jewish life in the modern world." Ashton, "Feminization of Jewish Education," 15.

39 Imhoff, "Myth of American Jewish Feminization."

40 Pollak, "Forty Years," 46.

41 As Shari Rabin has elucidated, to study nineteenth-century Judaism behind the walls of denominations obscures the mobility of American Jews as they forged new identities and constructions of Jewish belonging across the nascent religious spectrum. Rabin, *Jews on the Frontier*, 99.

42 As Melissa Klapper acknowledges, while the narratives of nineteenth-century Jewish youth offer a fascinating subject for analysis, sources produced by students in this era are slim and must be supplemented with prescriptive materials. Klapper, *Jewish Girls Coming of Age*, 9.

43 Lerner, *Majority Finds Its Past*, 179.

44 As Kathryn Lofton argues, religious communities manifest their identities through consumption. What they buy and how it is sold to them is as integral to understanding religious culture as analyses of their sacred texts and their creedal principles. See Lofton's *Consuming Religion*.

CHAPTER 1. JEWISH WOMEN ON THE EDUCATIONAL FRONTIER

1 The school was in the home of the Peixotto sisters, Simha and Rachel. Friends of Gratz's from their synagogue, Mikveh Israel, the Peixotto sisters ran an academy out of their home during the week. They served in the Sunday school as teachers and wrote some of its earliest original teaching materials.

2 There is some dispute about whether Gratz founded the first Sunday school for Jewish children. In two texts dated 1840 and 1888, Isaac Leeser suggested that a Sunday school in Richmond, Virginia, preceded the Philadelphia school and was organized by Isaac B. Seixas, with Leeser serving as his assistant. Leeser left Richmond in 1829. In his address at the second annual examination of Gratz's Philadelphia school, he noted that before 1838, "only in Richmond had the attempt been made, but with partial success, by the late Isaac B. Seixas"—implying that the Virginia Sunday school preceded Gratz's. In his eulogy at Seixas's funeral in 1839, Leeser recalled that "it was in the synagogue at Richmond where he [Seixas], feebly assisted by me, commenced teaching on the Sabbath and the first day, such children and youth as desired religious instruction. If the success was not so great as we at one time hoped, it was owing to the great difficulties we had to encounter." The school was, by Leeser's account, short-lived. Historians have therefore argued broadly that Gratz founded the first Hebrew Sunday school in

America, because it was the first to achieve any longevity. Isaac Leeser and Moses N. Nathan, "Second Annual Examination of the Sunday School for Religious Instruction of Israelites in Philadelphia," Congregation Mikveh Israel, 1840, Beth Ahabah Museum and Archives, Richmond, VA; "Proceedings of the Commemorative Celebration of the Fiftieth Anniversary of the Founding of Hebrew Sunday Schools in America," 1888, box 10, folder 16, Binswanger/Solis-Cohen Family Collection, ARC MS 18, Library at the Herbert D. Katz Center for Advanced Judaic Studies, University of Pennsylvania, Philadelphia.

3 According to Henry Morais, 50 children attended the school in 1838; by 1894 the number of enrolled students had risen to 1,800, and the school maintained multiple campuses. Morais, *Jews of Philadelphia*, 149.

4 Rosa Mordecai, "Recollections of the First Hebrew Sunday School," *Hebrew Watchword and Instructor*, no. 6 (February 1897): 5; Leeser and Nathan, "Second Annual Examination."

5 Hebrew Sunday School Society of Philadelphia, "Constitution and By-Laws of the Hebrew Sunday School Society of Philadelphia," 1858, Rare Am 1859 Phi Heb 75053.O, Library Company of Philadelphia.

6 Histories of American Jewish education prior to 1838 include Gartner, *Jewish Education in the United States*; Graff, *"And You Shall Teach"*; Chazan, Chazan, and Jacobs, *Cultures and Contexts of Jewish Education*; Sarna, "American Jewish Education"; Rauch, *Education of Jews and the American Community*; Fromer, "In the Colonial Period"; Grinstein, "In the Course of the Nineteenth Century."

7 Ashton notes that in 1818, Gratz created an informal at-home religious school for the women and children of her family. It never grew beyond her household, but Ashton estimates that it was the first such effort to bring children together for educational purposes outside the synagogue in Philadelphia. Ashton, *Rebecca Gratz*, 97.

8 E. Davis, *History of Rodeph Shalom Congregation*, 70–79.

9 Kaganoff, "Education of the Jewish Child," 146–47. As Shari Rabin has discussed in "Working Jews," to earn a viable living, hazanim in nineteenth-century Jewish America occupied a variety of roles, whether or not they were qualified for the tasks at hand.

10 Engelman, "Jewish Education in Charleston," 54.

11 Isaac Leeser, "Letter from Isaac Leeser to the Parnass and Members of K.K. Mikveh Israel," 1838, box 1, folder 8, Binswanger/Solis-Cohen Family Collection,

12 By 1860 midwestern and eastern states all had state-regulated tax-based school systems. Kaestle, *Pillars of the Republic*, 113.

13 As Sarna has observed, during these years the American Jewish community increased at a rate that was almost fifteen times that of the nation as a whole. Sarna, *American Judaism*, 63.

14 Jick, *Americanization of the Synagogue*, 57; Diner, *A Time for Gathering*, 50.

15 By 1850 New York City was home to a quarter of the nation's Jews, yet the majority were not members of a synagogue. Leibman, *Art of the Jewish Family*, 173.

16 Rabin has illustrated this is in *Jews on the Frontier*.

17 Child labor laws were not instituted in the United States until the 1870s.

18 See Butler, *Awash in a Sea of Faith*; Corrigan, "Cosmology," 29–48.

19 Isaac Leeser, "Jewish Children under Gentile Teachers," *Occident and American Jewish Advocate*, December 1, 1843, 409–14. Though he became a firm supporter of Gratz's initiative, Leeser also advocated for full-day Jewish schools; two years later, in 1845, he published a proposal for a union of communal Jewish schools that would support a comprehensive education in Jewish and secular subjects for both boys and girls. Leeser, "Union for the Sake of Judaism," *Occident and American Jewish Advocate*, August 1, 1848, 217–27.

20 Ashton, *Rebecca Gratz*, 142. Hasia Diner and Beryl Lieff Benderly note that while the actual threat to Jews posed by Christian evangelists is debatable, it was undoubtedly a motivating factor for Gratz. Diner and Benderly, *Her Works Praise Her*, 117.

21 As Ashton has shown, in the adversarial social context of 1830s Philadelphia restoring order and decorum by removing children from the streets and engaging them in productive activity was a desideratum of both the Christian and Jewish Sunday schools. Ashton, "Feminization of Jewish Education," 16.

22 Histories of the Protestant Sunday school include Lynn and Wright, *Big Little School*; Boylan, *Sunday School*; Carper and Hunt, *Religious Schooling in America*.

23 J. Marcus, *American Jewish Woman*, 44.

24 Ashton, *Rebecca Gratz*, 158.

25 This paralleled the gendered divisions in education for girls and boys in modern European Judaism. See Hyman, *Gender and Assimilation*, 10–49.

26 On women and religion in nineteenth-century American popular culture, see· McDannell, *The Christian Home in Victorian America*.

27 Schleiermacher, *On Religion*. On the interrelationship of women, religion, and sentiment, see Braude, *Radical Spirits*; Cruea, "Changing Ideals of Womanhood"; De Jong, *Sentimentalism in Nineteenth-Century America*; Ashton, *Rebecca Gratz*, 117.

28 Gilding, "Preserving Sentiments," 156–65; Clevinger, "'These Human Flowers.'"

29 Marion A. Kaplan, *Making of the Jewish Middle Class*, 64–84.

30 Hyman, *Gender and Assimilation*, 47–48.

31 Ashton, *Rebecca Gratz*, 23.

32 Elzas, *Jews of South Carolina*, 182. See also Moore, "Freedom's Fruits," 18; Zola, *Isaac Harby of Charleston*.

33 Association for the Moral Instruction of Children of the Jewish Faith, Meeting Minutes 1839–46, Congregation Shearith Israel Archives, New York, NY. See also Pool and Pool, *An Old Faith in the New World*, 363–66. The school closed in 1846 when a smallpox epidemic led the number of enrolled pupils to decline dramatically.

34 "Domestic News," *Reform Advocate*, May 19, 1906, 447.

35 "Hebrew School Fund Ball at Richmond, Va.," *Occident and American Jewish Advocate*, April 1, 1847, 45–46; Richman, "Jewish Sunday School Movement," 568;

M. Berman, *Richmond's Jewry*, 56; Hanft, "Mordecai's Female Academy," 79. Julia Richman lists Ellen Myers as cofounder of the Virginia Sunday school. The credit is more likely owed to Ella C. Myers, a prominent female member of the congregation and a relative of Emma Mordecai's. See Malcolm H. Stern, *First American Jewish Families*, 217. Also see Ezekiel and Lichtenstein, *History of the Jews of Richmond*, 49, 253.

36 The Shearith Israel school was led by Henrietta Hart. "New School in Charleston," *Occident and American Jewish Advocate*, June 1, 1844, 163–64; Engelman, "Jewish Education in Charleston," 59.

37 In synagogue contexts, women's auxiliaries paralleled those founded by, and restricted to, men. See Sochen, "Some Observations"; Diner, *A Time for Gathering*, 97. On Jewish women's engagement with clubs, see Wenger, "Jewish Women of the Club."

38 The teaching "all Israel is responsible for one another" is expounded in the Talmud; see BT Shavuot 39a. As Ashton explains, Gratz and the women of Congregation Mikveh Israel believed that because evangelists targeted the poor, Jewish women needed their own charitable societies. Ashton, *Rebecca Gratz*, 100.

39 As Laura Leibman has observed, women's engagement in benevolent causes fostered a new ideal of Jewish kinship in nineteenth-century America, one in which women could contribute to community life not only as producers of children but through affective bonds. Leibman, *Art of the Jewish Family*, 17.

40 Four dollars in 1863 would be $96 in 2022. Though the society was organized by women, in response to a call from Isaac Mayer Wise for Jewish women to support their indigent sisters, a group of men from the community elected themselves to serve as the society's first officers, insisting that the women of the community were ill equipped for leadership roles. Within a couple of months, the women had voted the men out of leadership, though men remained on an advisory council to the society. "Ladies Society for the Support of Hebrew Widows and Orphans in the State of Michigan, Constitution," 1865, box 3, folder, 1, Women's Organizations Collections, Leo M. Franklin Archives, Temple Beth El, Bloomfield Hills, MI.

41 Diner notes, for example, that new immigrant Jewish women often ran shops while their husbands traveled as peddlers. Diner, *Roads Taken*, 61.

42 "Hebrew Sunday School of Columbia, S.C.," *Occident and American Jewish Advocate*," May 1, 1844, 83–87; "Proceedings of Israelites at Columbia, S.C.," *Occident and American Jewish Advocate*," November 1, 1846, 387–89; Isaac Leeser, "News Items," *Occident and American Jewish Advocate*, January 1, 1844, 5). See also Rosengarten and Rosengarten, *A Portion of the People*, 95.

43 Burstyn, "Catharine Beecher"; Beecher, *Essay on the Education of Female Teachers*.

44 Shearith Israel was a common name for early American congregations and reflected its founders' understanding that the community represented a small minority in a new environment.

45 T.J.M., "Forming of a Congregation at Augusta, Ga.," *Occident and American Jewish Advocate*, November 1, 1846, 389–92; "Examination of the Sunday School

at Augusta, Ga.," *Occident and American Jewish Advocate*, August 1, 1848, 267–69. A similar trajectory can be seen in Atlanta, where two Jewish mothers began a religious school in their homes in the 1850s, long before a synagogue was organized in 1867. And in Sioux City, Iowa, women conducted the only Sabbath school in the city until 1898. Blumberg, *As but a Day to a Hundred and Twenty*, 1–2; Shuman, *A History*, 19.

46 Florance was the sister of Gershon Kursheedt, one of the officers of the new congregation and the executor of Touro's significant estate. On the establishment of Nefutsoth Yehudah, see "New Orleans," *Occident and American Jewish Advocate*, December 1, 1850, 48. Rebecca Florance's name was given incorrectly in that story, which the paper corrected in its next edition. See also Isaac Leeser, "The Consecration at New Orleans," *Occident and American Jewish Advocate*, June 1, 1850, 10–19.

47 Nathaniel Levin, "Address Delivered before the Society for the Instruction of Jewish Youth, in Charleston, S.C. on the Anniversary of the Society," *Occident and American Jewish Advocate*, July 1, 1843, 162–74.

48 "Examination of the Pupils of 'The Society for the Instruction of Jewish Doctrine,' Charleston, S.C.," *Occident and American Jewish Advocate*, June 1, 1845, 136–43.

49 As Riv-Ellen Prell and Karla Goldman have demonstrated, this ambivalence toward women's public leadership was characteristic of the American Reform movement. Prell, "Dilemma of Women's Equality"; Goldman, "Ambivalence of Reform Judaism," and "Longing for Jewish Homes."

50 Solis-Cohen, "Jacob S. Solis," 319; Fein, *Making of an American Jewish Community*.

51 "Hebrew Sunday School of Baltimore," *Occident and American Jewish Advocate*, January 1, 1857, 496.

52 "News Items," *Occident and American Jewish Advocate*, May 1, 1857, 103–104.

53 Fein, *Making of an American Jewish Community*, 186.

54 *Cleveland Plain Dealer*, January 6, 1847, 5.

55 Henry Loewenthal to Isaac Mayer Wise, August 17, 1859, in Rabin, *Jews on the Frontier*, 70; Editorial, *American Israelite*, October 4, 1878, 6.

56 Graff, "Public Schooling and Jewish Education," 70.

57 The congregation changed its name to Temple Emanu-El in 1927, following a merger.

58 Myer Stern, *Rise and Progress of Reform Judaism*.

59 See Sulzberger, *Fifty Years' Work*, 73.

60 Religious School Reports, 1866, box 21, folder 7, Congregation Bene Israel (Cincinnati, Ohio) Records, American Jewish Archives, Cincinnati, OH. In 1880 the Sabbath school became a "free school," open to all children, not only those whose parents were members of the congregation. "Annual Report," *American Israelite*, October 22, 1880, 134.

61 Lloyd Gartner has argued that by 1880 Jewish education in America was synonymous with Sunday school. Gartner, *Jewish Education in the United States*, 10. Writing in 1929, Rabbi Jacob P. Pollak estimated that by 1882 almost 90 percent of

congregations affiliated with the Reform movement's umbrella organization, the Union of American Hebrew Congregations, educated their children in Sunday schools. Pollak, "Forty Years," 404.

62 Union of American Hebrew Congregations, *Proceedings of the Second Annual Session of the Council* (Cincinnati, OH: Bloch, 1875), 142–44.

63 Union of American Hebrew Congregations, *Sixteenth Annual Report of the Union of American Hebrew Congregations* (Cincinnati, OH: Bloch, 1889), 2494.

64 Temple Education Committee School Board Minutes Book, 1871–93, Leo M. Franklin Archives.

65 Sarna has described this preference for supplemental education on the weekends as indicative of American Judaism's preference for a Protestant, rather than Catholic, model of religious educational training. Sarna, "American Jewish Education," 11.

66 Bodek, "Making Do," 158; McDannell, *Christian Home in Victorian America*, 7.

67 Henry Barnard, "Second Annual Report of the Board of Commissioners of Common Schools in Connecticut," 1840, cited in Kaestle, *Pillars of the Republic*, 123.

68 Kaestle, *Pillars of the Republic*, 220; Preston, "Domestic Ideology, School Reformers."

69 Duties and Powers of the Board of School Directors, 1866, carton 1, folder 18, Congregation Emanu-El, Religious Education Collection, MSS 2010/612, Bancroft Library, University of California, Berkeley.

70 Kohut, *My Portion (An Autobiography)*, 60.

71 As Melissa Klapper has explained, women embraced teaching roles in Jewish life at the same time that women embraced public education more broadly during the second half of the nineteenth century. Coeducational public schools emphasized educational opportunities for both genders, and higher education became increasingly accessible to women of means. Public lectures, vocational courses, and domestic arts classes provided opportunities for women's ongoing education as adults, and women increasingly sought paid employment as teachers. Klapper, *Jewish Girls Coming of Age*, 59–104.

72 Barbara Kirshenblatt-Gimblett has argued, for example, that fundraising fairs for Jewish causes provided opportunities for women to gain and display organizational prowess, as well as artistic and design skills. Kirshenblatt-Gimblett, "Moral Sublime."

73 Abrams, *Jewish Women Pioneering*, 103.

74 Bettol, "When Uptown Met Downtown," 50.

75 Kaestle, *Pillars of the Republic*, 131; Klapper, *Jewish Girls Coming of Age*, 96–97.

76 Temple Beth El Education Committee Annual Report, 1892, box 1, folder 48, Temple Beth El Education Committee Collection, Leo M. Franklin Archives

77 National Council of Jewish Women, *Proceedings of the First Convention of the National Council of Jewish Women* (New York: Jewish Publication Society, 1896), 121.

78 Diary, box 1, folder 2, Jennie Mannheimer [Jane Manner] Papers, 1880–1952, MS 259, American Jewish Archives.

79 Clara Lowenberg Moses, "My Memories," SC-8499, American Jewish Archives.

80 Mary Cohen kept a detailed series of scrapbooks in which she pasted prints of her writings, including many reprints of her work from the *Baptist Register*. Bound scrapbook of Mary M. Cohen, 1850–1912, box 4, folder 1, Charles and Mary Cohen Collection, ARC MS3, Library at the Herbert D. Katz Center. See also Ashton, "Crossing Boundaries."

81 Harby, "Penina Moïse."

82 Minutes of Congregation Ahawath Chesed, 1864–1972, 273, Central Synagogue Archives, New York, NY.

83 A Mr. B. Nurmser earned $25 per month, a Mr. A. Reiss earned $20 a month and a Mr. L. Rothenberg earned $15 per month. School Board Minutes Book, 1869–88, box 23, folder 11, Congregation Bene Israel, Cincinnati, Ohio Collection, MS-24, American Jewish Archives.

84 Greenstone, "Jewish Education in the United States," 113.

85 In 2022 dollars, $7.40 would be the equivalent of $249.

86 Minute Book, 1902–11, box 1, folder 1, Temple B'nai Israel, Galveston, Texas, Records, MS-530, American Jewish Archives. Congregation B'nai Israel formed in Galveston in 1868 and continues under that name, although it is listed under Temple B'nai Israel in the archives' records.

87 On the themes of rabbinic discourse in the nineteenth century, see N. Cohen, *What the Rabbis Said.*

88 Goldstein, *Price of Whiteness*, 35–50. On the late nineteenth-century Jewish revival, see Sarna, *A Great Awakening*; Fishbane, Fishbane, and Sarna, *Jewish Renaissance and Revival in America*; Schwartz, *Emergence of Jewish Scholarship in America*.

89 Rose Barlow, "The Jewish Woman as Teacher," March 15, 1891, Women's Club of Temple Beth El, National Council of Jewish Women, Greater Detroit Section Records, UR001647, Walter P. Reuther Library, Wayne State University. Rose Barlow Weinman later became a public school teacher and was known locally for her art and poetry in addition to her educational work. "Sinai Hospital to Get Bequest of $5,000 from Rose B. Weinman Estate," *Detroit Jewish News*, February 1, 1963, 32.

90 National Council of Jewish Women, *Proceedings of the First Convention*, 16. On the ambivalence in Kohler's writings on Jewish women, see Goldman, "Ambivalence of Reform Judaism," and "Longing for Jewish Homes."

91 See, for example, "Leaves from the Diary of a Jewish Minister," *Jewish Messenger*, June 24, 1864, 187; N. Cohen, *What the Rabbis Said*, 19–20.

92 Samson Raphael Hirsch, *Horeb: Versuche über Jissroels Pflichten in der Zersteuung* (Essays on the Duties of the Jewish People in the Diaspora), translated in Marion A. Kaplan, *Jewish Daily Life in Germany*, 237.

93 McDannell, *Christian Home in Victorian America*, 113–14.

94 An appellation extolling Jewish motherhood taken from Judges 5:7. On the use of the biblical "mother in Israel" trope to describe nineteenth-century American

Jewish women, see Josselit, " Special Sphere"; Lichtenstein, *Writing Their Nations*, 23–31; Nadell, *America's Jewish Women*, 55–108.

95 Special Report of the Sabbath School Committee, 1895, box 1, folder 3, Temple Beth El, Leo M. Franklin Archives.

96 Isaac Mayer Wise, "Religious Home Training," *American Israelite*, May 15, 1885, 4.

97 David Philipson, "The Ideal Jewess," *American Jewess* 4, no. 6 (March 1897): 257–62; Joselit, "Special Sphere."

98 See, for example, Tobias Schanfarber, "News and Views," *American Israelite*, June 29, 1885, 5.

99 "Jewish Women's Congress," *American Israelite*, September 14, 1893, 2. As Melissa Klapper has noted, a written symposium sponsored by the *Jewish Messenger* on the American Jewish woman featured a number of articles arguing that the primary purpose of Jewish education for women was to equip them for their roles as "mothers of the Jewish future." Klapper, *Jewish Girls Coming of Age*, 21. See also Diner and Benderly, *Her Works Praise Her*, 245.

100 Ruskay, *Hearth and Home Essays*.

101 See, for example, Ella E. Bartlett, "Ideal Motherhood," *American Jewess* 1, no. 6 (September 1895): 289–81. As Karla Goldman has written, Sonneschein believed that American Jewish leaders had devalued customs that had long been at the core of women's religiosity. Goldman, *Beyond the Synagogue Gallery*, 36. On the American Jewish women more generally, see Porter, "Rosa Sonnenschein and the *American Jewess*."

102 Rosa Sonneschein, "Editor's Desk," *American Jewess* 1, no. 5 (August 1895): 260.

103 Sabato Morais, "A Cooperative Work in Educational Institutions," box 13, folder 19, Sabato Morais Collection, ARC MS-8, Library at the Herbert D. Katz Center.

104 Sabato Morais, "On the Need of More Religious Schools," box 13, folder 19, Sabato Morais Collection.

CHAPTER 2. CATECHISMS, MASCULINITY, AND RATIONAL JEWISH RELIGION

1 "Children's Column," *American Hebrew*, December 16, 1881, 54. For the second installment of the story see "Children's Column," *American Hebrew*, December 23, 1881, 66.

2 On the development of textbooks for Jewish education in nineteenth-century America, see Krasner, "Representations of Self and Other"; Gold, *Making the Bible Modern*.

3 The Christian catechism was not an innovation of the Reformation. Distillations of Christian theology for the purpose of initiating children and new converts date to at least the second century with the Didache. Yet the format was revived and rejuvenated during the early modern period. For a concise summary of the history of catechisms in European Christianity, see Green, *Christian's ABC*; Faierstein, "Abraham Jagel's 'Leqaḥ Ṭov.'"

4 On the use of catechisms in American Christian Sunday schools, see Boylan, *Sunday School*, 40.

5 Rosa Mordecai, "Recollections of the First Hebrew Sunday School," *Hebrew Watchword and Instructor*, no. 6 (February 1897): 5.

6 Both of these volumes are analyzed in Sarna, "God Loves an Infant's Praise."

7 In the preface to her catechism Simha Peixotto recorded her gratitude to the Protestant Sunday School Union, writing, "An acknowledgment is due to the American Sunday School Union for the liberality they have manifested in permitting us to make their 'Child's Scripture Question Book' the basis of this production, and I, therefore, return them publicly my thanks for their kind permission." Peixotto, *Elementary Introduction to the Hebrew Scriptures*, 2.

8 Sarna, "God Loves an Infant's Praise," 82.

9 Leeser's influence upon later Jewish catechisms was recognized by contemporary commentators. See "Text Books," *American Hebrew*, September 9, 1881, 38.

10 Sarah Imhoff explores this topic at length in *Masculinity and the Making of American Judaism*. On the connection between reason and masculinity in European thought more broadly, see Lloyd, *Man of Reason*. On the idea of the individual rational self as masculine, and for a feminist framing of selfhood and modern Jewish thought, see Benjamin, *Obligated Self*.

11 Seidman, *Marriage Plot*, 254.

12 As Michael Meyer has observed, during the last quarter of the eighteenth century, European Jews across the nascent denominational spectrum began to call for catechisms, or "manuals of instruction," that could be used in Jewish children's education. Meyer, *Origins of the Modern Jew*, 125. The definitive survey to date of catechetical literature produced by Jews in Europe is Petuchowski, "Manuals and Catechisms of the Jewish Religion."

13 Altmann, "Articles of Faith." The demand for a systematically ordered textbook explaining the foundations of Judaism for the purposes of religious education was first voiced as part of the Josephinian reforms of 1781–82 in the Habsburg Empire. See von der Krone, "Old and New Orders of Knowledge," 67.

14 On the education of children in premodern Europe, see I. Marcus, *Rituals of Childhood*; Baumgarten, *Mothers and Children*.

15 On Jewish theological writing as a modern educational genre, see Stone, "Mussar Ethics." On Sephardic introduction to Judaism literature, see Fisher, *Amsterdam's People of the Book*.

16 Gotzmann, "Dissociation of Religion and Law." In some contexts catechisms were imposed upon Jews by secular authorities. See Miller, *Rabbis and Revolution*, 71–76.

17 Petuchowski, "Manuals and Catechisms of the Jewish Religion," 47.

18 On the development of Jewish publishing in America, see Sarna, *J.P.S.*, and "Two Ambitious Goals"; Singerman, *Judaica Americana*. On the development of books for children specifically, see Krasner, "Representations of Self and Other."

19 Rachel Mordecai to Samuel Mordecai, Warrenton, NC, July 27, 1817, Jacob Morde-
    cai Papers, William Perkins Library, Duke University, Durham, NC. M. Berman,
    Richmond's Jewry, 52–53.

20 Ibid.

21 Isaac Leeser, "The Season," *Occident and American Jewish Advocate*, September 1,
    1866, 16–18.

22 As Andreas Gotzmann observes, the belief in the pedagogical power of remote
    memorization was shared by European educators, including European Jews, par-
    ticularly in the context of learning through catechism. Gotzmann, "Dissociation
    of Religion and Law," 108.

23 "Examination of the Talmud Torah School of New York," *Occident and Ameri-
    can Jewish Advocate*, February 1, 1844, 550–51. The New York Talmud Torah and
    Hebrew Institute was organized as an all-day Hebrew and English school by S.
    M. Isaacs in 1842 and had enrolled eighty pupils, all boys, by 1843. While the
    Occident did not mention the title of the catechism used in the school, Hyman
    Grinstein reports that the most popular catechisms used in the first half of the
    nineteenth century in New York's all-day Jewish schools included *Lekah Tov*
    (Good Lesson) by the fifteenth- to sixteenth-century Kabbalist Abraham Jagel, the
    German *Yesode haTorah* (Fundamentals of the Torah) by Solomon Herxheimer,
    and *Derekh haEmunah* (The Road to Faith) by Henri Loeb, also in German. All
    these catechisms were initially printed in Europe and were reprinted multiple
    times in the United States, translated at various points into English, all signs of
    their popularity in American Jewish education. W. Gunther Plaut has estimated,
    for example, that Herxheimer's *Yesode HaTorah* was published in as many as
    twenty-nine editions, while Dov Rappel identifies eleven different publications of
    an English-language translation of Henri Loeb's *The Road to Faith*. See Grinstein,
    Rise of the Jewish Community, 232–57; Plaut, *Rise of Reform Judaism*, 147; Rappel,
    "A Bibliography." On Jacob's *Lekah Tov* specifically, see Faierstein, "Abraham Jagel's
    'Leqaḥ Ṭov.'"

24 Rappel, "A Bibliography,'" 40; "Textbooks," *American Hebrew*, September 9, 1881,
    147; "Sunday School Textbooks," *American Hebrew*, November 11, 1881, 38.

25 Kley, *Catechismus der Mosaichen Religion* (Catechism of the Mosaic Religion).
    Kley's catechism was based on an exemplar of its own, Joseph Albo's fifteenth-
    century *Sefer ha-Ikkarim* (Book of Principles). Albo proposed that religion in
    general could be reduced to three core principles—the existence of God, divine
    revelation, and reward and punishment—whereas Judaism in particular was
    defined by eight principles derived from this common core. Albo offered a
    pared-down alternative to more extensive lists of principles, notably Maimonides'
    thirteen principles of faith. See Weiss, *Joseph Albo on Free Choice*, 4–41; Ehrlich,
    "Albo, Joseph."

26 Leora Batnitzky has explored this in *How Judaism Became a Religion*.

27 Kant established this in the *Critique of Pure Reason*, published in 1781. He treated
    the topic of religion more thoroughly in his 1793 *Religion within the Bounds of*

Bare Reason, published ten years after Mendelssohn's *Jerusalem.* In the *Critique of Pure Reason* Kant responded to Mendelssohn's defense of Judaism, asserting that Judaism represented little more than slavery to a set of arcane laws. See Tomasoni, "Mendelssohn and Kant"; Pasternack, *Kant on Religion.*

28 Munk, "Mendelssohn and Kant on Judaism"; Stephen Palmquist, *Comprehensive Commentary on Kant's* Religion within the Bounds of Bare Reason.

29 Mendelssohn, *Jerusalem,* pt. 2.

30 As Michael Meyer argues in *Origins of the Modern Jew,* 25.

31 Ingrid Lohmann, "The Citizen of Jewish Faith as an Educational Ideal. Eduard Israel Kley's 'Treatise on the Israelite Elementary School,'" trans. Richard S. Levy, in *Key Documents of German-Jewish History,* August 9, 2017, https://jewish-history-online.net.

32 Kley, *Catechismus der Mosaichen Religion.* See questions 1, 2, 7, and 24.

33 Thus Malachi Haim Hacohen has suggested that Kley's catechism was little more than a "Jewish-inflected liberal Protestantism." Hacohen, *Jacob and Esau,* 232.

34 Leeser, "Catechism for Younger Children," vi.

35 Sussman, *Isaac Leeser,* 151.

36 While the majority of Leeser's catechism focused on philosophical questions, Leeser did not embrace his predecessor's conviction that Jewish education, even in a Sunday school context, could be reduced to theology alone. Leeser added to his catechism two appendixes—one titled "The Ceremonial Law," the other a translation of Maimonides' Thirteen Principles titled "The Jewish creed"—that set out the obligations of the traditional Jewish calendar. The appendixes affirmed his commitments to halacha even while his exploration of Jewish doctrine was anchored more centrally in the affordances of modern European religious thought.

37 Leeser, *Catechism for Younger Children,* 1, 6.

38 As Petuchowski notes—that the function and purpose of religion was to secure human happiness—*glück,* or *glückseligkeit,* was a common trope in European Jewish catechisms. Petuchowski, "Manuals and Catechisms of the Jewish Religion," 55.

39 N. Cohen, *Encounter with Emancipation,* 175–80.

40 Leeser, *Catechism for Younger Children,* 3–4.

41 Ibid., 6.

42 Leeser began work on his translation of *Jerusalem* in 1838. See Sussman, *Isaac Leeser,* 185.

43 Leeser, introduction to Moses Mendelssohn, *Jerusalem, a Treatise on Religious Power,* iv.

44 On the use of the Peixottos' and Pyke's catechisms outside Philadelphia, see, for example, "Hebrew Society for the Instruction of Jewish Youth, in Charleston," *Occident and American Jewish Advocate,* May 1, 1845, 94–96; T.J.M., "Examination of the Sunday School at Augusta, Ga.," *Occident and American Jewish Advocate,* August 1, 1847, 260–61.

45 Dov Rappel's survey of Jewish textbooks published in America between 1766 and 1919 offers an extensive list of catechisms, including reprints of earlier European works. Rappel, "A Bibliography."

46 "Juvenile Books Wanted," *Jewish Messenger*, July 1, 1867, 4.

47 David Philipson, "Confirmation in the Synagogue," *American Israelite*, October 9, 1890, 1.

48 "Sunday School Textbooks," *American Hebrew*, November 11, 1881, 147.

49 Mordecai, "Recollections," 4.

50 *American Israelite*, October 8, 1880, 118. Wise's catechism was considered particularly expensive. When the Sunday school at Congregation Beth Israel in Houston, Texas, ordered seventy-five copies of Wise's catechism for its students in 1873, it found the $50 invoice challenging to pay. A. Cohen, *Centenary History*, 25.

51 Dov Rappel has estimated that *Road to Faith* was reprinted at least eleven times in the United States. Rappel, "A Bibliography," 40.

52 Mordecai, "Recollections," 4.

53 DeSolla, *A Catechism of the Jewish Religion*, 3.

54 On rabbinic salaries in the nineteenth century, see Judson, *Pennies for Heaven*; Caplan, "In God We Trust."

55 Judson, *Pennies for Heaven*, 67–68. Jacobs had been a slaveowner before the Civil War, and his vexation at his financial situation was likely a Southern lament at the economic ramifications of emancipation as much as a complaint about his congregation's failures to increase his salary. See M. Berman, *Richmond's Jewry*, 177.

56 G. Jacobs, *Nativ HaEmet, the Path of Truth*.

57 Sunday School Minute Book, 1869–99, box 2, folder, 2, Congregation Shaaray Tefila (New York, NY) Records, American Jewish Archives, MS-367, Cincinnati, OH.

58 Rebecca G. Jacobs, "Literary Pilfering," *Jewish Messenger*, August 10, 1888, 3.

59 National Council of Jewish Women, *Proceedings of the First Convention of the National Council of Jewish Women* (New York: Jewish Publication Society, 1896), 208. Twenty years earlier the newly founded Union of American Hebrew Congregations found that of the twenty-six schools that responded to a survey of Sabbath school literature, most used either Benjamin Szold's *Reshit Da'at* or Wise's *Judaism*. Union of American Hebrew Congregations, *Proceedings of the Second Annual Session of the Council* (Cincinnati, OH: Bloch, 1875), 157.

60 On the use of catechisms written by authors who espoused a different approach to Judaism than was practiced by the congregations that they served, see National Council of Jewish Women, *Proceedings of the First Convention*, 208.

61 This arrangement followed the French rather than German style of catechism. See Petuchowski, "Manuals and Catechisms of the Jewish Religion," 47.

62 Lyons, *Sunday School Lessons*.

63 It was reprinted at least twice, each time by a Baltimore publisher. See B. Szold, *Reshit Da'at*. Also see Rappel, "A Bibliography," 45.

64 Elzas serialized his catechism monthly in the *Sabbath School Companion*, a periodical he edited for his congregational Sunday school from February through November 1896. The catechism was advertised in June 1896 as available for

purchase as a thirty-two-page pamphlet. See *Sabbath School Companion* 2, no. 6 (June 1896): 3.

65 Elzas, *Judaism*.

66 Rosenbaum and Rosenbaum, *Visions of Reform*, 73. DeSolla, *A Catechism of the Jewish Religion*, 7–8.

67 DeSolla, *A Catechism of the Jewish Religion*, 3.

68 Harry H. Mayer, "The Kansas City Experiment with Reform Judaism: The First Eighty Years of Congregation B'nai Jehudah, 1800–1950," SC-6066, American Jewish Archives.

69 "'The Jewish Religion,' a Dictation Given to Confirmation Classes Prepared by Rev. Dr. William Rosenau, Rabbi," Eutaw Place Temple, JMM 1990.089.022, Rabbi William Rosenau Collection, Jewish Museum of Maryland, Baltimore.

70 The prayer should read "Holy, Holy, Holy." Miriam Greenbaum's notebook from her confirmation class with Rabbi A. Guttmacher, 1988.209.008, Jewish Museum of Maryland.

71 Betsy Lowenstein, Confirmation Book, August 8, 186?, IHI-001–019, Elizabeth S. and Alvin I. Fine Museum, Temple Emanu-El, San Francisco.

72 Meyer, "Abraham Geiger's Historical Judaism," 3; Meyer, *Response to Modernity*, 89.

73 Heschel, *Abraham Geiger and the Jewish Jesus*, 105.

74 Elias Eppstein Nearprint, American Jewish Archives.

75 Public schools became widely available in Detroit in the 1860s, undoubtedly influencing the move toward part-time Jewish education. Katz, "Jewish Education,"; Garrett, "Development of Jewish Education in Detroit."

76 The lectures were given verbally, with the expectation that the students would copy his words verbatim.

77 The same year, for example, Bernhard Felsenthal, a Reform German émigré who was rabbi of the Chicago Verein, also published a catechism—but Felsenthal's catechism was in German, still the dominant language of his community.

78 Eppstein, *Confirmant's Guide to the Mosaic Religion*, iv. *Israel* was commonly used synonymously with *Jews* or *Judaism* by American rabbis during the nineteenth century.

79 Eppstein, *Confirmant's Guide*, 1.

80 Wise, "Apologetics of Judaism," 226, in *Selected Writings*, 221–27.

81 As Sefton D. Temkin explains, Wise's *Judaism: Its Doctrines and Duties* was a distillation of Wise's 1861 *The Essence of Judaism*, in which Wise attempted to articulate a theology that he hoped—perhaps naively—all American Jews could unite behind. Temkin, *Creating American Reform Judaism*, 156–57.

82 Wise, *Judaism*, 9.

83 Ibid., 9–10.

84 Ibid., 11. Protestant biblical theorists had long attempted their own repackaging of Christianity as an entirely rational religion with a radical reading of the New Testament that understood its miracles as merely imagined for an inner spiritual

meaning, or kerygma. Thomas Jefferson's Bible, *The Life and Morals of Jesus of Nazareth*, offers an iconic example, while the work of the Bible scholar Rudolph Bultmann (1884–1976) offers a more systematic historical treatment. Wise inverted the religion that these Protestant theorists wrote about to formulate his own critique of Christianity.

85 Emil Hirsch, "Judaism and Modern Religion," *Jewish Exponent*, July 24, 1903, 8. Jewish engagements with comparative religious studies were evident at the 1893 World's Parliament of Religions. See Union of American Hebrew Congregations, ed., *Judaism at the World's Parliament of Religions*.

86 Isaac Moses, "The Genesis of Religion," *American Israelite*, April 6, 1888, 4.

87 See, for example, "Local," *American Israelite*, March 26, 1903, 6.

88 See, for example, Morris Cohn, "Thoughts on the Science of Religion," *American Israelite*, March 26, 1903, 4, and another article on page 6.

89 Max Lilienthal, "Light, Love and Mutual Damnation: A Sermon Delivered April 21 at the Universalist Church, Plum Street," *Israelite*, April 26, 1872, 8.

90 Leeser referred to "false belief" and idolatry as the "error which men are guilty of when they imagine that anything can be possessed of divine power except the Great Creator alone," but he mentioned no other religious traditions by name or implication. Leeser, *Catechism for Younger Children*, 5.

91 Similarly, in his 1899 catechism, Max Landsberg, rabbi of Temple B'rith Kodesh in Rochester, New York, defined religion as "the science of a truly human life." Landsberg, *Outline of Jewish Religion*, 1.

92 Kohler, *Guide for Instruction in Judaism*, 15. As Sarah Imhoff has explored, Kohler's theological writings emphasized that while Judaism harmonized with reason, it had not lost sight of the heart. Imhoff, *Masculinity*, 36.

93 Kohler, *Heaven and Hell*. As Kohler wrote in a 1922 letter to Alfred M. Cohen, chair of the Board of Governors of Hebrew Union College, "The study of the Jewish religion in these days of historical research requires a thorough familiarity with all religious systems which either have been of influence upon, or have been influenced by Judaism, during its more than three thousand years of history. Therefore, several years ago, as some of you will remember, I advocated the creation of a chair for Comparative Religion alongside of that of Theology for the clarification and illumination of Judaism both in its relation to its two daughter religions, Christianity, and Islam, and to other systems of faith and religious practice." Kohler to Cohen, June 25, 1922, series A, subseries 1, box 1, folder 1, Kaufmann Kohler Papers, MS-29, American Jewish Archives.

94 "Our American Needs and Opportunities," sermon given at Temple Beth El, 1888, series B, box 1, folder 7, Kaufmann Kohler Papers, MS-29, American Jewish Archives.

95 Kohler, *Guide for Instruction in Judaism*, 11.

96 Ibid., 14–15. The emphasis is in the original.

97 "Text Books," *American Hebrew*, September 9, 1881, 38.

CHAPTER 3. HOW DO YOU SOLVE A PROBLEM LIKE SHAVUOT?

1 Clara Lowenberg Moses, "My Memories," SC-8499, American Jewish Archives, Cincinnati, OH.

2 Lindheim, *Parallel Quest*, 8.

3 *Sabbath School Visitor*, June 1874, 86.

4 Wilson, "Introduction," 376.

5 The first confirmation to be held in a synagogue was celebrated in 1822. On the institution of confirmation in the context of the German Jewish Reform movement, see Eliav, *Judische Erziehung in Deutschland [Jewish Education in Germany]*; Herrmann, "Jewish Confirmation Sermons."

6 The first synagogue confirmation ceremony to include girls was celebrated in 1844 under the auspices of the German Reform movement in Breslau. See Resnick, "Confirmation Education from the Old World," 217.

7 On the history of the bar mitzvah as a coming-of-age ceremony, see Hilton, *Bar Mitzvah*.

8 Ibid., 84; Meyer, *Response to Modernity*, 40.

9 Herrmann, "Jewish Confirmation Sermons," 104.

10 Isaac Leeser, "News Items," *Occident and American Jewish Advocate*, August 1, 1846, 259–60.

11 When Rabbi Max Lilienthal arrived in New York in 1845, the traditionalist leaders of the three congregations he served prohibited him from introducing a Reform agenda. He was, however, permitted to introduce a limited number of changes designed to inculcate decorum and heighten aesthetic experience, including an annual confirmation for both boys and girls, because he had given "convincing evidence that the ceremony of confirmation is in accordance with the strictest rules of orthodoxy, as laid down in the Talmud and Shulchan Aruch." Measseph, "Dr. Lilienthal," *Occident and American Jewish Advocate*, February 1, 1847, 551–56. See also J.K.G., "Installation of Rev. Dr. Lilienthal," *Occident and American Jewish Advocate*, February 1, 1846, 574–76.

12 Measseph, "Dr. Lilienthal," 552. On Max Lilienthal's educational work in New York, see Merowitz, "Max Lilienthal"; Grinstein, *Rise of the Jewish Community*, 249.

13 Isaac Leeser, "News Items," *Occident and American Jewish Advocate*, August 1, 1846, 256–64; Isaac Leeser, "Editorial Correspondence," *Occident and American Jewish Advocate*, October 1846, 344–50. Leeser's rejection of confirmation inaugurated a series of letters variously defending and rejecting the ceremony, beginning with Morris Nathan, rabbi in St. Thomas, in February 1847. Morris Nathan, "Confirmation in St. Thomas," *Occident and American Jewish Advocate*, February 1, 1847, 544–46.

14 Isaac Leeser, "News Items," *Occident and American Jewish Advocate*, July 1, 1853, 234.

15 Grinstein, *Rise of the Jewish Community*, 247–49.

16 For examples of nineteenth-century Children's Day services, see "Children's Day at Morristown," *Christian Advocate*, June 20, 1872, 196; E. O. Haven, "Children's Day," *Christian Advocate*, May 29, 1873, 170. On the history of Children's Day, see Presbyterian Historical Society, "Children's Sunday in the Presbyterian Church."

17 On the customs associated with Shavuot, see L. Jacobs, "Shavuot."

18 Orthodox detractors would critique this animus toward postbiblical literature and the concomitant emphasis on a *sola scriptura* (by scripture alone) approach to the Bible as little more than the Protestantizing of Judaism, if not a modern-day Karaism. Shavit and Eran, *Hebrew Bible Reborn*, 19.

19 Shavit and Eran, *Hebrew Bible Reborn, 19*; Levenson, *Making of the Modern Jewish Bible*. Within American Judaism specifically, Penny Schine Gold outlines ways that American Jewish educators "made the Bible modern," by editing and retelling the stories of the Tanakh (Hebrew Bible) in accordance with their particular religious-ideological positions. Gold, *Making the Bible Modern*.

20 McDannell, *Christian Home in Victorian America*, 127–49.

21 Ashton notes that in 1845 Aguilar's *The Spirit of Judaism* was the most popular book in the library of the Hebrew Sunday School in Philadelphia. Ashton, *Rebecca Gratz*, 163.h

22 Minutes of Congregation Ahawath Chesed, 1864–1972, 132, Central Synagogue Archives, New York, NY.

23 Report of the Sabbath School Committee to the President, Officers, and Members of Beth El, 1886, School Board Minutes Book, 1871–93, box 1, folder 4, Leo M. Franklin Archives, Temple Beth El, Bloomfield Hills, MI.

24 Sadie Baer, interview by Aviv Naamani, 1978, University of Louisville, https://ohc.library.louisville.edu.

25 Wise maintained that the Torah was of divine origin, whereas the Talmud was the work of human hands. See Temkin, *Creating American Reform Judaism*, 79–86.

26 See Schechter, *Seminary Addresses and Other Papers*, 23.

27 On the cautious embrace of biblical scholarship among American Jews, see N. Cohen, "Challenges of Darwinism and Biblical Criticism,"; Schwartz, *Emergence of Jewish Scholarship in America*.

28 On Kohler's embrace of biblical criticism, see "The Bible in Light of Modern Research," his 1887 lecture at Temple Beth-El in New York. Kohler, *Hebrew Union College*, 173–84.

29 Kaufmann Kohler, "What a Jewish Institution of Learning Should Be," *American Israelite*, October 22, 1903, 1.

30 N. Cohen, "Challenges of Darwinism and Biblical Criticism."

31 Maftir, "San Francisco: A Good Age Shabuoth," *American Israelite*, June 12, 1885, 6. I am grateful to Jonathan Sarna for pointing me to the identity of "Maftir." Robert Singerman's unpublished book manuscript on Choynski is included in the collection of his papers. Robert L. Singerman Papers, BANC MSS 2012/228, Bancroft Library, University of California, Berkeley.

32 Miriam Greenbaum's notebook from her confirmation class with Rabbi A. Guttmacher is document 1988.209.008 in the Jewish Museum of Maryland, Baltimore.

33 His letter appeared in the *American Israelite*, June 4, 1908, 4. The literal translation of Shavuot is "weeks." It marks the end of the counting of the Omer, a seven-week daily obligation that begins on Passover and ends on Shavuot. This counting of weeks has historically cultivated anticipation for the giving of the Torah on Shavuot.

34 Examples of confirmation ceremonies that eschewed a Torah service include those held by Kehilath Anshe Ma'ariv Synagogue in Chicago and Temple Emanu-El in New York. The latter abolished Torah reading by confirmands in 1849. See Confirmation Materials, box 1, folder 3, Isaac S. Moses Papers, MS-122, American Jewish Archives; Grinstein, *Rise of the Jewish Community*, 249.

35 Laminated program of Order of Ceremonies at the Confirmation on Shabuoth in the Hanover St. Temple on June 12, 1891, JMM 1992.233.032; Bulletin from the Confirmation Exercises of the Congregation Oheb Shalom, Eutaw Place Temple, JMM 1990.089.020; Confirmation Program from Har Sinai Temple, June 11, 1913, JMM 1983.019.007; Program for Confirmation and Shabuoth Service, Madison Avenue Temple, JMM 1991.127.038, all in Jewish Museum of Maryland.

36 Isaac Mayer Wise, "The Confirmation Day," *American Israelite*, May 21, 1880, 4; Wise, "Shabuoth, 5650 A.M.," *American Israelite*, May 22, 1890, 4.

37 Central Conference of American Rabbis, *Yearbook of the Central Conference of American Rabbis*, Vol. 1 (1891), 43–58.

38 The debate over the liturgy was a symptom of larger problems besetting American Reform Judaism in the nineteenth century and the significant rivalries within the movement that prevented the reaching of a consensus on theological issues. See Friedland, "Hebrew Liturgical Creativity."

39 "The beautiful confirmation service," it was noted, "is the work of Rabbi Abraham Cronbach. We are all the debtors of our colleague for his generous act in placing the service at the disposal of the conference." Central Conference of American Rabbis, *Yearbook of the Central Conference of American Rabbis*, Vol. 22 (1912), 35. A manuscript of the initial submission is included in box 8, folder 10, Central Conference of American Rabbis Records, MS-34, American Jewish Archives.

40 For a copy of the *Minister's Handbook*, see box 2, folder 18, David Philipson Collection, American Jewish Archives.

41 Isaac Mayer Wise, "Shabuoth in Cincinnati," *American Israelite*, June 11, 1875, 4.

42 "Shabuoth—Confirmation," *Jewish Exponent*, May 27, 1887, 6.

43 "Wit and Humor," *Jewish Exponent*, September 16, 1887, 12.

44 Gartner, *History of the Jews of Cleveland*, 196.

45 William Max Nathan Autobiographical Questionnaire, December 13, 1954, SC-8721, American Jewish Archives.

46 Herman, "From Priestess to Hostess," 161.

47 "New York—Congregation Temple Emanu-El," *Israelite*, May 27, 1871, 7.

48 See Eleff, *Who Rules the Synagogue?*

49 See Dennis, *Red, White, and Blue.*

50 Schmidt, *Consumer Rites,* 13.

51 On the turn toward ritual within some sectors of American Christianity in the second half of the nineteenth century, see Lofton, *Consuming Religion,* 61–101. On the elaborate celebration of Christian holidays in the period, see Schmidt, *Consumer Rites,* 192–243.

52 On the elevation of Jewish holidays in America through spending and consumer culture, see Ashton, *Hanukkah in America,* 112–14; Joselit, *Wonders of America.*

53 See A. Rose, *Victorian America and the Civil War,* 9–20, and *Voices of the Marketplace,* 7.

54 Boylan, *Sunday School,* 15; Sâanchez-Eppler, *Dependent States,* 207–208; Perry, *Young America,* 8.

55 McDannell, *Christian Home in Victorian America,* 130–32.

56 This also dovetailed with sentimental ideas about childhood found in traditional Judaism. As Ephraim Kanarfogel has observed, Jewish parents have historically delighted in educating the younger generation, encouraging them to participate in Jewish rituals, particularly the Passover Seder. Kanarfogel, *Jewish Education and Society,* 39.

57 Maurice Frankel, "Confirmation Speech," box 1, folder 3, Isaac S. Moses Papers, MS-122, American Jewish Archives.

58 J. Cohen, *Jewish Religious Music.*

59 I am grateful to Judah M. Cohen for conversations about nineteenth-century synagogue choirs.

60 Minutes of Congregation Ahawath Chesed, 1864–1972, p. 78, Central Synagogue Archives.

61 Bostonia, "Brieflets by Bostonia," *American Israelite,* June 8, 1883, 405.

62 Y. D'Awake, "Shabuoth: How It Was Observed at Various Points. Touro Synagogue," *American Israelite,* June 5, 1890, 3.

63 Drusus, "Baltimore," *American Israelite,* May 29, 1890, 2.

64 Minute Book, 1890–1900, box 1, folder 1, Temple Beth El History Collection, Leo M. Franklin Archives.

65 Board Minutes, 1884–1901, archives of Rodef Shalom Congregation, Pittsburgh.

66 See Eisenberg, *J.P.S. Guide to Jewish Traditions.* There can be no greater indication of the popularity of the custom than the fact that at least one halakhic authority tried to censure the practice. The Gaon of Vilna, Rabbi Eliyahu Kramer, opposed the custom, contending that because flowers and greens were widely used in church services and in non-Jewish cemeteries, Jews should abandon the custom of flowers and greens in the synagogue on Shavuot. The Gaon's opinion was taken up by the Jews of Lithuania but largely ignored by the rest of the Jewish world. See L. Jacobs, "Shavuot," 422–23.

67 Tice, *Gardening in America.*

68 See Ginzberg, *Women and the Work of Benevolence.* On the spirituality of nineteenth-century domesticity, see Clark, "Domestic Architecture as an Index."

69 On the turn toward ritual in American Protestantism, see Lofton, *Consuming Religion*, 61–81.

70 On the embrace of flowers in nineteenth-century American Easter celebrations, see Schmidt, *Consumer Rites*, 192–243.

71 See, for example, "Easter Flowers," *Harper's Monthly Magazine*, July 27, 1863, 189–94; "Flowers in the Church," *Christian Observer*, June 18, 1899, 2.

72 See, for example, Ella Rodman Church, "About Cut Flowers," *Harper's Bazaar*, September 19, 1896, 794.

73 Leibman, *Art of the Jewish Family*, 140–53.

74 Schmidt, *Consumer Rites*, 196–201.

75 For a broader description of the meanings attached to flowers in this era and their influence on contemporary aesthetic culture, see Seaton, *Language of Flowers*.

76 Y. D'Awake, "Shabuoth at Various Points."

77 Baal Ti Moore, "Baltimore," *American Israelite*, June 22, 1883, 418; Selag, "Nashville," *American Israelite*, June 22, 1883, 418.

78 Krauskopf, *Service Manual*.

79 William Rosenau Collection, JMM 1990.89.22, Jewish Museum of Maryland.

80 Manuscript of the *Minister's Handbook*.

81 Wise, *Hymns, Psalms, and Prayers*, 198.

82 Ibid., 199.

83 American Jews were cognizant that the confirmation ceremony was an import from Christianity, and, in the words of one reporter from Boston, "an imitation of the same rite as in the Christian church." Bostonia, "Brieflets by Bostonia."

84 Krauskopf, *Service Manual*.

85 This hymn, if not the liturgy as a whole, seems to have been adopted by other synagogues as well. For example, a newspaper report on the confirmation service at Temple Adath Israel, Louisville, Kentucky, in 1911, refers to its use. "Louisville Notes, *American Israelite*, June 8, 1911, 2.

86 Krauskopf, *Service Manual*, 480.

87 Episcopal Church, *The Book of Common Prayer, with the Psalter, or the Psalms of David*, 1836, 65; *Evangelical Episcopalian*, Chicago, March 1903, 127.

88 J. Cohen, *Jewish Religious Music*.

89 Maftir, "San Francisco Notes," *American Israelite*, June 4, 1880, 6.

90 Emily Seasongood, autobiography, SC-11128, American Jewish Archives.

91 Confirmation Collection, 1903, Leo M. Franklin Archives.

92 William Max Nathan Autobiographical Questionnaire, December 13, 1954, SC-8721, American Jewish Archives; Hebrew Benevolent Orphan Asylum Minutes, 1891, Jewish Historical Society of Greater MetroWest, Whippany, NJ.

93 *Israelite*, June 20, 1862, 406.

94 "Shabuoth at New Orleans: Synagogue Touro Temple Sinai," *American Israelite*, June 17, 1887, 3.

95 Maftir, "San Francisco Notes."

96 Emphasis in the original. Aliquis, "Wheeling, W.Va.," *American Israelite*, June 20, 1889, 2.

97 Reizenstein was a pun on the German *reizen*, meaning "irritate."

98 Ben Meir, "Mrs. Reizenstein's Remarks Concerning Carrie's Confirmation," *Jewish Exponent*, June 17, 1887, 4.

99 Henrietta Szold, "The Education of the Jewish Girl," *Maccabean* 5, no. 1 (July 1903): 6.

100 Max Heller, "Shabuoth," *American Israelite*, May 28, 1903, 4.

101 "Confirmation," *American Israelite*, June 20, 1889, 2.

102 Aliquis, "Wheeling, W.Va."; Selag, "Nashville."

103 See Goldman, *Beyond the Synagogue Gallery*, 110.

104 On ritual as a form of cultural performance, see Schechner, *Performance Theory*; Turner, *Anthropology of Performance*.

CHAPTER 4. EXPANDING THE EDUCATIONAL MARKETPLACE

1 Sâanchez-Eppler, *Dependent States*, 153.

2 Esther Weinstein, "Goshen, Ind.," *Sabbath Visitor*, February 15, 1891, 592–93.

3 In 1905 the total circulation of monthly periodicals in America had reached 64 million—an increase from 18 million in 1890. See Ohmann, "Diverging Paths," 103.

4 The Jewish Publication Society had two short-lived beginnings, from 1845 to 1851 and from 1871 to 1873, but the society's effort, begun in 1888, achieved longevity. Madison, *Jewish Publishing in America*; Sarna, "Two Ambitious Goals," and *J.P.S.*

5 Sarna, "Two Ambitious Goals," 377.

6 Avery, *Behold the Child*; Gross and Kelley, *An Extensive Republic*

7 Some adult Jewish newspapers also included a column for children, such as "Aunt Babette's Children's Corner" in the *American Israelite*. See, for example, "Children's Corner: Rosh Hashonah They Went Mushrooming How They Grow Our First and Still Another," *American Israelite*, September 22, 1892, 6.

8 Intended for children aged eleven to thirteen, *Young Israel* was printed originally in English and German and later only in English. In 1900 it changed its name to *Israel's Home Journal* and its audience to adult readers. Gottheil and Popper, "Periodicals."

9 Gottheil and Popper, "Periodicals"; Patz and Miller, "Jewish Religious Children's Literature"; Hirt-Manheimer, "A Critical History"; Kenny, "Contemporary Jewish American."

10 Rose L. Brown, "The Story of the Years in Colorado from 1890–1903," SC-1435, American Jewish Archives, Cincinnati, OH.

11 Louis Helbrun to the editor, *Sabbath School Visitor*, March 1874, 38.

12 On network culture and nineteenth-century American religion, see Supp-Montgomerie, *When the Medium Was the Mission*.

13 "Letter-Box," *Sabbath Visitor*, July 3, 1886, 185.

14 After Lilienthal's death in 1882, the *Visitor* was edited by a succession of lead-ing rabbis within the Reform movement, including Isaac Mayer Wise, Kaufman Kohler, and Jacob Voorsanger. See N. Cohen, *What the Rabbis Said*, 104–28; Patz and Miller, "Jewish Religious Children's Literature."

15 *Hebrew Sabbath School Visitor* 1, no. 1 (1874): 2.

16 In its later years the *Visitor* moved away from the child-centered nature of its earlier editions. It began to include lesson plans for Sabbath schools adapted from the Talmud Ylomdim Institute in Cincinnati and addressed content to teachers and parents as well as to children.

17 *Hebrew Sabbath School Visitor*, July 1874, 99.

18 "Minute Book, 1902–1911," box 1, folder 1, Temple B'nai Israel (Galveston, TX) Records, MS-530, American Jewish Archives.

19 The books published by the Hebrew Sabbath School Union of America (HSSUA) included Adolph Moses and I. S. Moses, *The Ethics of the Hebrew Scriptures* (Cincinnati, OH: Bloch, 1889) and *The Proverbs: School Edition* (Cincinnati, OH: Bloch, 1890); Moses Mielziner, *Selections from the Book of Psalms* (Cincinnati, OH: Hebrew Sabbath School Union of America, 1888). The pamphlets were Henry Berkowitz, *Plan of Religious Instruction for Sabbath Schools* (Cincinnati, OH: Hebrew Sabbath School Union of America), and *How to Organize a Jewish Sabbath School* (Cincinnati, OH: Hebrew Sabbath School Union of America). See Union of American Hebrew Congregations (hereafter UAHC), *Proceedings of the Sixteenth Annual Session of the Council* (Cincinnati, OH: Bloch, 1889), 2493.

20 Barnett Elzas, "Editorial Brevities," *Sabbath School Companion* 1, no. 3 (March 1895): 4. HSSUA president Moses Mielziner noted there was a common impression that the union sought to interfere with the independence of the Sabbath schools and with the religious and pedagogical views of the teachers. UAHC, Congregations, *Proceedings of the Sixteenth Annual Session*, 2491–502.

21 UAHC, *Proceedings of the Thirty-Second Session of the Council* (Cincinnati, OH: Bloch, 1905), 5393. As Kerry Marc Olitzky has observed, it was not until Emmanuel Gamoran took over Reform education in 1923 that the movement published books in any appreciable numbers. Olitzky, "A History," 13.

22 After three years the juvenile and pedagogic material published in *Young Israel* was divided, with "an 80 page monthly, devoted for the most part to Juvenile interests, and a 20 page weekly, consisting largely of Religious School material as an aid to teachers in religious schools." UAHC, *Proceedings of the Thirty-Seventh Annual Session of the Council* (Cincinnati, OH: Bloch, 1910), 6518.

23 "Advertisements," *Young Israel*, November 29, 1907, 18.

24 George Alexander Kohut, "Editorial Column," *Young Israel* 1, no. 1 (1907): 1.

25 UAHC, *Proceedings of the Thirty-Eighth Annual Session of the Council* (Cincinnati, OH: Bloch, 1911), 6853–64.

26 *Sabbath Visitor*, June 17, 1881, 191.

27 By including advertising in periodicals for American Jewish children, Jewish publishers mirrored the design of Christian and other mass-market children's literature in the United States. See Jacobson, *Raising Consumers*.

28 *Young Israel* 2, no. 9 (1872), published by the New York Hebrew Orphan Asylum.

29 "Advertisements," *Young Israel* 1, no. 1 (1907): 30–31, published in Detroit by the Union of American Hebrew Congregations.

30 On the late nineteenth-century piano craze, see Joselit et al., *Getting Comfortable in New York*, 35.

31 On the manifestation of these dynamics within popular Christian children's literature of the era, see Kooistra, "Home Thoughts and Home Scenes"; Jacobson, *Raising Consumers*, 16–55.

32 Christian and secular children's periodicals began to include advertisements for largely the same reasons. See Jacobson, *Raising Consumers*, 16–55.

33 As Melissa Klapper notes, periodicals had highly variable circulation rates and may not have reached as wide an audience as they often claimed. Klapper, *Jewish Girls Coming of Age*, 9.

34 Richman, "Jewish Sunday School Movement," 575.

35 Sarna, *J.P.S.*, 143.

36 See Krasner, "Representations of Self and Other."

37 Sarna, "Two Ambitious Goals," 387.

38 See Bloch Publishing Company, "Marriage Certificate and Ketubbah," 80.21.1, Magnes Collection, University of California, Berkeley; Bloch Printing Company, "Marriage Contract," JM 1–49, Jewish Museum, New York.

39 Gordon, *Saturated World*, 4.

40 D. P. Sanford, *Eddy's Tickets: A Tale for the Little Ones* (New York: General Protestant Episcopal Sunday School Union, 1864).

41 Greenspoon, "Sunday School Prizes and Books," 87.

42 Jewish Chautauqua Society, *Second Summer Assembly of the Jewish Chautauqua Society: Official Account*, ed. Solomon Foster (Atlantic City, NJ: Jewish Chautauqua Society, 1898), 46, YIVO Library, Center for Jewish History, New York, NY.

43 Josephine Grauman Marks, "A Little Religious School in a Little Town: Read before the Kentucky Convention of Religious Schools at Louisville," *American Israelite*, February 3, 1916, 1.

44 Mordecai, "Recollections," 5.

45 Ashton, *Rebecca Gratz*, 153.

46 Isaac Leeser, "School Books," *Occident and American Jewish Advocate*, October 1866, 5. Maimonides' Thirteen Principles were included in the catechism published by Isaac Leeser in 1839 and titled "The Creed."

47 Minnie, "Charleston Letter: The Sunday-School, William Cullen Bryant, Dr. George Prince Azor," *American Israelite*, July 5, 1878, 2.

48 Board Minutes, 1884–1901, archives of Rodef Shalom Congregation, Pittsburgh.

49 "Lafayette, Ind.," *American Israelite*, May 28, 1891, 7; "Philadelphia," *American Israelite*, July 22, 1897, 2.

50 "Local and Domestic: Cincinnati the First Response, St. Louis Hebrew Free School, a Golden Wedding, YMHA," *American Israelite*, February 27, 1880, 6.

51 "Our Sunday Schools. Shearith Israel and Bnai Jeshurun Closing Exercises," *Jewish Messenger*, June 17, 1876, 5.

52 See, for example, letter to the editor, *American Israelite*, March 2, 1877, 6.

53 A. Cohen, *Centenary History*, 27.

54 Ashton, *Hanukkah in America*, 81–83.

55 Dwyer-Ryan, Porter, and Davis, *Becoming American Jews*, 25; "Wilson Avenue Temple Notes," *Jewish Review and Observer*, November 24 1899, 2.

56 Mathilda M. Lemlein, "Interest without Prizes," in *Record of the Third Jewish Chautauqua Summer Assembly* (Atlantic City, NJ: Jewish Chautauqua Society, 1899), 2–3, YIVO Library, Center for Jewish History, New York, NY; "Our Sabbath Schools," *Jewish Messenger*, October 12, 1888, 4.

57 Julia Richman, "What Are Proper Incentives in Religious School Work?" in Jewish Chautauqua Society, *Second Summer Assembly*, 46–47.

58 Though the JCS was nondenominational, the outsize presence of Reform rabbis and scholars within its intellectual leadership nevertheless led to persistent accusations that it was a Reform institution. See Pearlstein, "Understanding through Education." On the twentieth-century activities of the Jewish Chautauqua movement, see also L. Berman, *Speaking of Jews*, 11–33.

59 M. Berkowitz, *Beloved Rabbi*, 152. See also Pearlstein, "Assemblies by the Sea."

60 From the first year of the society's existence, it recognized that its most important work lay in discussions of pedagogy and the organization of religious schools. See "Summer Assembly: Notable Gathering of Jewish Educators," *Jewish Exponent*, July 30, 1897, 1.

61 Complete records of the summer assemblies have not been published. Excerpts from papers and proceedings of assemblies appeared in the Anglo Jewish press. The Philadelphia-based newspaper the *Jewish Exponent* published a special supplement, "Jewish Chautauqua Assembly Record" during the early summer assemblies held at Atlantic City, and the *American Hebrew* printed the activities of the JCS in a periodic section of the paper from 1895 to 1897. From 1901 the *Menorah Monthly* newspaper, published by B'nai Brith, became the official organ of the JCS. B'nai Brith terminated its connections with *Menorah Monthly* in 1902, but the paper survived and published the records of the JCS assemblies until 1907.

62 H. Berkowitz, "Jewish Chautauqua Society," in *Beloved Rabbi*, 165–66.

63 National Council of Jewish Women, "Sabbath-School Reform," *Jewish Messenger*, February 12, 1897, 5.

64 Jewish Chautauqua Society, *Second Summer Assembly*, 9–10.

65 Gordon, *Saturated World*, 53.

66 Jewish Chautauqua Society, *Second Summer Assembly*, 46.

67 Jewish Chautauqua Society, *First Summer Assembly: Official Account* (Atlantic City, NJ: Jewish Chautauqua Society, 1897).

68 "Jottings," *American Israelite*, December 28, 1893, 6; Maggid, "Philadelphia," *American Israelite*, March 12, 1886, 7; "National Council of Jewish Women: Philadelphia Section, Denver Section, Brooklyn, N.Y. Section," *American Israelite*, March 18, 1897, 6.

69 Almost thirty years earlier, Rabbi Max Lilienthal had promoted object teaching within secular education and co-authored a graded primer for use in Cincinnati public schools. There is little evidence, however, that his proposals were adopted by his colleagues working in American Jewish education. Lilienthal and Allyn, *Object Lessons*. See also Ruben, *Max Lilienthal*, 165.

70 Wajda, "And a Little Child"; Carter, *Object Lessons*; Knupfer, "Learning to Read."

71 Jewish Chautauqua Society, *Second Summer Assembly*, 24.

72 Quimby, "Use of Costumes, Objects and Models"; Lindquist, "Slow Time and Sticky Media."

73 Lemlein, "Interest without Prizes," 7–8.

74 Jewish Chautauqua Society, *Second Summer Assembly*, 23–24.

75 M. Berkowitz, *Beloved Rabbi*, 165–66.

76 "Jewish Chautauqua Society: Work of the Educational Council, Changes in the Summer Assembly, Provisions for Religious School Teachers, Lectures on Jewish Biography," *American Israelite*, October 13, 1904, 8.

77 Including an extensive series of textbooks and correspondence courses. For a critique of the JCS's failings, see Krasner, "Jewish Chautatuqua, Jewish History."

78 Originally written in the thirteenth century, an abridged version of "Maoz Tzur" was published by American rabbis Marcus Jastrow and Gustav Gottheil in 1896. It was given the popular Christian title "Rock of Ages" rather than the Hebrew one, and the lyrics were altered to emphasize cheery celebrations of God saving the Jewish people, rather than the destruction of the temple. Ashton, *Hanukkah in America*, 85–87.

79 Cronbach later became a rabbi, receiving ordination at the Hebrew Union College in 1906. Abraham Cronbach, Autobiography, p. 17, MF-435, American Jewish Archives.

80 On stereopticon shows as dramatic narratives, see Borton and Borton, *Before the Movies*.

81 The later stereopticon projector used photographic slides. Musser, "Stereopticon," 52–79.

82 See, for example, "Advertisements," *Youth's Companion*, October 27, 1887, 463; "Advertisements," *Ladies' Home Journal*, November 1889, 1; T. H. McAllister, *Catalogue of Stereopticons, Dissolving View Apparatus, and Magic Lanterns with Extensive List of Slides*" (Boston, 1899).

83 See, for example, "Advertisements," *American Hebrew*, July 7, 1882, 99. Stereopticon projectors were often featured as prizes at raffles and competitions held by Jewish organizations. See Roger Williams, "Providence, R.I.," *American Israelite*, March 13, 1890, 1.

84 Sherith Israel Religious School Committee Reports, 1899–1935, carton 55, folder 1, Sherith Israel Records, BANC MSS 2021/720, Bancroft Library, University of California, Berkeley.

85 "Philadelphia City News," *Jewish Exponent*, January 10, 1890, 6.

86 "Chanuccah Celebrations," *Jewish Exponent*, December 23, 1887, 10.

87 As Jonathan Krasner notes, the popularity of the stereopticon still abounded among educators in the early twentieth century. Samson Benderly used slides to teach Hebrew vocabulary and Bible lessons in Baltimore beginning in 1903. Later, stereopticon slide shows would be used as a recruitment device for the New York Bureau of Education. Krasner, *Benderly Boys*, 33, 2.

88 Jewish Chautauqua Society, *Second Summer Assembly*, 24.

89 "Philadelphia City News: Dies, Jeanette Miriam Goldberg," *Jewish Exponent*, March 8, 1935, 11; Weiner, "Goldberg, Jeannette Miriam."

90 Tobias Schanfarber, "News and Views," *American Israelite*, June 29, 1905, 5.

91 Minute Book, 1902–11, box 1 folder 1, Temple B'nai Israel (Galveston) Records, MS-530, American Jewish Archives.

92 While stereopticon exhibits for American Jewish children were routinely referenced in the American Jewish press, few actual slides remain in the collections of American Jewish archives and museums. By the midtwentieth century the stereopticon had become obsolete technology. I am grateful to three synagogues' archival collections that fortuitously preserved the stereopticon slides used in their religious schools and shared them with me: Temple Israel of Boston, Congregation Rodeph Shalom in Philadelphia, and Temple Beth El in Bloomfield Hills, Michigan.

93 "Bulletin No. 18," T. H. McAllister, Manufacturing Optician, 49 Nassau Street, New York, December 1890, Harvard University Library, Cambridge, MA.

94 T. H. McAllister advertised its lantern slides regularly in the *American Israelite* beginning in 1885. See, for example, "Classified Advertisements," *American Israelite*, October 12, 1888, 3; "Classified Advertisements," *American Israelite*, November 4, 1887, 8. I am grateful to Susan L. Porter and Lisa Fagin Davis of Temple Israel in Boston for sharing the script for their exhibit of the Temple Israel stereopticon slide collection, "Projecting Palestine: Lantern Slides of the Holy Land, 1880–1915."

95 Ogden William Butler, "Four Days in Petra, with Photographs Taken by Mr William. H, Rau," *Journal of the American Geographical Society of New York* 20, no. 1 (1888): 137; "William H. Rau, the Photographer and the Man," *Bulletin of Photography: The Weekly Magazine for the Professional Photographer*, August 29, 1917, 213–15; Edward L. Wilson, "A Photographer's Visit to Petra," *Century Illustrated Magazine*, November 1885, 3.

96 William H. Rau, "Photographer Lantern Slides," microfilm reel 150, no. 1663, Smithsonian Institution.

97 As Mark Noll shows, American Protestant interest in the old lands of the Bible drew in large part from a belief that the United States was built upon its own biblical blueprint. Noll, *Old Religion in a New World*. On nineteenth-century

Orientalist enthusiasm for "Bible lands," see J. Davis, *Landscape of Belief*; Rogers, *Inventing the Holy Land*. On nineteenth-century Jewish Orientalism and the "Bible lands," see Carr, *Hebrew Orient*, 70–74; Silver-Brody, *Documentors of the Dream*.

98 Ari, "Spiritual Capital and the Copy"; Hallote, "Photography and the American Contribution."

99 She attributed this trend to participation in secular higher education and therefore to men who had access to it. Rosa Sonneschein, "Review of the National Council of Jewish Women," *American Jewess* 1, no. 4 (July 1895): 189.

100 Schorsch, "Art as Social History."

101 Julian Werner, "Correspondence: New York," *American Israelite*, December 2, 1881, 178.

102 "The Woman Who Talks," *American Jewess* 7, no. 5 (September 1898): 53–57.

103 As Sarna has explored, images of Zion in the United States have historically said more about American Jewish aspirations and ideals than about Eretz Israel. Sarna, "A Projection of America."

104 Mordecai, "Recollections," 5.

105 See, for example, "The Ideal," *Israelite*, February 10, 1871, 8; Occasional, "Sunday-School Talk by a Layman," *American Israelite*, June 25, 1875, 6. Krasner notes that when Samson Benderly attempted to introduce magic lantern slides in Bible classes at the West Side branch of New York's Uptown Talmud Torah in the second decade of the twentieth century, his more Orthodox opponents complained that the images were irreverent and sacrilegious, violating the biblical injunction against graven images. Krasner, *Benderly Boys*, 52–53.

106 Fein, *Making of an American Jewish Community*, 186.

CHAPTER 5. RELIGIOUS EDUCATION AS AMERICANIZATION

1 Gurock, "Orthodox Synagogue," 43.

2 Union of American Hebrew Congregations, *Proceedings of the Sixteenth Annual Session of the Council* (Cincinnati, OH: Bloch, 1889), 2468–2502.

3 Greenstone, *Statistical Data*, 4.

4 Samson Benderly, "The Problem of Educating the Jewish Girl," *American Hebrew and Jewish Messenger*, January 6, 1911, 278.

5 See Klapper, *Ballots, Babies, and Banners of Peace*. On Protestant women's work as child welfare and educational activists, see Ginzberg, *Women and the Work of Benevolence*, 174–213.

6 Congregation B'nai Jeshurun Minutes, 1887–92, Jewish Historical Society of MetroWest Archives, Whippany, NJ; Jewish Women's Organizations Collection, box 1, folder 1, Leo M. Franklin Archives, Temple Beth El, Bloomfield Hills, MI.

7 Jewish Women's Organizations Collection, box 1, folder 1, Leo M. Franklin Archives.

8 Jenna Weissman Joselit notes that by 1900, there were at least sixteen sisterhood groups in New York City, with a combined membership of several thousand.

Joselit, "Special Sphere," 209. On the development of sisterhoods, see Goldman, "Public Religious Lives"; Herman, "From Priestess to Hostess."

9 Kohut, *My Portion (An Autobiography)*, 246.

10 Solomon, *Fabric of My Life*, 95.

11 Sarah Kussy, "The Story of Miriam Auxiliary of Oheb Shalom," 1940, p. 2, Sarah Kussy Papers, American Jewish Historical Society, New York.

12 "The Story of Oheb Shalom: Sixty-Five Years in Retrospect," 1945, pp. 2–3, Kussy Papers, P-4;; "Story of Miriam Auxiliary."

13 Goldman, "Public Religious Lives," 122.

14 Program: Sabbath School Festival, Held at California Theatre, Presenting "The Merry Company," 1895, IHI:001–025, Individual Historic Items, Congregation Emanu-El Collection, Elizabeth S. and Alvin I. Fine Museum, Temple Emanu-El, San Francisco.

15 "Hanukkah Festival of Emanu-El Religious School to be held at California Club Rooms," December 20, 1908, Religious School/Holidays: Chanukah, Congregation Emanu-El Collection.

16 Ashton, *Hanukkah in America*, 91–92.

17 Sherith Israel Religious School—Board Resolutions, March 2, 1896, carton 522, folder 22, Congregation Sherith Israel Collection, BANC MSS 2021/720, Bancroft Library, University of California, Berkeley.

18 J. Berman, "Jewish Education," 263.

19 "Practical Mission Work," *American Hebrew*, December 10, 1880, 44.

20 Joselit et al., *Getting Comfortable in New York*, 25.

21 *Second Annual Report of the United Jewish Charities of Cincinnati, Ohio*, p. 52, Klau Library, Hebrew Union College, Cincinnati, OH.

22 Brosterman, *Inventing Kindergarten*, 35–88, 93.

23 See, for example, "Editorial Article," *Jewish Exponent*, October 26, 1888, 4.

24 Noech, "Louisville, KY," *American Israelite*, July 7, 1892, 2.

25 *Second Annual Report*, 47.

26 "Kindergartens in Jewish Schools," *Jewish Exponent*, November 1, 1895, 4.

27 On the history of the NCJW, including its founding as a protest against the lack of representation of women within the Jewish Denominational Congress at the 1893 World's Columbian Exposition, see Rogow, *Gone to Another Meeting*; Elwell, "Founding and Early Programs"; Korelitz, "'A Magnificent Piece of Work.'"

28 Klapper, *Ballots, Babies, and Banners of Peace*, 3; McCune, *Whole Wide World, without Limits*, 22.

29 The NCJW's commitment to a religious articulation of its work is illustrated in the case of Henrietta Szold, who refused to participate in the NCJW because she saw religion as a private affair, not a cause for public activism.

30 National Council of Jewish Women, *Proceedings of the First National Convention*, 21.

31 Congregation Bene Israel Yearbook, box 24, folder 2, Congregation Bene Israel (Cincinnati) Records, MS-24, American Jewish Archives, Cincinnati, OH.

32 National Council of Jewish Women, *Proceedings of the First National Convention*, 66–67, 97.

33 *Reform Advocate*, December 5, 1896, 244.

34 Korelitz, "'A Magnificent Piece of Work'"; Sochen, "Some Observations."

35 Victoria Cooper, *The Story of NCJW San Francisco Section: 115 Years of Courage, Compassion, and Community Service* (San Francisco: National Council of Jewish Women, San Francisco Section, 2015), 28, 30.

36 National Council of Jewish Women, *Proceedings of the First National Convention*, 74, 83; NCJW, Pittsburgh Section, and Ailon Shiloh, *By Myself, I'm a Book!*, 66–67, 74. Sue Levi Elwell has estimated that by 1902, sixteen council sections were supporting eighteen mission schools with 162 teachers and an attendance of 2,500 students. Elwell, "Founding and Early Programs," 206–207.

37 Wenger, "Federation Men."

38 *Jewish Review and Observer*, May 9, 1924, 1, 8.

39 Female teachers were also paid considerably less than their male counterparts, as described in chapter 1. On women's entry into teaching in the nineteenth century, see Clifford, "'Daughters into Teachers.'"

40 Scrapbook, 1894–1945, oversize vol. 1, National Council of Jewish Women Records 1894–1967, MSS 3620, Cleveland Historical Society, Cleveland, OH; Minutes, container 1, folder 2, Cleveland Section, NCJW Records, MSS 3620, Cleveland Historical Society; Elwell, "Founding and Early Programs," 118.

41 National Council of Jewish Women, *Proceedings of the First National Convention*, 365. Hahn was active in the Sunday school movement both in her own city of Philadelphia and nationally. She would become president of the NCJW and of the Hebrew Sunday School Society before her death in 1907. "Died: Mrs. Clara Hahn," *Jewish Exponent*, January 4, 1907, 11.

42 See, for example, Henrietta Szold, "The Education of the Jewish Girl," *Maccabean* 5, no. 1 (July 1903): 6. Szold was a trenchant critic of the limited curriculum of the Sunday school. She had pedagogical credentials—she taught at a Jewish day school and founded a night school for new immigrants—yet she also kept a traditionally observant home and was heavily involved in efforts to rejuvenate traditional Jewish observance. Thus her antagonism toward an institution that by the end of the nineteenth century was broadly associated with Reform is also hardly surprising.

43 Pollak, "Forty Years"; Greenstone, *Statistical Data*.

44 F. de Sola Mendes, "Woman's Awakening," *American Hebrew*, January 18, 1895, 323.

45 Rosa Sonneschein, "Editor's Desk," *American Jewess*, vol. 2, no. 1 (October 1895): 63. See also Diner and Benderly, *Her Works Praise Her*, 121.

46 Elwell, "Founding and Early Programs," 105.

47 Ibid., 110.

48 Ibid., 112.

49 Minutes, container 1, folder 2, Cleveland Section, National Council of Jewish Women Records, 1894–1967, MSS 3620, Cleveland Historical Society.

50 Minutes of Executive Committee, 1896–1901, NCJW Records, Baltimore Section, MS 124, JMM, 2002.107.1, Jewish Museum of Maryland, Baltimore.

51 "National Council of Jewish Women," *American Hebrew*, January 18, 1895, 333.

52 Kaufmann Kohler, "Esther or Woman in the Synagogue," *American Hebrew*, March 23, 1900, 605.

53 On Kohler's ambivalent attitudes toward women, see Goldman, "Ambivalence of Reform Judaism," and *Beyond the Synagogue Gallery*, 151–71. As Dvora HaCohen notes, nineteenth-century Jewish women were rarely credited for their expert knowledge of content. Henrietta Szold received little credit for her work at the Jewish Publication Society, even though it required intensive Jewish content knowledge and significant linguistic expertise. HaCohen, *To Repair a Broken World*, 63.

54 Temple Education Committee Administrative Reports, 1892, Leo M. Franklin Archives.

55 Appeal from the Hebrew Education Society of Newark, New Jersey, November 21, 1889, Jewish Historical Society of Greater MetroWest, Whippany, NJ.

56 Helmreich, *Enduring Community*, 24.

57 Berrol, "When Uptown Met Downtown."

58 National Council of Jewish Women, *Proceedings of the First National Convention*, 207.

59 Richman, "Jewish Sunday School Movement," 574–75.

60 Meyer was ordained in the 1901 class of the Hebrew Union College and received a doctoral degree in history from Columbia in 1906. He served as both a congregational rabbi at Congregation Emanu-El in San Francisco and as lecturer in Jewish history at the University of California, Berkeley, from 1911 until his death in 1925. Meyer spoke about his time living in Palestine at the Jewish Chautauqua Society's summer institute in 1902, describing the Jewish community of the "unholy city" as impoverished and easy prey for Christian missionaries. L. I. Newman, "Martin A. Meyer," 179–81; Pearlstein, "Assemblies by the Sea."

61 Patz and Miller, "Jewish Religious Children's Literature," 22. On didactic instruction supplied to new immigrants by German American Jews, see Joselit et al., *Getting Comfortable in New York*.

62 National Council of Jewish Women, *Proceedings of the First National Convention*, 363–66.

63 Sâanchez-Eppler, *Dependent States*, 212.

64 L. M. Newman, *White Women's Rights*, 14.

CHAPTER 6. FROM THEOLOGY TO RELIGION

1 Flexner's address was published as "Religious Training of Children." See also Henrietta Szold, "Knowledge vs. Spirituality in the Curriculum of the Jewish Religious School," paper presented at the First Summer Assembly of the Jewish Chautauqua Society, in *First Summer Assembly of the Jewish Chautauqua Society: Official Account* (Atlantic City, NJ: Jewish Chautauqua Society, 1897), 1.

2 See, for example, Occasional, "Sunday-School Talk by a Layman," *American Israelite*, June 25, 1875, 6; "What the Jewish Religious School Teacher Should Know: Address Delivered July 15, 1903, before the Jewish Chautauqua Society, at Atlantic City, N.J. by Rabbi David Philipson, D.D., President of the Hebrew Sabbath School Union, of America," *American Israelite*, August 13, 1903, 4; "Our Sabbath Schools," *Jewish Messenger*, October 12, 1888, 4.

3 Grossman, *Aims of Teaching in Jewish Schools*, 53.

4 Congregation Bene Israel Yearbook, 1904, box 24, folder 2, Congregation Bene Israel (Cincinnati, Ohio) Records, MS-24, American Jewish Archives, Cincinnati, OH.

5 Sherith Israel Religious School Committee Reports, 1899–1935, carton 55, folder 1, Congregation Sherith Israel Records, BANC MSS 2021/720, Bancroft Library, University of California, Berkeley.

6 Jacob, *Changing World of Reform Judaism*, 97.

7 Teaching by using catechism still was frequent in public school education through the end of the century. William Torrey Harris, the US commissioner of education, wrote in 1891 that the chief criticism of US public schools was still an overemphasis on memorization. Reese, *America's Public Schools*, 115.

8 Sabato Morais, "An Appeal on Behalf of the Hebrew Sunday School," box 13, folder 9, Sabato Morais Collection, ARC MS-8, Library at the Herbert D. Katz Center for Advanced Judaic Studies, University of Pennsylvania, Philadelphia.

9 Leeser, "Catechism for Younger Children."

10 *Sabbath School Visitor*, January 1874, 2.

11 See, for example, *Sabbath School Visitor*, February 1874, 20.

12 Prov. 19:20 appeared in both English and Hebrew on the masthead of the magazine.

13 Emphasis in the original. Kaufmann Kohler, "Instruction in Biblical History," in Philipson, *Guide*, 10.

14 Reese, *America's Public Schools*, 79.

15 Chinn, *Inventing Modern Adolescence*, 33–34, 75; Reese, *America's Public Schools*, 79; Sâanchez-Eppler, *Dependent States*, xx.

16 See Zelizer, *Pricing the Priceless Child*; Friedman, *These Are Our Children*, 60–63.

17 Carter, *Object Lessons*, 27–52.

18 Catherine Ward Beecher's *Domestic Economy*, for example, was reprinted every year between 1841 and 1856. See Clement, *Growing Pains*, 10.

19 Reese, *America's Public Schools*, 79.

20 Tyack and Cuban, *Tinkering toward Utopia*, 18–21.

21 Hulbert, "Century of the Child," 17.

22 Diary entry, March 15, 1880, box 1, folder 1, Elias Eppstein Diaries, MS-220, American Jewish Archives. See F. Adler, *Roots in a Moving Stream*, 44.

23 Kaufman, *Shul with a Pool*, 13.

24 Bernard Shuman, *A History*, 21–22.

25 The HSSUA published a series of graded textbooks and pamphlets, all focused on the Bible. "Hebrew Sabbath School Union of America: Seat of Executive Committee in Cincinnati," *American Jewish Yearbook* 1 (1889): 5.

26 Philipson first raised the idea of these leaflets in 1894, but it was not until 1897 that they became reality. Union of American Hebrew Congregations (hereafter UAHC), *Twenty-First Annual Report of the Union of American Hebrew Congregations* (Cincinnati, OH: Bloch, 1894), 3419; *Twenty-Fifth Annual Report of the Union of American Hebrew Congregations* (Cincinnati, OH: Bloch, 1898), 3958–59. One of the continual problems faced by the HSSUA was a lack of commitment by its members that frequently hampered its ability to function effectively. Periodic pleas to the members of the HSSUA to answer requests made by committee chairs were published in the *American Israelite*. See, for example, *American Israelite*, July 29, 1887, 4.

27 UAHC, *Twenty-Fifth Annual Report*, 3958–59. See also "Sabbath School Leaflets," *American Israelite*, December 22, 1898, 6.

28 UAHC, *Twenty-Fifth Annual Report*, 3958–59; and *Proceedings of the Twenty-Seventh Annual Report of the Union of American Hebrew Congregations* (Cincinnati, OH: Bloch, 1901), 4291–92. See also Philipson, *My Life*, 98. The leaflets were later serialized as lessons in *Young Israel*, a periodical issued by the UAHC beginning in 1907.

29 "The World's First Week," *Leaflets on Biblical History Series* 1, no. 1 Hebrew Sabbath School Union of America Nearprint File, American Jewish Archives.

30 See UAHC, *Twenty-Fifth Annual Report*, 3958–59.

31 Central Conference of American Rabbis, *Yearbook of the Central Conference of American Rabbis*, Vol. 12 (1902), 188.

32 It should also be noted that while the account of creation occurs first in the order of the Tanakh, a longstanding minhag (custom) has study of the Torah for young children begin not with the book of Genesis but with Leviticus, on the basis of a midrash (explanation) that the purity of children aligns with the purity of the sacrifices discussed in the text. See Safrai et al., "Education and the Study of the Torah," 945.

33 "Prospectus: First Summer Assembly of the Jewish Chautauqua Society," Atlantic City, NJ, July 25–August 8,1897.

34 "The Jewish Chautauqua," *American Hebrew*, October 16, 1896, 600.

35 H. Berkowitz, *Open Bible*, 3–4.

36 H. Berkowitz, "Chautauqua Round Table," paper presented at the Chautauqua Summer Assembly, in *First Summer Assembly*, 10.

37 The JCS Bible course was described as the "foundation of all our reading courses in the Jewish Chautauqua Society." It took four years to complete, with participants receiving a certificate on completion. See "Prospectus," *Third Summer Assembly of the Jewish Chautauqua Society: Official Account* (Philadelphia: Jewish Chautauqua Society, 1899), 17.

38 Pearlstein, "Understanding through Education," 117.

39 Montefiore, *Bible for Home Reading*, iv, 562. Montefiore's words were also included in abridged form in advertisements for the volume that appeared in the American Jewish press. "Advertisements—the Bible for Home Reading," *American Hebrew*, June 19, 1896, 167.

40 Montefiore, "Should Biblical Criticism", and "Recent Criticism upon Moses." See also Shavit and Eran, *Hebrew Bible Reborn*, 128.

41 Montefiore, *Bible for Home Reading*, 560–61, 70.

42 Ibid., vii.

43 The term "primitive" is used in this chapter to replicate the discourse of nineteenth-century American Jews who engaged with hierarchical schemas for mapping human culture. I use it here mindful of its pejorative connotations, and the fact that it has been used in justification of racism and discrimination, in order to engage the reality that American Jews contributed to the production of discourse that classified human culture in these pejorative ways. It was a term that was prevalent in nineteenth-century American popular culture, including among American Jews. See Shuttleworth, *Mind of the Child*, 39

44 H. Szold, "Knowledge vs. Spirituality in the Curriculum," 85–86.

45 Jewish Chautauqua Society, *First Summer Assembly*, 16.

46 Ibid., 11. Other opponents of historical criticism saw the JCS's alignment with Montefiore as sufficient reason to dismiss the society as a dogmatic institution, concerned with propagating a radical Reform approach to Judaism. Peggy Pearlstein notes that the (minority) Orthodox participants in the JCS continued their opposition to Montefiore's magnum opus at least twenty years later. See Pearlstein, "Understanding through Education," 117.

47 Sabato Morais, "Claude Montefiore's Bible," *American Hebrew*, July 10, 1896, 247.

48 Richard Gottheil, "Judaica," *Jewish Messenger*, July 17, 1896, 5.

49 National Council of Jewish Women, *Proceedings of the First National Convention*. See also "Montefiore's *Bible for Home Reading*," *Jewish Exponent*, January 15, 1897, 8.

50 Henry Berkowitz, "Claude Montefiore's New Book: *The Bible for Home Reading* Completed," *American Israelite*, October 26, 1899, 4.

51 On the proliferation of the child-savage trope from the Victorian era to the present day, see Wesseling, *Child Savage, 1890–2010*, 184–99.

52 See Sâanchez-Eppler, *Dependent States*, 186–220. On the child-savage equation, see J. Rose, *Case of Peter Pan*.

53 "The Religious Training of Children," *American Hebrew*, November 29, 1901, 43.

54 Blanch, *Educational Imagination*, 156.

55 Hall, "Introductory Remarks," 5.

56 Recapitulation had existed as an idea since the Romantic period. The work of Darwin and other evolutionary biologists, however, offered a new biological framework to scientifically ground the analogy of childhood and human evolution.

57 The theory of recapitulation was succinctly captured in the title of a book published by Alexander Chamberlain, one of Hall's students, *The Child: A Study in the Evolution of Man*.

58 Shuttleworth, *Mind of the Child*, 269.

59 Bederman, *Manliness & Civilization*, 77–120.

60 Sarah Imhoff suggests that most American Jews ignored recapitulation. In the context of Jewish education, however, there was considerable interest. Imhoff, *Masculinity and the Making of American Judaism*, 131–32.

61 Kohut, *My Portion (An Autobiography)*, 298.

62 See, for example, "Literary," *American Hebrew*, December 29, 1893, 271; "Educational Works of the Year," *American Hebrew*, December 2, 1892, 155.

63 See, for example, Henry Berkowitz's sermon, "Nature in Education," box 4, folder 7:N, Henry Berkowitz Papers, MS-25, American Jewish Archives; "Kansas City: Summer Sayings," *American Israelite*, June 29, 1888, 9. Iris Idelson-Shein has demonstrated that the image of the child as savage is pervasive in maskilic pedagogical literature, serving as an illustration of the importance and the possibilities of modern education. Idelson-Shein, "Beginning of the End."

64 Edward Calisch, "How to Teach Biblical History in the Primary Grades," in Philipson, *Guide*, 81–90.

65 Hall returned the admiration, contributing an introduction to Grossman's 1919 volume on pedagogy in which Hall described the work as "the best treatise on religious pedagogy anywhere yet appeared," taking for the first time "adequate account of our new knowledge of child nature and life." Hall, introduction to Grossman, *Aims of Teaching in Jewish Schools*, 13–15.

66 "Notes and Fragments," box 2, folder 6, Louis Grossman Papers, MS 92, American Jewish Archives.

67 Jewish Chautauqua Society, *First Summer Assembly*, 14.

68 Louis Grossman, "The Essential place of Religion in Education," n.d., box 1, folder 10, Grossman Papers.

69 Montague N.A. Cohen, "The Religious Influences of Childhood on Adolescence," *Yearbook of the Central Conference of American Rabbis*, Vol. 17 (1907), 239–51.

70 For a concise exposition of Hall's definition of adolescence in relation to religion, see Hall, "Moral and Religious Training of Children."

71 Macleod, *Age of the Child*, 139–40.

72 "Rodef Shalom: Dr. Berkowitz on the Irreligion of Youth," *Jewish Exponent*, March 2, 1905, 11.

73 See, for example, *Yearbook of the Central Conference of American Rabbis*, vol. 17 (1907), 239–51.

74 Ibid., 136.

75 Louis Grossman, "The Week," *American Israelite*, May 23, 1901, 4.

76 See Bender, *New Metaphysicals*, 10.

77 James, *Varieties of Religious Experience*, 31.

78 For an analysis of the ways in which the foundational scholars within academic religious studies were entangled in Protestant truth claims, see Masuzawa, *Invention of World Religions*; McCutcheon, *Manufacturing Religion*.

79 Klapper, *Jewish Girls Coming of Age*, 145.

80 On competing definitions of Judaism in the early twentieth century, see Levitt, "Impossible Assimilations, American Liberalism"; Greene, *Jewish Origins of Cultural Pluralism*, 5–12.

CONCLUSION: IS JUDAISM A RELIGION?

1 *Yearbook of the Central Conference of American Rabbis*, vol. 10 (1900), 150.
2 Pew Research Center, *Jewish Americans in 2020*, May 11, 2021, and *A Portrait of Jewish Americans: Findings from a Pew Research Center Survey of American Jews*, October 1, 2013, both at www.pewresearch.org.
3 Gamoran, "General Situation," 25.
4 Kaplan, *Judaism as a Civilization*, 345.
5 Krasner, *Benderly Boys*, 5.
6 Ibid., 91–94, 138.
7 In the survey of Jewish education conducted before the founding of the New York Bureau of Jewish Education, Mordecai Kaplan and Bernard Cronson stressed the faults of both extremes of the educational spectrum—Sunday schools and cheders—in order to promote an alliance with the Talmud Torahs. Kaplan and Cronson, "Report of Committee on Jewish Education."
8 Ingall, *Women Who Reconstructed*, 18–19.
9 Benderly died in 1944.
10 In 2020 the Pew Research Center found that while one in four American Jews attended a full-time Jewish day school or yeshiva, six in ten reported attending a supplemental educational program such as a Hebrew school or Sunday school. Pew Research Center, *Jewish Americans in 2020*.
11 *B-mitzvah* is used by Jews who prefer a gender-neutral alternative to the binary gender options of bar (son) and bat (daughter) mitzvah. Ethnographic studies of bar and bat mitzvahs, and the Hebrew schools that prepare students for them, include Schoem, *Ethnic Survival in America*; Munro, *Coming of Age in Jewish America*; Schoenfeld, "Folk Judaism, Elite Judaism."
12 See, for example, Cohen and Kotler-Berkowitz, "Impact of Childhod Jewish Education"; Pew Research Center, Jewish Americans in 2020; Wertheimer, *New American Judaism*; Sklare and Greenblum, *Jewish Identity on the Suburban Frontier*. For two recent critiques of the sociological tendency to equate Jewish identity with religious identity, see Levisohn and Kelman, *Beyond Jewish Identity*; Gross, *Beyond the Synagogue*.
13 Levitt, "Impossible Assimilations, American Liberalism," and "Other Moderns, Other Jews."
14 Secularism, of course, was itself a product of the idea of religion. By describing Jewish religion as a phenomenon located primarily in the individual human person, rabbis and modern Jewish thinkers simultaneously created secularism as the opposite of Jewish religious belief. When American Jews named Judaism as a religion, they also named the possibility of secularism defined as rejection of Jewish religion, even though alternative models of Jewish secularism, mainly imported

from Europe, offered frameworks for Jewish nontheism that were rooted in Jewish cultural belonging. Cady and Fessenden, *Religion, the Secular, and the Politics*, 4–24; Curtis, *Production of American Religious Freedom*, 1–6.

15 Rauch, *Education of Jews and the American Community*, 304–308; Meyer, *Response to Modernity*, 286; Graff, "And You Shall Teach," 27–28; Gartner, *Jewish Education in the United States*, 9; Grinstein, "In the Course of the Nineteenth Century," 27; Chazan, Chazan, and Jacobs, *Cultures and Contexts of Jewish Education*, 95–100.

16 Imhoff, *Myth of American Jewish Feminization*.

17 Berman, Rosenblatt, and Stahl, "Continuity Crisis."

BIBLIOGRAPHY

MANUSCRIPT COLLECTIONS
American Jewish Archives, Cincinnati, OH
    Henry Berkowitz Papers
    Rose L. Brown, Autobiography
    Central Conference of American Rabbis Records
    Congregation Bene Israel (Cincinnati, OH) Records
    Congregation Shaaray Tefila (New York, NY) Records
    Abraham Cronbach, Autobiography
    Elias Eppstein Diaries
    Elias Eppstein Nearprint
    Louis Grossman Papers
    The Kansas City Experiment with Reform Judaism: The First Eighty Years of Congregation B'nai Jehudah, 1800–1950
    Kaufmann Kohler Papers
    David Philipson Collection
    Jennie Mannheimer/Jane Manner Papers
    Clara Lowenberg Moses Nearprint
    Isaac S. Moses Papers
    Emily Seasongood, Autobiography
    Temple B'nai Israel (Galveston, TX) Records

American Jewish Historical Society, New York, NY
    Chautauqua Records
    Sarah Kussy Papers

Archives of Rodef Shalom Congregation, Pittsburgh
    Board Minutes, 1884–1961
    Sunday School Collection

Bancroft Library, University of California, Berkeley
    Sherith Israel Records
    Robert L. Singerman Collection
    Temple Emanu-El Records

Beth Ahabah Museum and Archives, Richmond, VA
    Congregation Beth Shalome Records
    Isaac Leeser Records

Central Synagogue Archives, New York, NY
    Congregation Ahawath Chesed Minutes, 1864–72

Cleveland Historical Society, Cleveland, OH
    Cleveland Section, National Council of Jewish Women Records

Congregation Shearith Israel, New York, NY
    Association for the Moral Instruction of Children of the Jewish Faith Meeting
        Minutes, 1839–46

The Elizabeth S. and Alvin I. Fine Museum, Congregation Emanu-El, San Francisco
    Individual Historic Items
    Betsy Lowenstein Papers
    Religious School/Holidays Records

Jewish Historical Society of MetroWest, Whippany, NJ
    Congregation B'nai Jeshurun Records
    Congregation Oheb Shalom Records
    Hebrew Benevolent Orphan Asylum Minutes
    Hebrew Education Society of Newark Records

Jewish Museum of Maryland, Baltimore
    Eutaw Place Temple Papers
    Miriam Greenbaum Papers
    Hanover Street Temple Papers
    Har Sinai Papers
    Madison Avenue Temple Papers
    Rabbi William Rosenau Collection

Library at the Herbert D. Katz Center for Advanced Judaic Studies, University of
    Pennsylvania, Philadelphia
    Binswanger/Solis-Cohen Family Collection
    Charles and Mary Cohen Collection
    Isaac Leeser Collection
    Sabato Morais Collection

Library Company of Philadelphia, Philadelphia
    Hebrew Sunday School Society of Philadelphia Papers

Rabbi Leo M. Franklin Archives, Temple Beth El, Bloomfield Hills, MI
  Confirmation Collection
  Jewish Women's Organizations Collection
  Temple Beth El History Collection
  Temple Education Committee School Board Minutes

Walter P. Reuther Library, Wayne State University, Detroit
  National Council of Jewish Women, Greater Detroit Section Papers

NEWSPAPERS AND PERIODICALS
American Hebrew
American Jewess
American Jewish Yearbook
Christian Advocate
Christian Observer
Harper's Bazaar
Harper's Monthly Magazine
Hebrew Watchword and Instructor
Helpful Thoughts
Israelite
Jewish Exponent
Jewish Home
Jewish Messenger
Jewish Review and Observer
Maccabean
Occident and American Jewish Advocate
Reform Advocate
Sabbath Visitor/ Hebrew Sabbath School Visitor/Visitor
Young Israel

CONFERENCE PROCEEDINGS
Proceedings of the First National Convention of the National Council of Jewish Women
Proceedings of the Union of American Hebrew Congregations
Yearbook of the Central Conference of American Rabbis

PUBLISHED PRIMARY SOURCES

Beecher, Catherine. *Essay on the Education of Female Teachers for the United States.*
  New York: Van Nostrand & Dwight, 1835.
Berkowitz, Henry. *The Open Bible: Helps for the Bible Reader. Arranged According to the
  Chautauqua System of Education.* Philadelphia: Jewish Chautauqua Society, 1896.
Berkowitz, Max. *The Beloved Rabbi: An Account of the Life and Works of Henry Berkow-
  itz.* New York: Macmillan, 1932.

Bricker, Harry, and Simon Marcson. *Jewish Education in Chicago*. Chicago: Jewish Charities of Chicago, 1940.

Chamberlain, Alexander. *The Child: A Study in the Evolution of Man*. London: W. Scott, 1900.

Davis, Ed. *The History of Rodeph Shalom Congregation, Philadelphia, 1803–1926*. Philadelphia: Edward Stern, 1926.

DeSolla, Jacob Mendes. *A Catechism of the Jewish Religion*. San Francisco: Bacon, 1871.

Elzas, Barnett. *The Jews of South Carolina, from the Earliest Times to the Present Day*. Philadelphia: J. B. Lippincott, 1905.

———. *Judaism: An Exposition in Question and Answer*. Charleston, SC: Daggett Printing, 1896.

Eppstein, Elias. *Confirmant's Guide to the Mosaic Religion*. Detroit: F. A. Schober, 1868.

Ezekiel, Herbert T., and Gaston Lichtenstein. *The History of the Jews of Richmond from 1769–1917*. Richmond, VA: Herbert T. Ezekiel, 1917.

Flexner, Abraham. "The Religious Training of Children." *International Journal of Ethics* 7, no. 3 (1897): 314–28.

Gamoran, Emanuel. "The General Situation in the Jewish Sunday School." *Jewish Education* 1, no. 1 (1929): 25–33.

Gottheil, Richard, and William Popper. "Periodicals." In *The Jewish Encyclopedia*, edited by Isidore Singer, 616–40. New York: Funk and Wagnalls, 1916.

Greenstone, Julius. "Jewish Education in the United States." *American Jewish Yearbook* 16 (1914): 90–127.

———. *Statistical Data of the Jewish Religious Schools of Baltimore, Maryland, and Pittsburgh, Pennsylvania for 1908–1909*. Philadelphia: Gratz College, 1909.

Grossman, Louis. *The Aims of Teaching in Jewish Schools: A Handbook for Teachers*. Cincinnati, OH: Teacher's Institute of the Hebrew Union College, 1919.

Hall, G. Stanley. "Introductory Remarks," *Paidologist* 1, no. 1 (1899): 5.

———. "The Moral and Religious Training of Children." *Princeton Review*, January 1882, 26–48.

Harby, Lee C. "Penina Moïse: Woman and Writer." *American Jewish Yearbook* 7 (1905): 17–31.

Jacobs, George. *Nativ HaEmet, The Path of Truth: A Catechism for Instruction in the Tenets and Observances of the Mosaic Faith*. Philadelphia: Potsdamer, 1879.

James, William. *The Varieties of Religious Experience: A Study in Human Nature*: New York: Longmans, Green, 1920.

Kaplan, Mordecai M. *Judaism as a Civilization: Toward a Reconstruction of American Jewish Life*. Rev. ed. Philadelphia: Jewish Publication Society, 2010.

Kaplan, Mordecai M., and Bernard Cronson. "Report of Committee on Jewish Education of the Kehillah (Jewish Community) Presented at Its First Annual Convention, New York, February 27, 1910." *Jewish Education* 20, no. 3 (1949): 113–16.

Kley, Eduard. *Catechismus der Mosaichen Religion* (Catechism of the Mosaice Religion). Berlin: Maurerschen, 1814.

Kohler, Kaufmann. *Guide for Instruction in Judaism: A Manual for Schools and Homes.* New York: Philip Cowen, 1898.

———. *Heaven and Hell in Comparative Religious Tradition.* New York: Macmillan, 1923.

———. *Hebrew Union College and Other Addresses.* Cincinnati: Ark, 1916.

———. *Studies, Addresses and Personal Papers.* New York: Alumni Association of the Hebrew Union College, 1931.

Kohut, Rebekah Bettelheim. *My Portion (An Autobiography).* New York: T. Seltzer, 1925.

Krauskopf, Joseph. *The Service Manual.* Philadelphia: Edward Stern, 1892.

Landsberg, Max. *Outline of Jewish Religion.* Rochester, NY: Atlas Press, 1899.

Leeser, Isaac. *Catechism for Younger Children Designed as a Familiar Exposition of the Jewish Religion.* Philadelphia: Adam Wadlie, 1839.

———. Introduction to Moses Mendelssohn, *Jerusalem, a Treatise on Religious Power and Judaism.* Translated by Isaac Leeser. Philadelphia: C. Sherman, 1852.

Lilienthal, Max, and Robert Allyn. *Object Lessons: Things Taught: Systematic Instruction in Composition and Object Lessons.* Cincinnati, OH: Sargent, Wilson & Hinkle, 1862.

Lindheim, Irma L. *Parallel Quest: A Search of a Person and People.* New York: Thomas Yoseloff, 1962.

Lyons, Jacques Judah. *Sunday School Lessons for Young Israelites.* New York: T. B. Harrison, 1864.

Mendelssohn, Moses. *Jerusalem, or, on Religious Power and Judaism.* Translated by Allan Arkush. Waltham, MA: Brandeis University Press, 1983.

Montefiore, Claude G. *The Bible for Home Reading: With Comments and Reflections for the Use of Jewish Parents and Children.* London: MacMillan, 1896.

———. "Recent Criticism upon Moses and the Pentateuchal Narratives of the Decalogue." *Jewish Quarterly Review* 3, no. 2 (1891): 251–91.

———. "Should Biblical Criticism Be Spoken of in Jewish Pulpits?" *Jewish Quarterly Review* 18 (1906): 302–16.

Morais, Henry S. *The Jews of Philadelphia: Their History from the Earliest Settlements to the Present Time; a Record of Events and Institutions, and of Leading Members of the Jewish Community in Every Sphere of Activity.* Philadelphia: Levytype, 1894.

National Council of Jewish Women, Pittsburgh Section, and Ailon Shiloh. *By Myself, I'm a Book! An Oral History of the Immigrant Jewish Experience in Pittsburgh.* Waltham, MA: American Jewish Historical Society, 1972.

Newman, Louis I. "Martin A. Meyer." *Publications of the American Jewish Historical Society,* no. 29 (1925): 171–85.

Peixotto, Simha. *Elementary Introduction to the Hebrew Scriptures for the Use of Hebrew Children.* Philadelphia: Haswell, Barrington and Haswell, 1840.

Philipson, David. *My Life as a Young American Jew.* Cincinnati, OH: John G. Kidd and Son, 1941.

———, ed. *Guide for Jewish Sabbath School Teachers.* Cincinnati, OH: Bloch, 1890.

Pollak, Jacob B. "Forty Years of Reform Jewish Education." *CCAR Yearbook* 34 (1929): 402–33.

Pyke, Mrs. Eliezer. *Scriptural Questions for the Use of Sunday Schools for the Instruction of Israelites.* Philadelphia: L. R. Bailey, 1843.

Richman, Julia. "The Jewish Sunday School Movement in the United States." *Jewish Quarterly Review* 12, no. 4 (1900): 563–601.

Schechter, Solomon. *Seminary Addresses and Other Papers.* Cincinnati, OH: Ark, 1915.

Solomon, Hannah G. *Fabric of My Life: The Autobiography of Hannah G. Solomon,* New York: Bloch, 1946.

Stern, Myer. *The Rise and Progress of Reform Judaism, Embracing a History Made from the Official Records of Temple Emanu-El of New York, with a Description of Salem Field Cemetery, Its City of the Dead, with Illustrations of Its Vaults, Monuments, and Landscape Effects, in Connection with the Celebration of the Fiftieth Anniversary of the Founding of the Congregation, April 1895.* New York: M. Stern, 1895.

Szold, Benjamin. *Reshit Da'at.* Baltimore: Museham & Seimars, 1873.

Union of American Hebrew Congregations. *Judaism at the World's Parliament of Religions: Comprising the Papers on Judaism Read at the Parliament at the Jewish Denominational Congress, and at the Jewish Presentation.* Cincinnati, OH: Robert Clarke, 1894.

Wise, Isaac Mayer. *Hymns, Psalms, and Prayers in English and German.* Cincinnati, OH: Bloch, 1868.

———. *Judaism: Its Doctrines and Duties.* Cincinnati, OH: Office of the Israelite, 1872.

———. *The New American Jew: American Jewish Life as Seen from Albany, New York, September 1847.* Translated by Sefton D. Temkin. Albany, NY: Congregation Beth Emeth, 1977.

———. *Selected Writings of Isaac Mayer Wise.* Edited by David Philipson and Louis Grossman. Cincinnati, OH: Robert Clarke, 1900.

SECONDARY SOURCES

Abrams, Jeanne E. *Jewish Women Pioneering the Frontier Trail: A History in the American West.* New York: New York University Press, 2006.

Ackerman, Walter. "The Americanization of Jewish Education." *Judaism* 24, no. 416–35 (1975): 416–35.

Adler, Eliyana R. *In Her Hands: The Education of Jewish Girls in Tsarist Russia.* Detroit: Wayne State University Press, 2011.

Adler, Eliyana R., and Antony Polonsky, eds. *Jewish Education in Eastern Europe.* Liverpool: Liverpool University Press, 2018.

Adler, Frank J. *Roots in a Moving Stream: Centennial History of Congregation B'nai Jehudah.* Kansas City, MO: The Temple, Congregation B'nai Jehuda.

Altmann, Alexander. "Articles of Faith." In *Encyclopedia Judaica,* edited by Cecil Roth and Geoffrey Wigoder, 654–60. Jerusalem: Macmillan, 1972.

Ari, Nisa. "Spiritual Capital and the Copy: Painting, Photography, and the Production of the Image in Early Twentieth-Century Palestine." *Arab Studies Journal* 25, no. 2 (2017): 60–99.

Asad, Talal. *Genealogies of Religion: Discipline and Reasons of Power in Christianity and Islam.* Baltimore: Johns Hopkins University Press, 1993.

Ashton, Dianne. "Crossing Boundaries: The Career of Mary M. Cohen." *American Jewish History* 83, no. 2 (1995): 153–76.

———. "The Feminization of Jewish Education." *Transformations: The Journal of Inclusive Scholarship and Pedagogy* 3, no. 2 (1992): 15–23.

———. *Hanukkah in America: A History.* New York: New York University Press, 2013.

———. *Rebecca Gratz: Women and Judaism in Antebellum America.* Detroit: Wayne State University Press, 1997.

Avery, Gillian. *Behold the Child: American Children and Their Books, 1621–1922.* Baltimore: Johns Hopkins University Press, 1994.

Batnitzky, Leora Faye. *How Judaism Became a Religion: An Introduction to Modern Jewish Thought.* Princeton, NJ: Princeton University Press, 2011.

Baumgarten, Elisheva. "Judaism." In *Children and Childhood in World Religions: Primary Sources and Texts,* edited by Don S. Browning and Marcia J. Bunge, 15–82. New Brunswick, NJ: Rutgers University Press, 2009.

———. *Mothers and Children: Jewish Family Life in Medieval Europe.* Princeton, NJ: Princeton University Press, 2004.

Bederman, Gail. *Manliness & Civilization: A Cultural History of Gender and Race in the United States, 1880–1917.* Chicago: University of Chicago Press, 1995.

Bender, Courtney. *The New Metaphysicals: Spirituality and the American Religious Imagination.* Chicago: University of Chicago Press, 2010.

Benjamin, Mara H. *The Obligated Self: Maternal Subjectivity and Jewish Thought.* Bloomington: Indiana University Press, 2018.

Berman, Jeremiah J. "Jewish Education in New York City, 1860–1900." *YIVO Annual of Jewish Social Science* 9 (1954): 247–75.

Berman, Lila Corwin. *Speaking of Jews: Rabbis, Intellectuals, and the Creation of an American Public Identity.* Berkeley: University of California Press, 2009.

Berman, Lila Corwin, Kate Rosenblatt, and Ronit Y. Stahl. "Continuity Crisis: The History and Sexual Politics of an American Jewish Communal Project." *American Jewish History* 104, no. 2/3 (April–July 2020): 167–94.

Berman, Myron. *Richmond's Jewry, 1769–1976: Shabbat in Shockoe.* Charlottesville: University Press of Virginia for the Jewish Community Federation of Richmond, 1979.

Berrol, Selma. "When Uptown Met Downtown: Julia Richman's Work in the Jewish Community of New York, 1880–1912." *American Jewish History* 70, no. 1 (1980): 35–51.

Beyer, Peter. *Religions in Global Society.* London: Routledge, 2006.

Blumberg, Janice Rothschild. *As but a Day to a Hundred and Twenty, 1867–1987.* Atlanta: Hebrew Benevolent Congregation, 1987.

Bodek, Evelyn. "Making Do: Jewish Women and Philanthropy." In *Jewish Life in Philadelphia, 1830–1940*, edited by Murray Friedman, 143–62. Philadelphia: Institute for the Study of Human Issues, 1983.

Borton, Terry, and Deborah Borton. *Before the Movies: American Magic-Lantern Entertainment and the Nation's First Great Screen Artist, Joseph Boggs Beale*. London: John Libbey, 2014.

Boylan, Anne M. *Sunday School: The Formation of an American Institution, 1790–1880*. New Haven, CT: Yale University Press, 1988.

Braude, Ann. *Radical Spirits: Spiritualism and Women's Rights in Nineteenth-Century America*. Boston: Beacon Press, 1989.

Brosterman, Norman. *Inventing Kindergarten*. New York: H. N. Abrams, 1997.

Burstyn, Joan N. "Catharine Beecher and the Education of American Women." *New England Quarterly* 47, no. 3 (1974): 386–403.

Butler, Jon. *Awash in a Sea of Faith: Christianizing the American People*. Cambridge, MA: Harvard University Press, 1990.

Cady, Linell E., and Tracy Fessenden. *Religion, the Secular, and the Politics of Sexual Difference*. New York: Columbia University Press, 2013.

Caplan, Kimmy. "In God We Trust: Salaries and Income of American Orthodox Rabbis, 1881–1924." *American Jewish History* 86 (1998): 77–106.

Carper, James C., and Thomas C. Hunt. *Religious Schooling in America*. Birmingham, AL: Religious Education Press, 1984.

Carr, Jessica L. *The Hebrew Orient: Palestine in Jewish American Visual Culture, 1901–1938*. Albany: State University of New York Press, 2020.

Carter, Sarah Anne. *Object Lessons: How Nineteenth-Century Americans Learned to Make Sense of the Material World*. New York: Oxford University Press, 2018.

Chazan, Barry, Robert Chazan, and Benjamin M. Jacobs. *Cultures and Contexts of Jewish Education*. New York: Springer, 2017.

Chinn, Sarah E. *Inventing Modern Adolescence: The Children of Immigrants in Turn-of-the-Century America*. New Brunswick, NJ: Rutgers University Press, 2009.

Clark, Clifford. "Domestic Architecture as an Index to Social History: The Romantic Revival and the Cult of Domesticity in America, 1840–1870." In *Material Life in America, 1600–1860*, edited by Robert Blair St. George, 535–49. Boston: Northeastern University Press, 1986.

Clement, Priscilla Ferguson. *Growing Pains: Children in the Industrial Age, 1850–1890*. New York: Twayne, 1997.

Clevinger, Kara B. ""These Human Flowers": Sentimentalizing Children and Fashioning Maternal Authority in *Godey's Lady's Book*." In *Sentimentalism in Nineteenth-Century America: Literary and Cultural Practices*, edited by Mary G. De Jong and Paula Bernat Bennett, 15–28. Madison, NJ: Fairleigh Dickinson University Press; Lanham, MD: Rowman & Littlefield, 2013.

Clifford, Geraldine Jonçich. "'Daughters into Teachers': Educational and Demographic Influences on the Transformation of Teaching into 'Women's Work' in America." In *Women Who Taught: Perspectives on the History of Women and Teaching*, edited by

Alison Prentice and Marjorie R. Theobald, 136–69. Toronto: University of Toronto Press, 1991.

Cohen, Anne Nathan. *The Centenary History, Congregation Beth Israel of Houston, Texas 1854–1954.* Houston, TX: Congregation Beth Israel, 1955.

Cohen, Judah M. *Jewish Religious Music in Nineteenth-Century America: Restoring the Synagogue Soundtrack.* Bloomington: Indiana University Press, 2019.

Cohen, Naomi W. "The Challenges of Darwinism and Biblical Criticism to American Judaism." *Modern Judaism* 4, no. 2 (1984): 121–57.

———. *Encounter with Emancipation: The German Jews in the United States, 1830–1914.* Philadelphia: Jewish Publication Society, 1984.

———. *What the Rabbis Said: The Public Discourse of Nineteenth-Century American Rabbis.* New York: New York University Press, 2008.

Cohen, Steven M., and Laurence Kotler-Berkowitz. *The Impact of Childhood Jewish Education on Adults' Jewish Identity: Schooling, Israel Travel, Camping and Youth Groups.* New York: United Jewish Communities, 2004..

Cooper, Victoria. *The Story of NCJW. San Francisco Section: 115 Years of Courage, Compassion, and Community Service.* San Francisco: National Council of Jewish Women, San Francisco Section, 2015.

Cooperman, Jessica. *Making Judaism Safe for America: World War I and the Origins of Religious Pluralism.* New York: New York University Press, 2018.

Corrigan, John. "Cosmology." In *Religion in American History*, edited by Amanda Porterfield and John Corrigan, 29–48. Malden, MA: Wiley-Blackwell, 2010.

Cruea, S. M. "Changing Ideals of Womanhood during the Nineteenth-Century Woman Movement." *ATQ* 19 (2005): 187–204.

Curtis, Finbarr. *The Production of American Religious Freedom.* New York: New York University Press, 2016.

Dash Moore, Deborah. "Freedom's Fruits: The Americanization of an Old Time Religion." In *A Portion of the People: Three Hundred Years of Southern Jewish Life*, edited by Theodore Rosengarten and Dale Rosengarten, 10–21. Columbia: University of South Carolina Press, 2002.

Dash Moore, Deborah. *To the Golden Cities: Pursuing the American Jewish Dream in Miami and L.A.* New York: Free Press, 1994.

Davis, John. *The Landscape of Belief: Encountering the Holy Land in Nineteenth-Century American Art and Culture.* Princeton, NJ: Princeton University Press, 1996.

De Jong, Mary. *Sentimentalism in Nineteenth-Century America: Literary and Cultural Practices.* Madison, NJ: Fairleigh Dickinson University Press; Lanham, MD: Rowman & Littlefield, 2013.

Dennis, Matthew. *Red, White, and Blue Letter Days: An American Calendar.* Ithaca, NY: Cornell University Press, 2002.

Diner, Hasia R. *A Time for Gathering: The Second Migration, 1820–1880.* Baltimore: Johns Hopkins University Press, 1992.

———. *Roads Taken: The Great Jewish Migrations to the New World and the Peddlers Who Forged the Way.* New Haven, CT: Yale University Press, 2018.

Diner, Hasia R., and Beryl Lieff Benderly. *Her Works Praise Her: A History of Jewish Women in America from Colonial Times to the Present.* New York: Basic Books, 2002.

Dreyfus, Hannah. "Steven M. Cohen, Shunned by Academy after Harassment Allegations, Makes Stealthy Comeback—and Provokes Uproar." *Forward*, March 23, 2021.

Dwyer-Ryan, Meaghan, Susan L. Porter, and Lisa Fagin Davis. *Becoming American Jews: Temple Israel of Boston.* Waltham, MA: Brandeis University Press, 2009.

Ehrlich, Dror. "Albo, Joseph." In *Encyclopaedia Judaica*, edited by Michael Berenbaum and Fred Skolnik, 593–95. Detroit : Macmillan Reference USA, 2007.

Eisenberg, Ronald L. *The JPS Guide to Jewish Traditions.* Philadelphia: Jewish Publication Society, 2004.

Eisner, Elliot. *The Educational Imagination: On the Design and Evaluation of School Programs.* 3rd ed. New York: Macmillan, 1994.

Eleff, Zev. *Who Rules the Synagogue? Religious Authority and the Formation of American Judaism.* New York: Oxford University Press, 2016.

Eliav, Moshe. *Judische Erziehung in Deutschland im Zeitalter der Aufklarung und der Emanzipation* (Jewish Education in Germany in the Age of Enlightenment and Emancipation). Münster, DE: Waxman, 2001.

Elwell, Ellen Sue Levi. "The Founding and Early Programs of the National Council of Jewish Women: Study and Practice as Jewish Women's Religious Expression." PhD diss., Indiana University, 1982.

Endelman, Todd M. *Broadening Jewish History: Towards a Social History of Ordinary Jews.* Oxford: Littman Library of Jewish Civilization, 2011.

Engelman, Uriah Zevi. "Jewish Education in Charleston, South Carolina during the Eighteenth and Nineteenth Centuries." *Publications of the American Jewish Historical Society* 42, no. 1 (1952): 43–70.

Faierstein, Morris M. "Abraham Jagel's 'Leqaḥ Tov' and Its History." *Jewish Quarterly Review* 89, no. 3/4 (1999): 319–50.

Fein, Isaac M. *The Making of an American Jewish Community: The History of Baltimore Jewry from 1773 to 1920.* Philadelphia: Jewish Publication Society of America, 1971.

Fessenden, Tracy. *Culture and Redemption: Religion, the Secular, and American Literature.* Princeton, NJ: Princeton University Press, 2007.

Fishbane, Leah Levitz, Eitan P. Fishbane, and Jonathan D. Sarna. *Jewish Renaissance and Revival in America: Essays in Memory of Leah Levitz Fishbane.* Waltham MA: Brandeis University Press, 2011.

Fisher, Benjamin E. *Amsterdam's People of the Book: Jewish Society and the Turn to Scripture in the 17th Century.* Cincinnati, OH: Hebrew Union College Press, 2020.

Fitzgerald, Timothy. *The Ideology of Religious Studies.* New York: Oxford University Press, 2000.

Friedland, Eric L. "Hebrew Liturgical Creativity in Nineteenth-Century America." *Modern Judaism* 1, no. 3 (1981): 323–36.

Friedman, Reena Sigman. *These Are Our Children: Jewish Orphanages in the United States, 1880–1925.* Hanover, NH: University Press of New England for Brandeis University Press, 1994.

Fromer, Seymor. "In the Colonial Period." In *A History of Jewish Education in America*, edited by Judah Pilch, 1–24. New York: National Curriculum Research Institute of the American Association for Jewish Education, 1969.

Garrett, Morris. "The Development of Jewish Education in Detroit." *Michigan Jewish History* 5, no. 2 (1965): 4–10.

Gartner, Lloyd P. *History of the Jews of Cleveland*. Cleveland, OH: Western Reserve Historical Society, 1978.

———. *Jewish Education in the United States: A Documentary History*. New York: Teachers College Press, 1969.

Gilding, Anna Luker. "Preserving Sentiments: American Women's Magazines of the 1830s and the Networks of Antebellum Print Culture." *American Periodicals* 23, no. 2 (2013): 156–71.

Ginzberg, Lori D. *Women and the Work of Benevolence: Morality, Politics, and Class in the Nineteenth-Century United States*. New Haven, CT: Yale University Press, 1990.

Gold, Penny Schine. *Making the Bible Modern: Children's Bibles and Jewish Education in Twentieth-Century America*. Ithaca, NY: Cornell University Press, 2004.

Goldman, Karla. "The Ambivalence of Reform Judaism: Kaufmann Kohler and the Ideal Jewish Woman." *American Jewish History* 79, no. 4 (1990): 477–99.

———. *Beyond the Synagogue Gallery: Finding a Place for Women in American Judaism*. Cambridge, MA: Harvard University Press, 2000.

———. "The Longing for Jewish Homes, Jewish Babies, and the Trouble with Jewish Women." *American Jewish History* 104, no. 2/3 (April–July 2020): 195–200.

———. "The Public Religious Lives of Cincinnati's Jewish Women." In *Women and American Judaism: Historical Perspectives*, edited by Pamela S. Nadell and Jonathan D. Sarna, 107–27. Hanover, NH: University Press of New England, 2001.

Goldstein, Eric L. *The Price of Whiteness: Jews, Race, and American Identity*. Princeton, NJ: Princeton University Press, 2006.

Gordon, Beverly. *The Saturated World: Aesthetic Meaning, Intimate Objects, Women's Lives, 1890–1940*. Knoxville: University of Tennessee Press, 2006.

Gotzmann, Andreas. "The Dissociation of Religion and Law in Nineteenth-Century German-Jewish Education." *Leo Baeck Institute Year Book* 43, no. 1 (1998): 103–26.

Graff, Gil. *"And You Shall Teach Them Diligently": A Concise History of Jewish Education in the United States, 1776–2000*. New York: Jewish Theological Seminary of America, 2008.

———. "Public Schooling and Jewish Education, 1915–1970: A Contemporary Perspective." *Journal of Jewish Education* 69, no. 1 (2003): 69–76.

Green, I. M. *The Christian's ABC: Catechisms and Catechizing in England c. 1530–1740*. New York: Oxford University Press, 1996.

Greene, Daniel. *The Jewish Origins of Cultural Pluralism: The Menorah Association and American Diversity*. Bloomington: Indiana University Press, 2011.

Greenspoon, David. "Sunday School Prizes and Books in Early Nineteenth-Century America." In *Creating Religious Childhoods in Anglo-World and British Colonial*

Contexts, 1800–1950, edited by Hugh Morrison and Mary Clare Martin, 87–102. London: Routledge, 2017.

Grinstein, Hyman B. "In the Course of the Nineteenth Century." In *A History of Jewish Education in America*, edited by Judah Pilch, 25–50. New York: National Curriculum Research Institute of the American Association for Jewish Education, 1969.

———. *The Rise of the Jewish Community of New York, 1654–1860*. Philadelphia: Porcupine Press, 1976.

Gross, Rachel B. *Beyond the Synagogue: Jewish Nostalgia as Religious Practice*. New York: New York University Press, 2021.

Gross, Robert A., and Mary Kelley. *An Extensive Republic: Print, Culture, and Society in the New Nation, 1790–1840*. Chapel Hill: American Antiquarian Society and University of North Carolina Press, 2010.

Gurock, Jeffrey S. "The Orthodox Synagogue." In *The History of the Synagogue in America*, edited by Jack Wertheimer, 37–84. New York: Cambridge University Press, 1988.

HaCohen, Dvora. *To Repair a Broken World: The Life of Henrietta Szold, Founder of Hadassah*. Cambridge, MA: Harvard University Press, 2021.

Hacohen, Malachi Haim. *Jacob and Esau: Jewish European History between Nation and Empire*. New York: Cambridge University Press, 2019.

Hallote, Rachel. "Photography and the American Contribution to Early 'Biblical' Archaeology, 1870–1920." *Near Eastern Archaeology* 70, no. 1 (2007): 26–41.

Hanft, Sheldon. "Mordecai's Female Academy." *American Jewish History* 72–93, no. 1 (1989): 72–93.

Helmreich, William B. *The Enduring Community: The Jews of Newark and MetroWest*. New Brunswick, NJ: Transaction, 1999.

Herberg, Will. *Protestant, Catholic, Jew; An Essay in American Religious Sociology*. New York: Doubleday, 1955.

Herman, Felicia. "From Priestess to Hostess: Sisterhoods of Personal Service in New York City, 1887–1936." In *Women and American Judaism*: Historical Perspectives, edited by Pamela S. Nadell and Jonathan D. Sarna, 148–81. Hanover, NH: University Press of New England, 2001.

Herrmann, Klaus. "Jewish Confirmation Sermons in Nineteenth-Century Germany." In *Preaching in Judaism and Christianity: Encounters and Developments from Biblical Times to Modernity*, edited by Alexander Deeg, Walter Homolka, and Heinz-Günther Schöttler, 91–112. Berlin: Walter de Gruyter, 2008.

Heschel, Susannah. *Abraham Geiger and the Jewish Jesus*. Chicago: University of Chicago Press, 1998.

Hess, Jonathan M. *Germans, Jews, and the Claims of Modernity*. New Haven, CT: Yale University Press, 2002.

Hilton, Michael. *Bar Mitzvah: A History*. Lincoln: University of Nebraska Press, 2014.

Hirt-Manheimer, Aron. "A Critical History of Reform Youth Magazines." MA thesis, Hebrew Union College, 1970.

Hulbert, Ann. "The Century of the Child." *Wilson Quarterly* 23, no. 1 (1999): 14–29.

Hyman, Paula. *Gender and Assimilation in Modern Jewish History: The Roles and Representation of Women.* Seattle: University of Washington Press, 1995.

Idelson-Shein, Iris. "The Beginning of the End: Jews, Children and Enlightenment Pedagogy." *Jewish Quarterly Review* 106, no. 3 (2016): 383–95.

Imhoff, Sarah. *Masculinity and the Making of American Judaism.* Bloomington: Indiana University Press, 2017.

———. "The Myth of American Jewish Feminization." *Jewish Social Studies* 21, no. 3 (2016): 126–52.

Ingall, Carol K. *The Women Who Reconstructed American Jewish Education, 1910–1965.* Waltham, MA: Brandeis University Press, 2010.

Jacob, Walter. *The Changing World of Reform Judaism: The Pittsburgh Platform in Retrospect: Papers Presented on the Occasion of the 100th Anniversary of the Pittsburgh Platform, February, 1985 and the Proceedings of 1885.* Pittsburgh: Rodef Shalom Congregation, 1985.

Jacobs, Louis. "Shavuot." In *Encyclopedia Judaica*, edited by Michael Berenbaum and Fred Skolnik, 422–23. Detroit: Macmillan Reference, 2007.

Jacobson, Lisa. *Raising Consumers: Children and the American Mass Market in the Early Twentieth Century.* New York: Columbia University Press, 2004.

Jick, Leon A. *The Americanization of the Synagogue, 1820–1870.* Hanover, NH: University Press of New England for Brandeis University Press, 1976.

Joselit, Jenna Weissman. "The Special Sphere of the Middle-Class American Jewish Woman: The Synagogue Sisterhood, 1890–1940." In *American Synagogue: A Sanctuary Transformed*, edited by Jack Wertheimer, 206–30. Waltham, MA: Brandeis University Press, 1987.

———. *The Wonders of America: Reinventing Jewish Culture, 1880–1950.* New York: Hill and Wang, 1994.

Joselit, Jenna Weissman, Barbara Kirshenblatt-Gimblett, Irving Howe, and Susan L. Braunstein. *Getting Comfortable in New York: The American Jewish Home, 1880–1950.* New York: Jewish Museum, 1990.

Judson, Daniel. *Pennies for Heaven: The History of American Synagogues and Money.* Waltham, MA: Brandeis University Press, 2018.

Kadar, Naomi Prawer. *Raising Secular Jews: Yiddish Schools and Their Periodicals for American Children, 1917–1950.* Waltham, MA: Brandeis University Press, 2017.

Kaestle, Carl F. *Pillars of the Republic: Common Schools and American Society, 1780–1860.* New York: Hill and Wang, 1983.

Kaestle, Carl F., and Janice A. Radway, eds. *Print in Motion: The Expansion of Publishing and Reading in the United States, 1880–1940.* Chapel Hill: University of North Carolina Press, 2009.

Kaganoff, Nathan. "The Education of the Jewish Child in the District of Columbia, 1861–1915." In *The Jews of Washington, D.C., A Communal History Anthology*, edited by David Altshuler, 146–54. Washington, DC: Jewish Historical Society of Greater Washington, 1985.

Kanarfogel, Ephraim. *Jewish Education and Society in the High Middle Ages*. Detroit: Wayne State University Press, 1992.

Kaplan, Marion A. *Jewish Daily Life in Germany, 1618–1945*. Oxford: Oxford University Press, 2005.

———. *The Making of the Jewish Middle Class: Women, Family, and Identity in Imperial Germany*. New York: Oxford University Press, 1991.

Katz, Irving I. "Jewish Education at Temple Beth El, Detroit: 1850–1880." *Michigan History* 52, no. 3 (Fall 1968): 218–28.

Kaufman, David. *Shul with a Pool: The "Synagogue-Center" in American Jewish History*. Hanover, NH: University Press of New England, 1999.

Kenny, Deborah Ann. "Contemporary Jewish American Children's Periodicals: Origins and Content." PhD diss., Columbia University, 1994.

Kirshenblatt-Gimblett, Barbara. "The Moral Sublime: Jewish Women and Philanthropy in Nineteenth-Century America." In *Writing a Modern Jewish History: Essays in Honor of Salo Wittmayer Baron*, edited by Barbara Kirshenblatt-Gimblett, 36–56. New York: Jewish Museum; New Haven, CT: Yale University Press, 2006.

Klapper, Melissa R. *Ballots, Babies, and Banners of Peace: American Jewish Women's Activism, 1890–1940*. New York: New York University Press, 2013.

———. *Jewish Girls Coming of Age in America, 1860–1920*. New York: New York University Press, 2005.

Knupfer, Peter B. "Learning to Read While Reading to Learn: Marcius Willson's Basal Readers, Science Education, and Object Teaching, 1860–1890." *Paedagogica Historica* (2021): 1–20. https://doi.org/10.1080/00309230.2020.1864423.

Kooistra, Lorraine Janzen. "Home Thoughts and Home Scenes: Packaging Middle-Class Childhood for Christian Consumption." In *The Nineteenth-Century Child and Consumer Culture*, edited by Dennis Denisoff, 151–72. Aldershot, UK: Ashgate, 2008.

Korelitz, Seth. "'A Magnificent Piece of Work': The Americanization Work of the National Council of Jewish Women." *American Jewish History* 83, no. 2 (1995): 177–293.

Krasner, Jonathan. *The Benderly Boys & American Jewish Education*. Waltham, MA: Brandeis University Press, 2011.

———. "Jewish Chautauqua, Jewish History and a Jewish Correspondence School." *American Jewish Archives Journal* 56 (2004): 57–93.

———. "Representations of Self and Other in American Jewish History and Social Studies Schoolbooks: An Exploration of the Changing Shape of American Jewish Identity." PhD diss., Brandeis University, 2002.

Leibman, Laura Arnold. *The Art of the Jewish Family: A History of Women in Early New York in Five Objects*. New York: Bard Graduate Center, 2020.

Lerner, Gerda. *The Majority Finds Its Past: Placing Women in History*. New York: Oxford University Press, 1979.

Levenson, Alan T. *The Making of the Modern Jewish Bible: How Scholars in Germany, Israel, and America Transformed an Ancient Text*. Lanham, MD: Rowman & Littlefield, 2011.

Levisohn, Jon A., and Ari Y. Kelman. *Beyond Jewish Identity: Rethinking Concepts and Imagining Alternatives.* Brookline, MA: Academic Studies Press, 2019.

Levitt, Laura. "Impossible Assimilations, American Liberalism, and Jewish Difference: Revisiting Jewish Secularism." *American Quarterly* 59, no. 3 (2007): 807–32.

———. "Other Moderns, Other Jews: Revisiting Jewish Secularism in America." In *Secularisms*, edited by Janet R. Jakobsen and Ann Pellegrini, 107–38. Durham, NC: Duke University Press, 2008.

Lichtenstein, Diane. *Writing Their Nations: The Tradition of Nineteenth-Century American Jewish Women Writers.* Bloomington: Indiana University Press, 1992.

Lindquist, Benjamin. "Slow Time and Sticky Media: Frank Beard's Political Cartoons, Chalk Talks, and Hieroglyphic Bibles, 1860–1905." *Winterthur Portfolio* 53, no. 1 (2019): 41–84.

Lloyd, Genevieve. *The Man of Reason: "Male" and "Female" in Western Philosophy.* 2nd ed. Minneapolis: University of Minnesota Press, 1993.

Lofton, Kathryn. *Consuming Religion.* Chicago: University of Chicago Press, 2017.

Lynn, Robert W., and Elliott Wright. *The Big Little School: Two Hundred Years of the Sunday School.* 2nd ed. Birmingham, AL: Religious Education Press, 1980.

Macleod, David I. *The Age of the Child: Children in America, 1890–1920.* New York: Twayne, 1998.

Madison, Charles Allan. *Jewish Publishing in America: The Impact of Jewish Writing on American Culture.* New York: Sanhedrin Press, 1976.

Marcus, Ivan G. *Rituals of Childhood: Jewish Acculturation in Medieval Europe.* New Haven, CT: Yale University Press, 1996.

Marcus, Jacob Rader. *The American Jewish Woman, 1654–1980.* New York: Ktav, 1981.

Masuzawa, Tomoko. *The Invention of World Religions, or, How European Universalism Was Preserved in the Language of Pluralism.* Chicago: University of Chicago Press, 2005.

McCune, Mary. *The Whole Wide World, without Limits: International Relief, Gender Politics, and American Jewish Women, 1893–1930.* Detroit: Wayne State University Press, 2005.

McCutcheon, Russell T. *Manufacturing Religion: The Discourse on Sui Generis Religion and the Politics of Nostalgia.* New York: Oxford University Press, 1997.

McDannell, Colleen. *The Christian Home in Victorian America, 1840–1900.* Bloomington: Indiana University Press, 1986.

Merowitz, Morton. "Max Lilienthal: Jewish Educator in Nineteenth-Century America." *YIVO Annual of Jewish Social Science* 15 (1974): 46–65.

Meyer, Michael A. "Abraham Geiger's Historical Judaism." In *New Perspectives on Abraham Geiger*, edited by Jacob Petuchowski, 3–16. Cincinnati, OH: Hebrew Union College Press, 1975.

———. *The Origins of the Modern Jew: Jewish Identity and European Culture in Germany, 1749–1824.* Detroit: Wayne State University Press, 1979.

———. *Response to Modernity: A History of the Reform Movement in Judaism.* Detroit: Wayne State University Press, 1995.

Miller, Michael Laurence. *Rabbis and Revolution: The Jews of Moravia in the Age of Emancipation*. Stanford, CA: Stanford University Press, 2011.

Mott, Frank Luther. *A History of American Magazines, 1741–1850*. New York: D. Appleton, 1930.

Munk, Reinier. "Mendelssohn and Kant on Judaism." *Jewish Studies Quarterly* 13, no. 3 (2006): 215–22.

Munro, Patricia Keer. *Coming of Age in Jewish America: Bar and Bat Mitzvah Reinterpreted*. New Brunswick, NJ: Rutgers University Press, 2016.

Musser, Charles. "The Stereopticon: Plaform or New Media Form?" In *Politicking and Emergent Media: U.S. Presidential Elections of the 1890s*, 52–79. Oakland: University of California Press, 2016.

Nadell, Pamela. *America's Jewish Women: A History from Colonial Times to Today*. New York: W. W. Norton, 2019.

Nadell, Pamela S., and Jonathan D. Sarna, eds. *Women and American Judaism: Historical Perspectives*. Hanover, NH: University Press of New England, 2001.

Neusner, Jacob. "Defining Judaism." In *The Blackwell Companion to Judaism*, edited by Jacob Neusner and Alan J. Avery-Peck, 3–19. Malden, MA: Blackwell, 2000.

———. *Take Judaism, for Example: Studies toward the Comparison of Religions*. Atlanta: Scholars Press, 1992.

Newman, Louise Michele. *White Women's Rights: The Racial Origins of Feminism in the United States*. New York: Oxford University Press, 1999.

Noll, Mark A. *The Old Religion in a New World: The History of North American Christianity*. Grand Rapids, MI: Eerdmans, 2002.

Ohmann, Richard. "Diverging Paths: Books and Magazines in the Transition to Corporate Capitalism. " In Carl F. Kaestle and Janice A. Radway, *Print in Motion: The Expansion of Publishing and Reading in the United States, 1880–1940*, 102–15. Chapel Hill: University of North Carolina Press, 2009.

Olitzky, Kerry M. "A History of Reform Jewish Education during Emanuel Gamoran's Tenure as Educational Director of the Commission on Jewish Education of the Union of American Hebrew Congregations, 1923–1958." PhD diss., Hebrew Union College, 1984.

Palmquist, Stephen. *Comprehensive Commentary on Kant's Religion within the Bounds of Bare Reason*. Hoboken, NJ: Wiley, 2015.

Pasternack, Lawrence. *Kant on Religion within the Boundaries of Mere Reason*. London: Routledge, Taylor & Francis, 2014.

Patz, Naomi M., and Philip E. Miller. "Jewish Religious Children's Literature in America: An Analytical Survey." *Phaedrus*, spring–summer 1980, 19–29.

Pearlstein, Peggy. "Assemblies by the Sea: The Jewish Chautauqua Society in Atlantic City, 1897–1907." *Jewish Political Studies Review* 10, no. 1/2 (1998): 5–17.

———. "Understanding through Education: One Hundred Years of the Jewish Chautauqua Society, 1893–1993." PhD diss., George Washington University, 1993.

Perry, Claire. *Young America: Childhood in Nineteenth-Century Art and Culture*. New Haven, CT: Yale University Press and the Iris & B. Gerald Cantor Center for Visual Arts, Stanford University, 2006.

Petuchowski, Jacob. "Manuals and Catechisms of the Jewish Religion in the Early Period of Emancipation." In *Studies in Nineteenth-Century Jewish Intellectual History*, edited by Alexander Altmann, 47–64. Cambridge, MA: Harvard University Press, 1964.

Pew Research Center. *A Portrait of Jewish Americans: Findings from a Pew Research Center Survey of American Jews*. Washington, DC: Pew Research, 2013.

———. *Jewish Americans in 2020*. Washington, DC: Pew Research, 2021. www.pewforum.org.

Pilch, Judah, ed. *A History of Jewish Education in America*. New York: National Curriculum Research Institute of the American Association for Jewish Education, 1969.

Plaut, W. Gunther. *The Rise of Reform Judaism: A Sourcebook of Its European Origins*. Lincoln: University of Nebraska Press, 2015.

Pool, David de Sola, and Tamar de Sola Pool. *An Old Faith in the New World: Portrait of Shearith Israel 1654–1954*. New York: Columbia University Press, 1955.

Porter, Jack Nusan. "Rosa Sonnenschein and *The American Jewess*: The First Independent English-Language Jewish Women's Journal in the United States." *American Jewish History* 68, no. 1 (1978): 57–63.

Prell, Riv-Ellen. "The Dilemma of Women's Equality in the History of Reform Judaism." *Judaism* 30, no. 4 (1981): 418–26.

Presbyterian Historical Society. "Children's Sunday in the Presbyterian Church." *Journal of Presbyterian History* 83, no. 1 (2005): 84–89.

Preston, Jo Anne. "Domestic Ideology, School Reformers, and Female Teachers: Schoolteaching Becomes Women's Work in Nineteenth-Century New England." *New England Quarterly* 66, no. 4 (1993): 531–51.

Quimby, Chester Warren. "The Use of Costumes, Objects and Models in Teaching Bible." *Journal of Bible and Religion* 13, no. 3 (1945): 152–76.

Rabin, Shari. *Jews on the Frontier: Religion and Mobility in Nineteenth-Century America*. New York: New York University Press, 2017.

———. "Working Jews: Hazanim and the Labor of Religion in Nineteenth-Century America." *Religion and American Culture: A Journal of Interpretation* 25, no. 2 (2015): 178–217.

Rappel, Dov. "A Bibliography of American Jewish Textbooks, 1766–1919." *Studies in Bibliography and Booklore* 18 (1993): 27–62.

Rauch, Eduardo L. *The Education of Jews and the American Community: 1840 to the New Millennium*. 2nd ed. Tel Aviv: Jaime and Joan Constantiner School of Education, 2006.

Reese, William J. *America's Public Schools: From the Common School to "No Child Left Behind."* Updated ed. Baltimore: Johns Hopkins University Press, 2011.

Resnick, David. "Confirmation Education from the Old World to the New: A 150-Year Follow-Up." *Modern Judaism* 31 (2011): 213–28.

Rock, Howard B. *Haven of Liberty: New York Jews in the New World, 1654–1865*. New York: New York University Press, 2013.

Rodrigue, Aron. *French Jews, Turkish Jews: The Alliance Israélite Universelle and the Politics of Jewish Schooling in Turkey, 1860–1925*. Bloomington: Indiana University Press, 1990.

Rogers, Stephanie Stidham. *Inventing the Holy Land: American Protestant Pilgrimage to Palestine, 1865–1941*. Lanham, MD: Lexington Books, 2011.

Rogow, Faith. *Gone to Another Meeting: The National Council of Jewish Women, 1893–1993*. Tuscaloosa: University of Alabama Press, 1993.

Rose, Anne C. *Victorian America and the Civil War*. New York: Cambridge University Press, 1992.

———. *Voices of the Marketplace: American Thought and Culture, 1830–1860*. New York: Twayne, 1995.

Rose, Jacqueline. *The Case of Peter Pan, or, the Impossibility of Children's Fiction*. Philadelphia: University of Pennsylvania Press, 1993.

Rosenbaum, Fred, and Fred Rosenbaum. *Visions of Reform: Congregation Emanu-El and the Jews of San Francisco, 1849–1999*. Berkeley, CA: Judah L. Magnes Museum, 2000.

Rosengarten, Theodore, and Dale Rosengarten. *A Portion of the People: Three Hundred Years of Southern Jewish Life*. Columbia: University of South Carolina Press and McKissick Museum, 2002.

Ruben, Bruce. *Max Lilienthal: The Making of the American Rabbinate*. Detroit: Wayne State University Press, 2011.

Ruskay, Esther J. *Hearth and Home Essays*. Philadelphia: Jewish Publication Society of America, 1902.

Sânchez-Eppler, Karen. *Dependent States: The Child's Part in Nineteenth-Century American Culture*. Chicago: University of Chicago Press, 2005.

Safrai, Shmuel, M. Stern, David Flusser, and W. C. van Unnik. "Education and the Study of the Torah." In *The Jewish People in the First Century: Historical Geography, Political History, Social, Cultural and Religious Life and Institutions*, edited by S. Safrai, D. Flusser, and W. C. van Unnik, 945–70. Leiden, NE: Brill, 1976.

Sarna, Jonathan. *A Great Awakening: The Transformation That Shaped Twentieth-Century American Judaism and Its Implications for Today*. New York: Council for Initiatives in Jewish Education, 1995.

———. "American Jewish Education in Historical Perspective." *Journal of Jewish Education* 64, no. 1–2 (1998): 8–21.

———. *American Judaism: A History*. 2nd ed. New Haven, CT: Yale University Press, 2019.

———. "A Projection of America as It Ought to Be: Zion in the Mind's Eye of American Jews." In *Envisioning Israel: The Changing Ideals and Images of North American Jews*, edited by Allon Gal, 41–59. Jerusalem: Magnes Press; Detroit: Wayne State University Press, 1996.

———. "'God Loves an Infant's Praise': Cultural Borrowing and Cultural Resistance in Two Nineteenth-Century American Jewish Sunday-School Texts." *Jewish History* 27, no. 1 (2013): 73–89.

———. *J.P.S.: The Americanization of Jewish Culture, 1888–1988*. Philadelphia: Jewish Publication Society, 1989.

———. "Two Ambitious Goals: American Jewish Publishing in the United States." In Carl F. Kaestle and Janice A. Radway, *Print in Motion: The Expansion of Publishing and Reading in the United States, 1880–1945*, 376–91. Chapel Hill: University of North Carolina Press, 2009.

Schechner, Richard. *Performance Theory*. Revised and expanded edition. New York: Routledge, 1988.

Schleiermacher, Friedrich. *On Religion: Speeches to Its Cultured Despisers*. Translated by Richard Crouter. Cambridge: Cambridge University Press, 1996.

Schmidt, Leigh Eric. *Consumer Rites: The Buying & Selling of American Holidays*. Princeton, NJ: Princeton University Press, 1995.

Schoem, David Louis. *Ethnic Survival in America: An Ethnography of a Jewish Afternoon School*. Atlanta: Scholars Press, 1989.

Schoenfeld, Stuart. "Folk Judaism, Elite Judaism and the Role of Bar Mitzvah in the Development of the Synagogue and Jewish School in America." *Contemporary Jewry* 9, no. 1 (1987): 67–85.

Schorsch, Ismar, ed. "Art as Social History: Moritz Oppenheim and the German Jewish Vision of Emancipation." In *From Text to Context: The Turn to History in Modern Judaism*, 93–112. Hanover, NH: University Press of New England, 1994.

Schwartz, Shuly Rubin. *The Emergence of Jewish Scholarship in America: The Publication of the Jewish Encyclopedia*. Cincinnati, OH: Hebrew Union College Press, 1991.

Seaton, Beverly. *The Language of Flowers: A History*. Charlottesville: University of Virginia Press, 1995.

Seidman, Naomi. *The Marriage Plot: Or How Jews Fell in Love with Love, and Literature*. Stanford, CA: Stanford University Press, 2016.

———. *Sarah Schenirer and the Bais Yaakov Movement: A Revolution in the Name of Tradition*. London: Littman Library of Jewish Civilization andLiverpool University Press, 2019.

Shavit, Jacob, and Mordechai Eran. *The Hebrew Bible Reborn: From Holy Scripture to the Book of Books: A History of Biblical Culture and the Battles over the Bible in Modern Judaism*. Berlin: Walter de Gruyter, 2007.

Sheedy, Matt. "Making the Familiar Strange: On the Influence of J. Z. Smith." *Journal of the American Academy of Religion* 87, no. 1 (2019): 41–46.

Shuman, Bernard. *A History of the Sioux City Jewish Community 1860–1969*. Sioux City, IA: Jewish Federation, 1969.

Shuttleworth, Sally. *The Mind of the Child: Child Development in Literature, Science, and Medicine, 1840–1900*. Oxford: Oxford University Press, 2010.

Silver-Brody, Vivienne. *Documentors of the Dream: Pioneer Jewish Photographers in the Land of Israel, 1890–1933*. Lincoln: University of Nebraska Press, 1999.

Singerman, Robert. *Judaica Americana: A Bibliography of Publications to 1900*. New York: Greenwood Press, 1990.

Sklare, M., and J. Greenblum. *Jewish Identity on the Suburban Frontier.* New York: Basic Books, 1967.

Smith, Jonathan Z. *Imagining Religion: From Babylon to Jonestown.* Chicago: University of Chicago Press, 1982.

———. *Map Is Not Territory: Studies in the History of Religions.* Chicago: University of Chicago Press, 1993.

———. *Relating Religion: Essays in the Study of Religion.* Chicago: University of Chicago Press, 2004.

Sochen, June. "Some Observations on the Role of American Jewish Women as Communal Volunteers." *American Jewish History* 70, no. 1 (1980): 22–34.

Solis-Cohen, J. "Jacob S. Solis: Traveling Advocate of American Judaism." *American Jewish Historical Quarterly* 52, no. 4 (1963): 310–19.

Stanislawski, Michael. *For Whom Do I Toil? Judah Leib Gordon and the Crisis of Russian Jewry.* New York: Oxford University Press, 1988.

Stern, Malcolm H. *First American Jewish Families: 600 Genealogies, 1654–1988.* 3rd ed. Baltimore: Ottenheimer, 1991.

Stern, Miriam Heller. "'A Dream Not Quite Come True': Reassessing the Benderly Era in Jewish Education." *Journal of Jewish Education* 70, no. 3 (September 2004): 16–26.

Stone, Ira. "Mussar Ethics and Other Nineteenth-Century Jewish Ethical Theories." In *The Oxford Handbook of Jewish Ethics and Morality,* edited by Elliot N. Dorff and Jonathan K. Crane, 118–33. New York: Oxford University Press, 2016.

Sulzberger, David. *Fifty Years' Work of the Hebrew Education Society of Philadelphia: 1848–1898.* Philadelphia: Hebrew Education Society of Philadelphia, 1899.

Supp-Montgomerie, Jenna. *When the Medium Was the Mission: The Atlantic Telegraph and the Religious Origins of Network Culture.* New York: New York University Press, 2021.

Sussman, Lance Jonathan. *Isaac Leeser and the Making of American Judaism.* Detroit: Wayne State University Press, 1995.

Temkin, Sefton D. *Creating American Reform Judaism: The Life and Times of Isaac Mayer Wise.* Portland, OR: Littman Library of Jewish Civilization, 1998.

Tice, Patricia M. *Gardening in America, 1830–1910.* Rochester, NY: Strong Museum, 1984.

Tomasoni, Francesco. "Mendelssohn and Kant: A Singular Alliance in the Name of Reason." *History of European Ideas* 30, no. 3 (2004): 267–94.

Turner, Victor W. *The Anthropology of Performance.* New York: PAJ, 1986.

Tyack, David B., and Larry Cuban. *Tinkering toward Utopia: A Century of Public School Reform.* Cambridge, MA: Harvard University Press, 1995.

von der Krone, Kerstin. "Old and New Orders of Knowledge in Modern Jewish History." *Bulletin of the German Historical Institute* 59 (2016): 59–82.

Wajda, Shirley Teresa. "'And a Little Child Shall Lead Them': American Children's Cabinets of Curiosities." In *Acts of Possession: Collecting in America,* edited by Leah Dilworth, 42–65. New Brunswick, NJ: Rutgers University Press, 2003.

Weiner, Hollace Ava. "Goldberg, Jeannette Miriam." In *Encyclopaedia Judaica*, edited by Michael Berenbaum and Fred Skolnik, 693. Detroit: Macmillan Reference USA, 2007.

Weiss, Shira. *Joseph Albo on Free Choice: Exegetical Innovation in Medieval Jewish Philosophy*. New York: Oxford University Press, 2017.

Wenger, Beth S. "Federation Men: The Masculine World of New York Jewish Philanthropy." *American Jewish History* 101, no. 3 (July 2017): 377–99.

———. "Jewish Women of the Club: The Changing Public Role of Atlanta's Jewish Women (1870–1930)." *American Jewish History* 76, no. 3 (1987): 311–33.

Wertheimer, Jack. *The New American Judaism: How Jews Practice Their Religion Today*. Princeton, NJ: Princeton University Press, 2018.

———, ed. *The American Synagogue: A Sanctuary Transformed*. Waltham, MA: Brandeis University Press, 1987.

Wesseling, Elisabeth. *The Child Savage, 1890–2010: From Comics to Games*. New York: Routledge, 2016.

Wilson, Kathleen. "Introduction: Three Theses on Performance and History." *Eighteenth-Century Studies* 48, no. 4 (2015): 375–90.

Wolf, Edwin, and Maxwell Whiteman. *The History of the Jews of Philadelphia from Colonial Times to the Age of Jackson*. Philadelphia: Jewish Publication Society, 1956.

Zalḳin, Mordekhai. *Modernizing Jewish Education in Nineteenth-Century Eastern Europe: The School as the Shrine of the Jewish Enlightenment*. Boston: Brill, 2016.

Zelizer, Viviana A. Rotman. *Pricing the Priceless Child: The Changing Social Value of Children*. New York: Basic Books, 1985.

Zola, Gary Phillip. *Isaac Harby of Charleston, 1788–1828: Jewish Reformer and Intellectual*. Tuscaloosa: University of Alabama Press, 1994.

INDEX

Page numbers in *italics* indicate photos.

Abraham (prophet), 153–54
Adler, Nathan Marcus, 33
Adler, Samuel, 64
adolescence, 160–62
advertisements, 106–7, 120, 206n94, 213n39
Aguilar, Grace, 76, 197n21
Ahawath Chesed Congregation, 36, 40, 76
Albo, Joseph, 191n25
American, Sadie, 136, 139
American Hebrew (newspaper), 48, 69, 204n61
American Israelite (newspaper), 43, 60, 108, 121, 125–26, 201n7; on confirmation ceremonies, 78, 79, 85, 90, 94, 96
Americanization, 27; gender in, 129; of Jewish immigrants, 128–30, 133–35, 141–44; NCJW in, 135–40; UAHC on, 128–29; women as activists in, 129, 130–35, *133*
American Jewess (periodical), 44–45, 125
American Jewish community growth, 19, 183n13
American Jewish press, 17. *See also specific publications*
American major holidays, 82, 83, 99, 101, 113
anthropology, 20
archival sources, 17
Asad, Talal, 8
Ashton, Dianne, 183n7, 184n21, 185n38, 197n21

Assimilation, Jewish, 19, 26, 42, 125, 126, 181n26, 184n25
Atlantic City, 115, 117, 204n61

Baer, Sadie, 76
Baltimore, 135, 137, 140; confirmation ceremonies in, 79, 85–86, 90; educational aids in, 127; without Jewish education, 129
Baltimore Hebrew Sunday School Society, 32
Barlow, Rose, 41
bar mitzvahs, 72, 73, 79, 81–82, 129, 215n11; confirmation ceremonies compared to, 72, 73, 79
Barnard, Henry, 35
baths, 133, 138
bat mitzvahs, 79, 215n11
Batnitzky, Leora, 181n26
Beard, Charles, 118
Beecher, Catherine Ward, 30, 211n18
Beitman, Jennie, 102
Benderly, Beryl Lieff, 179n20
Benderly, Samson, 6, 46, 168–69, 179n16, 206n87
Berkowitz, Henry, 114–15, 118, 126, 161; on Bible, 152–53, 155
Beyer, Peter, 180n20
Bible, 75–76, 152–53, 155. *See also* Tanakh
The Bible for Home Reading (Montefiore), 153–54, 213n39
Bible history, 76–78, 158, 197n25

bikkurim (first fruits), 75, 84, 86, 91
Bird's Eye View of Samaria, 123, *123*
Bloch Publishing Company, 60, 61, 63, 100, 106; confirmation certificates by, 108–9, 110, *110*
blue laws, 9
B'nai Brith, 204n61
Boston, 114, *124*
Bricker, Harry, 5
Brown, Rose, 101
Buffalo, 137
Bultmann, Rudolph, 194n84

California, 36, 210n60. *See also* San Francisco
Calisch, Edward, 158
cantors (hazanim), 22, 23, 33; compensation of, 60–61, 183n9
Carvalho, Sarah Nunes, 32
catechisms, 18, 48, 54, 70, 190n16, 211n7; criticism of, 147–48; for Orthodox Jews, 53
catechisms, gender, and rationalism, 190n9, 191n27; Christianity related to, 56, 189n3; for end-of-year ceremonies, 54; European Jewish catechisms in, 50; genus and species of American Judaism in, 54–59; German-style catechisms in, 50–51; halacha in, 51–52; legion of catechisms in, 59–61, *62,* 63–64; male authors in, 70; male-coded categories in, 51; memorization in, 54, 70, 191n22; Mendelssohn in, 55–56; Orthodox orientation of, 61, 63, 193n61; Protestant Reformation related to, 49–50, 189n3, 190n7; reforming religion in, 65–69; Reform orientation of, 63–64; "some excellent, majority mediocre" in, 69–70; transatlantic Jewish instruction in, 52–54, 190nn12–13, 190n16. *See also* Leeser, Isaac
Catholics, 114–15, 181n30, 187n65
Central Conference of American Rabbis (CCAR), 46, 79, 80, 160

Chamberlain, Alexander, 213n57
charitable societies, 134–35, 185nn38–39
Charleston, South Carolina, 27, 31–32, 63, 100–101; confirmation in, 112–13, *113;* Kahal Kadosh Beth Elohim in, 22, 39, 87, *87*
Chicago, 44, 84, 135, 198n34, 208n27
child, primitive. *See* primitive text and primitive child
child labor laws, 184n17
child psychology, science of, 145, 146, 148
Children's Day, 74, 82–83, 92
Children's periodicals, 99–108
child spirituality, 158–59. *See also* primitive text and primitive child
Choynski, Isidore Nathan (Maftir), 78, 93
Christian evangelists, 24, 134, 184n20, 185n38
Christianity, 8–9, 56, 87, 88–89, 91–92, 200n83
Christian missionaries, 3, 184n20, 184n21
Christian publications, 39, 188n80
Christian religious education, 98–100, 118–19
Christian schools, 184n21
Christian visitors to synagogues, 96–97
Christmas, 82, 99, 101, 113
Cincinnati, Ohio, 34, 93, 132, 186n60, 202n16, 205n69; kindergartens in, 134–35
Cleveland, Ohio, 33, 81, 94, 137–39, 140
Cohen, Gustav, 94
Cohen, Henry, 121
Cohen, Henry A., 40–41
Cohen, Jacob, 53
Cohen, Joseph A., 22
Cohen, Mary, 39, 188n80
Cohen, Miriam Moses, 24
Cohen, Montague, 160
Colorado, 136
comparative religious studies, 11, 67–69, 77, 162, 171, 195n85

compensation: for men, 1, 60–61, 179n2, 183n9; for women, 39, 40, 209n39
Confirmant's Guide (Eppstein), 65, 67
confirmation ceremonies, 4, 73, 86, 102, 196n5; *American Israelite* on, 78, 79, 85, 90, 94, 96; bar mitzvah compared to, 72, 73, 79; catechisms in, 70; criticism of, 92–96; in cross-denominational appeal, 80–81; divine revelation related to, 78; of flower children of 1860s, 83–92, *89*; in Germany, 72; girls in, 72–74, 196n6; invention of, 18–19; Leeser against, 73, 196n13; Lilienthal on, 72–73, 82, 196n11; in Mississippi, 71; in Missouri, 90; in New York, 72–73, 81–82, 85; opulence and extravagance of, 92–96; for Orthodox Jews, 72–73, 82, 94; primitive text and primitive child related to, 161–62; at Reform synagogues, 74, 196n6, 196n11; rituals of, 71–74; theater in, 92–93; Torah related to, 18; in West Virginia, 94–95
congregational education boards, 14–16, 22, 32, 35–36, 40–41, 46, 60, 81, 85, 93, 104, 108, 111–12, 132, 136–37, 139, 141, 146, 150
congregational records, 17
Congregation Bene Israel (Cincinnati), 34, 40
Congregation Beth El Religious School (Detroit), 37, *37*
Congregation Emanu-El (San Francisco), 36
Congregation Kahal Kadosh Beth Elohim (Charleston), 22, 39, 87, *87*
Connecticut, 35
Cooperman, Jessica, 181n33
Corwin-Berman, Lila, 172
criticism, 93, 155, 212n26, 213n46; of catechisms, 147–48; of confirmation ceremonies, 92–96; of Kohler, 140, 147; of NCJW, 136, 139, 208n27, 208n29
Cronbach, Abraham, 119, 198n39, 205n79

Cronson, Bernard, 12, 16, 215n7
cultural progress: American values as, 143–44; didactic moralism in, 142; patronization in, 141; Protestants related to, 143; un-American and, 142
curriculum, 20, 147; in Hebrew Sunday school, 2–3, 27, 49, 171; from men, 18; secularism in, 2, 13, 21, 52, 115, 145, 184n19, 205n69, 207n99

Darwin, Charles, 67
DeSolla, Jacob Mendes, 60, 63–64
Detroit, 141, 188n89, 194n75; Beth El Religious School, 37, *37*, 65–66; confirmation ceremonies in, 86, 94; leadership in, 131; Temple Beth El, 34–35, 37, 41, 43, 76, 86
Didache, 189n3
Diner, Hasia, 184n20, 185n41
Domestic Economy (Beecher), 211n18

educational aids, 19, 127. *See also* educational marketplace
Educational Alliance of the Lower East Side, 44
educational marketplace: Christian religious education related to, 98–100; Christmas in, 99; consumer market in, 98–99; entertainment in, 98; home from home in, 99–108, 101nn3–4, 101n8; HSSUA in, 105, 202nn19–20; Jewish youth movements in, 103; lesson plans in, 105–6; magic lanterns in, 119–26, *123*, *124*; model child paradigm in, 102–4; object lessons in, 114–19, 204n58, 205n69, 205n77; omnipresent teacher in, 103; prizes and paraphernalia in, 108–14, *110*, *113*; professional material resources in, 98; *Sabbath School Companion* in, 104; *Sabbath Visitor* in, 103–4; Sunday schools and, 100–108; *Young Israel* in, 104
Einhorn, David, 32

Elements of the Jewish Faith (Cohen, Jacob), 53
Ellis Island, 135
Elwell, Sue Levi, 209n36
Elzas, Barnett, 63, 104, 105, 193n64
embrace, of Jewish religious emotion: content knowledge in, 163–64; scientific theories of childhood in, 165; universality in, 164
emotion, religious, 160–65
emotional education, 45–46
Endelman, Todd, 180n25
English language, 2, 23, 44, 48, 53, 63, 75
entertainment, 98, 132, 138
Eppstein, Elias, 65–67, 150
ethnic identity, Judaism as, 5, 8, 9, 10, 164, 167, 170, 180n25
European anti-Semitism, 143
Eutaw Place Temple (Baltimore), 79
extracurriculars, 146

Fechner, Gustav, 156
Felling, Louis, 43, 141
Felsenthal, Bernhard, 194n77
female students. *See* girls
female superintendents, 4
feminization, of American Jewish education: emotional education in, 6, 12–16, 45–47, 171–73; Gratz in, 45; male authors in, 47; Morais on, 45
First Amendment, 9
first fruits (bikkurim), 75, 84, 86, 91
Fitzgerald, Timothy, 8
Flexner, Abraham, 145, 210n1
Florance, Rebecca, 31, 186n46
flower ceremony, 90–91
flowers, 82–88; bikkurim of, 86, 91–92; in Christianity, 82–83, 87, 88–89, 91–92, 200n83; confirmation ceremonies of, 83–92, 89; consumer culture in, 83; covenant of, 83–84; flowers of, 85–92, 87, 89, 199n66; formulaic model of, 84, 199n56; gender-neutral accessory for,

88; in Gilded Age, 82; music of, 84–85, 91–92, 200n85; ostentation and, 82–83; prosperity of, 82–83, 87–88; symbolisms for, 89–90; Victorian era floral culture of, 86–88, 87
Frank, Ray (Rachel), 36, 44
Frankel, Maurice, 84
Free Religious Association, 66–67
Froebel, Friedrich, 134
Fry, Grace A., 134–35
fundraising, 187n72; for Christian religious education, 74; Hebrew Benevolent Society for, 30; in Michigan, 29; by NCJW, 138; from Touro's estate, 34; by women activists, 130, 131–32

Gamoran, Emmanuel "Benderly boy," 164, 202n21
Gaon of Vilna. *See* Kramer, Eliyahu
Gartner, Lloyd, 186n61
Geiger, Abraham, 65, 67, 72
gender, 14–16, 72, 88, 179n16; in Americanization, 129; Hebrew Sunday school and, 25–26, 184n25; in Jewish religion invention, 10–11; teacher ratio related to, 182n37. *See also* catechisms, gender, and rationalism; feminization, of American Jewish education
Genesis, 153–54, 212n32
Georgia, 30–31, 33, 102, 185n45
gifts, 85, 93–95, 99, 111; for Hanukkah, 113–14
Ginsberg, Bernard, Mrs., 131
girls, 179n16; in confirmation ceremonies, 72–74, 196n6; in Reform Sunday schools, 14
God: belief in, 57, 66; catechisms on, 63, 67
Godey's Lady's Book (periodical), 26, 39
Gold, Penny Schine, 197n19
Goldberg, Jeanette Miriam, 121, 138
Goldman, Karla, 186n49, 189n101
gold rush, 94

Gottheil, Gustav, 130, 155, 205n78
Gotzmann, Andreas, 191n22
Gratz, Rebecca, 18, 21, 25, 27, 182nn1–2; at-home religious school of, 2, 183n7; charitable societies and, 185n39; Christian missionaries and, 3, 184n20, 184n21; initiative of, 24, 184n19; Victorian culture related to, 45. *See also* Hebrew Sunday school
Greenbaum, Miriam, 64, 78, 194n70, 198n32
Greenstone, Julius, 40, 129
Gries, Moses M. J., 137
Grinstein, Hyman, 191n23
Grossman, Louis, 131, 159, 162, 214n65
Guide for Instruction in Judaism (Kohler), 68–69
Guide for Sabbath School Teachers (HSSUA), 157–58
Guiterman, Emma, 134
Guttmacher, Adolph, 64, 194n70, 198n32

HaCohen, Dvora, 210n53
Hacohen, Malachi Haim, 192n33
Hahn, Clara, 139, 143, 209n41
halacha (Jewish law), 8; adaptation of, 142; education on, 51–52
Hall, G. Stanley, 156–57, 160–61, 214n65
Hanukkah, 100, 106; in catechisms, 48; European anti-Semitism related to, 143; festivals for, 132; gifts for, 113–14; hymn for, 119; magic lantern for, 120
Harris, William Torrey, 211n7
Hart, Henrietta, 184n36, 185n36
Haskalah (Jewish enlightenment), 8, 55
hazanim. *See* cantors
Hearth and Home Essays (Ruskey), 44
Hebrew Bible (Tanakh), 75, 168, 197n19, 212n32
Hebrew Free School, 112, 141
Hebrew Sabbath School Union of America (HSSUA), 145, 202n20; books published by, 105–6, 202n19, 212n25;

priceless American Jewish child and, 150, 212nn25–26; on primitive text and primitive child, 157–58
Hebrew schools, 6, 159, 164, 215nn10–11
Hebrew Sunday school (Philadelphia): Americanization in, 27; attendance at, 24–25; cost of, 21; curriculum in, 2–3, 27, 49, 171; denominationalism related to, 24–25; gender and, 25–26, 184n25; individualistic belief in, 25; Leeser related to, 3, 75–76; opening of, 2, 21; plans for, 24; prizes at, 111; Protestantism related to, 25, 27, 49–50; volunteer female teachers at, 14, 26–27
Hebrew Union College, 38, 68, 181n35
Helbrun, Louis, 101
Heller, Max, 78, 96
Helpful Thoughts (monthly), 100–101, 107, 142
Herberg, Will, 181n30
Herxheimer, Solomon, 191n23
Heschel, Susannah, 65
Hess, Emanuel, 64
Hess, Jonathan, 180n23
Hirsch, Samson Raphael, 42
historical criticism, 155, 213n46
Holy Land. *See* Israel
home from home, 201n3; advertisements in, 106–7; children's magazines for, 104–8; *Helpful Thoughts* in, 100–101, 107; Jewish Publication Society for, 100, 201n4; periodicals for, 99–104; subscriptions for, 107–8; *Young Israel* for, 100, 201n8
home religious schools, 183n7, 185n46
Houston, Texas, 94
How Judaism Became a Religion (Batnitzky), 181n26
HSSUA. *See* Hebrew Sabbath School Union of America
Hulbert, Ann, 149
Hyman, Paula, 26

Ibn Paquda, Bahya, 52
Idelson-Shein, Iris, 214n63
Imhoff, Sarah, 13–14, 190n10, 195n92
Indiana, 99, 102, 106, 119
Ingersoll, Robert, 162
Iowa, 150, 185n45
Isaacs, Abram Samuel, 125–26
Isaacs, S. M., 191n23
Israel, 66, 194n78; in magic lanterns, 121–
    25, *123, 124*; mothers in, 41–45, 188n94,
    189n99
Israelite (monthly), 99–100

Jacobs, Ella, 115–19, 121
Jacobs, George, 60–61, 62, *62, 193n55*
Jacobs, Rebecca, 61
Jagel, Abraham, 191n23
James, William, 162
Jastrow, Marcus, 205n78
JCS. *See* Jewish Chautauqua Society
JCS Bible course, 153, 212n37
Jefferson, Thomas, 194n84
Jerusalem (Mendelssohn), 8, 55, 58
Jewish Bible (Leeser), 75–76
Jewish Chautauqua Society (JCS), 204n58,
    205n77; founding of, 114–15; *Jewish Ex-
    ponent* on, 204n61; Meyer, at, 210n60;
    target of, 115; Teachers' Institute at,
    115–18
Jewish child, as priceless. *See* priceless
    American Jewish child
Jewish continuity, 12, 43, 83, 96, 172, 181n35
Jewish customs and practices (Yiddish-
    keit), 42
Jewish day schools, 184n19; in Cincin-
    nati, 34; in New York, 33–34, 54; in
    Philadelphia, 21–22, 23; Sunday school
    compared to, 169–70, 215n10
Jewish Denominational Congress, 208n27
Jewish Education in the United States
    (Gartner), 186n61
Jewish Exponent, 80–81, 95, 201n97,
    204n61

Jewish immigrants, 3–4, 19; American-
    ization of, 128–30, 133–35, 141–44;
    deficiencies of, 143; diversity among,
    5–6, 23; women, 185n41
Jewish law (halacha), 8, 142, 151–52
Jewish Messenger (periodical), 59, 61,
    189n99
Jewish Museum of Maryland, 198n35
Jewish Publication Society, 100, 201n4
Jewish religion: anti-Jewish discrimina-
    tion and, 9; blue laws in, 9; Christian-
    ity related to, 8–9; Europe compared
    to, 11; First Amendment and, 9;
    gender in, 10–11; Haskalah in, 8; hier-
    archy related to, 11; postwar Chris-
    tians and, 10; post-World War II,
    9–10; syntheses of, 11–12; universalist
    movements and, 11; Western religion
    definitions in, 7–8
Jewish revival organizations, 164
Jewish women educators: Christian
    evangelism and, 23–24; congrega-
    tional schools and, 21–22; corporal
    punishment and, 22; finances related
    to, 22–23; free public education and,
    23; Hebrew Sunday School Society of
    Philadelphia from, 21; Jewish immi-
    gration and, 23
Jews of Jerusalem at Abraham's Vineyard,
    124, *124*
Joselit, Jenna Weissman, 134, 176, 207n8
Josephinian reforms, 190n13
Judaism (Wise), 61, 67
Judaism, as religion, 69, 181n26, 181n30;
    affordable Jewish education in, 168;
    Benderly in, 168–69; catechism in,
    167, 168; free public schooling and,
    168; inauthenticity of, 167–68; Jewish
    Sunday school in, 169–70; peoplehood
    in, 169; suburban synagogues in, 169;
    teenagers in, 170; Victorian cult related
    to, 168
Judaism as a Civilization (Kaplan), 169

Judaism definitions, 10, 167, 180n25
Judges 5:7, 188n94

Kanarfogel, Ephraim, 199n56
Kansas City, 64, 90, 150, 151
Kant, Immanuel, 55, 191n27
Kaplan, Mordecai M., 12, 16, 169
Kehilath Anshe Ma'ariv Synagogue (Chicago), 198n34
Kentucky, 134–35, 145
kindergartens, 134–35
Kirshenblatt-Gimblett, Barbara, 187n72
Klapper, Melissa, 163–64, 182n42, 187n71, 189n99
Kley, Eduard, 55, 56–57, 191n25, 192n33
Kohler, Kaufmann, 42, 68–69, 148, 195n92–93; on Bible history, 77, 158; criticism of, 140, 147
Kohut, George Alexander, 142–43
Kohut, Rebekah, 36, 131, 157
Kramer, Eliyahu (Gaon of Vilna), 199n66
Krasner, Jonathan, 6, 206n87, 207n105
Krauskopf, Joseph, 91–92
Kursheedt, Gershon, 186n46

Ladies Hebrew Benevolent Society, 38
Landsberg, Max, 195n91
leaflets, 150–51, 212n26, 212n28
Leeser, Isaac, 24, 30, 182n2, 184n19, 192n42; appendixes from, 192n36; catechism of, 50–51, 68; against confirmation ceremonies, 73, 196n13; definitions from, 55; Eppstein compared to, 66; on 'false belief,' 195n90; Hebrew Sunday school related to, 3, 75–76; instructional sessions by, 30; Jewish Bible by, 75–76; Kley compared to, 56–57; Mendelssohn and, 58; at Mikveh Israel, 3, 38, 50, 179n8; paradigm from, 50–51, 190n9; school of, 34
Lehman, A., 33
Leibman, Laura Arnold, 88, 185n39
Lemlein, Mathilda, 119

Lerman, Gerda, 16–17
Leviticus, 212n32
Lilienthal, Max, 34, 68, 103, 205n69; on confirmation ceremonies, 72–73, 82, 196n11
Lindheim, Irma, 71
Loeb, Henri, 60, 183n51, 191n23
Loewenthal, Henry, 33
Lofton, Kathryn, 182n44
Lopez, Sally, 27, 31
Los Angeles, 96
Loth, Ella, 110, 110
Louis, Minnie D., 133–34
Louisiana, 112
Louisville, Kentucky, 76, 134–35, 200n85
Lowenberg, Clara, 38–39
Lowenstein, Betsy, 64
Luzzatto, Moshe Chaim, 52
Lyon, Jacques Judah, 61, 63

Maftir. See Choynski, Isidore Nathan
magic lanterns, 206n87; advertisements for, 120, 206n94; American Israelite related to, 121, 125–26; contemporary Palestine in, 122–23, 123, 124; Cronbach and, 119–20; electricity related to, 120; Holy Land in, 121–25, 123, 124; images in, 119–20, 205n80; obsolescence of, 206n92; Orthodox opponents of, 207n105; photographic slides for, 205n81; as prizes, 205n83; in Texas, 121; traditional Judaism with, 126, 207n103
Maimonides, 52, 111, 191n25, 192n36, 203n46
male authors, 47. See also men
Manhattan, 130
Mannheimer, Jennie, 98
"Maoz Tzur" ("Rock of Ages"), 119, 205n78
Marcus, Jacob Rader, 89, 89
Marks, Josephine Grauman, 111
Masculinity, 10, 15, 47; in Jewish catechisms, 48–70
Masuzawa, Tomoko, 8

McAllister, T. H., 122, 206n94

McCutcheon, Russell, 8

memorization, 54, 70, 191n22; in religion from theology, 147–48

men, 14, 47, 51; catechisms from, 18, 70; curriculum from, 18; leadership by, 35–36, 130–31, 137; as teachers, 40, 188n83, 209n39

Mendelssohn, Moses, 8, 55–56, 58, 180n23, 191n27

Menorah Journal, 164

Menorah Monthly (newspaper), 204n61

Menorah Society, 41

Messing, Aron J., 94

Meyer, Harry, 151

Meyer, Martin A., 142, 210n60

Meyer, Michael, 180n17, 190n12

Meyers, Elijah, 123–25, 124, 124

Michigan, 29, 37, 37. *See also* Detroit

midrash (explanation), 212n32

Mielziner, Moses, 202nn19–20

Mikveh Israel, 21, 179n8, 182n1, 185n38; Leeser at, 3, 38, 50; Morais at, 45

minhag (custom), 212n32

Minister's Handbook (CCAR), 80

Mississippi, 38–39, 188n86

Moise, Penina, 39

Moise, Sarah Ann, 27, 30–31

Montefiore, Claude G., 153–55, 156, 158, 213n39, 213n46

Morais, Henry, 183n3

Morais, Sabato, 38, 45, 147

Mordecai, Emma, 28, 184n35

Mordecai, Rachel, 53

Mordecai, Rosa, 49, 59–60, 111, 126–27

Mordecai, Sam, 53

Mordecai academy (North Carolina), 53

Moses, Clara Lowenberg, 71

Moses, Isaac, 68

music, 39, 84–85, 200n85, 205n78; "The Floral Offering" hymn as, 91–92; "Maoz Tzur" as, 119–20

Myers, Ella C., 184n35

Nashville, 90, 97

Natchez, Mississippi, 71

Nathan, Morris, 196n13

National Council of Jewish Women (NCJW), 13, 19, 42, 61, 188n90; criticism of, 136, 139, 208n27, 208n29; early programs of, 209n36; Hahn in, 209n41; for Jewish immigrants, 135; for Sunday schools, 135–40; without Jewish knowledge, 139–40

Nefutsoth Yehudah, 31

Neusner, Jacob, 8

Newark, New Jersey, 130–31, 132, 141

New Orleans, 31, 85, 94

Newport, Rhode Island, 9

New York, 100, 112, 137, 140; Ahawath Chesed in, 36, 40, 76; American movement in, 27–28, 184n33; confirmation ceremonies in, 72–73, 81–82, 85; Emanu-El in, 33–34, 130, 186n57, 198n34; Jewish day schools in, 33–34, 54; Jewish education in, 129, 131, 133–34; population/synagogue membership in, 23, 183n15; sisterhood groups in, 207n8; teachers in Israel in, 36, 40

New York Bureau of Jewish Education, 7

New York Kehillah, 129

New York Talmud Torah and Hebrew Institute, 191n23

Noll, Mark, 206n97

Nurmser, B., 188n83

object lessons, 114, 204n58; in Christian religious school, 118–19; decorations in, 117; Lilienthal for, 205n69; material goods in, 117; Teachers' Institute in, 115–17; textbooks and correspondence courses in, 205n77

Occident and American Jewish Advocate (newspaper), 3, 24, 31–32, 179n8; confirmation ceremonies in, 72, 73; didactic gifts in, 111; Jewish catechisms in, 54; national reach of, 99–100; women authors in, 39, 188n80

Ohio, 114

Olitzky, Kerry Marc, 202n21

The Open Bible (Berkowitz), 153, 155

Oppenheim, Moritz Daniel, 125, 126

opulence and extravagance, of confirmation ceremonies: criticism of, 93; gifts in, 93–95; rivalry in, 95–96; as theater, 92–93

"Oriental," 72; term use of, 8, 180n25

Orthodox congregational schools, 13

Orthodox Jews, 28, 32, 42, 81, 129, 207n105; catechism for, 53; confirmation ceremonies for, 72–73, 82, 94; orientation of, 61, 63, 193n61; Sabbath school for, 76, 137

Paidologist (journal), 156

Parliament of World Religions, 11

Pearlstein, Peggy, 213n46

Peixotto, Rachel, 182n1

Peixotto, Simha, 49, 182n1, 190n7

peoplehood, 169

periodicals, 99–104

personal spirituality, 164

Pestalozzi, Johann, 117, 149

Petuchowski, Jacob, 52, 192n38

Pew Research Center, 167

Philadelphia, 117, 143, 204n61, 209n41; confirmation ceremonies in, 90; congregational school in, 22; curriculum from, 20; primitive text and primitive child in, 161. *See also* Hebrew Sunday school

Philadelphia Jewish Foster Home and Orphan Asylum, 120

Philipson, David, 59, 79, 136, 146, 150, 212n26

Pittsburgh, 86, 111–12, 125, 137, 209n36

Pittsburgh Platform, 66

Plaut, W. Gunther, 191n23

Plaut Memorial Hebrew Free School, 141

Pollak, Jacob P., 186n61

Portland, Oregon, 133, *133*

praise, 31–32

Prell, Riv-Ellen, 186n49

priceless American Jewish child: child-rearing theories related to, 149–50; Creation related to, 151–52, 212n32; grade levels separation for, 150–51, 212n25; HSSUA and, 150, 212nn25–26; instructional leaflets for, 150–51, 212n26, 212n28; popular culture of, 148–49; Romanticism of, 149

primitive text and primitive child: adolescence in, 161–62; Christianity related to, 156; confirmation ceremony related to, 161–62; Creation story in, 156, 157–58; HSSUA on, 157–58; paternalism related to, 158–59; in Philadelphia, 161; "primitive" term meaning in, 154, 213n43; recapitulation in, 156–57, 159, 213nn56–57, 214n60; Reform movement and, 157, 162–63; savage child in, 156–57, 214n63

private tutors, 22, 129

prizes and paraphernalia: for Christian religious education, 109, 111; confirmation certificates as, 108–9, 110, *110*; didactic gifts as, 111; donations for, 112; for Hanukkah, 113–14; medals as, 112–13, *113*

prophetic mission, 69

Protestant groups, 29, 185n38

Protestantism, 8, 42, 180n23, 181n30, 182n51; Hebrew Sunday school related to, 25, 27, 49–50; vocabulary and ideology related to, 4, 5, 7; women as activists in, 130; women in, 26; women's religion related to, 13

Protestant Reformation, 49–50, 180n20, 189n3, 190n7

Protestant religious education, 109

Protestants, 181n30; American movement and, 29, 185n38; Bible lands related to, 206n97; cultural progress related to, 143

Proverbs 19:20, 148, 211n12

public school teachers, 36, 121, 138, 188n89

Pyke, Rachel, 49–50, 60

Rabbinical Association of the Jewish Theological Seminary, 46

rabbis, 14, 94–95, 140

Rabin, Shari, 182n41, 183n9, 183n16

Rappel, Dov, 192n45, 193n51

Rau, William H., 122–23, 123

Rauch, Eduardo, 180n17

recapitulation, 156–57, 159, 213nn56–57, 214n60

Reform movement, 14, 16, 65–69, 128, 157, 180n17, 204n58; catechisms in, 63–64; in Jewish religion invention, 9–10; primitive text and primitive child and, 162–63; Sunday schools related to, 4–5

Reform synagogues, 63, 65, 74, 78, 81, 132, 150

Religion, definitions of, 7–8, 57–59, 67, 70, 195n91

religious emotion, embrace of, 160–65

Richman, Julia, 36, 37, 107–8, 119, 184n35; JCS and, 114, 115–16

The Road to Faith (Loeb), 60, 193n51

Rockdale Temple Sabbath School (Cincinnati, Ohio), 38

"Rock of Ages" ("Maoz Tzur"), 119, 205n78

Rodef Shalom (Pittsburgh), 125

Rodeph Shalom (Philadelphia), 22, 73

Romanticism, 149

romanticization, 125

Rosenau, William, 155, 194n69

Rosenblatt, Kate, 172

Ruskay, Esther, 44, 45

Sabbath School Companion (monthly), 100–101, 104, 105, 107

Sabbath School Festival, 132

Sabbath Schools, 4–5, 34, 35, 186n60. See also Hebrew Sunday school

Sabbath School Visitor (magazine), 71, 101–2

Sabbath Visitor (magazine), 99, 100–101, 103–4, 148, 202n14, 202n16, 211n12

St. Thomas, 72

Samaria, Bird's Eye View, 123, 123

San Francisco, 36, 94, 120, 132, 146, 210n60; NCJW in, 136–37

Sarna, Jonathan, 108, 183n13, 187n66, 207n103

Schechter, Solomon, 77

Schleiermacher, Friedrich, 10, 26

science, of child psychology, 145, 146, 148

scientific childhood theories, 165

Seasongood, Emily, 93

secularism, 203n32, 215n14; in American Jewish population, 152, 160, 163, 171, 180n25; in curriculum, 2, 13, 21, 52, 115, 145, 184n19, 205n69, 207n99

Seixas, Isaac B., 182n2

Seixas, Moses, 9

sexual assault, 181n35

Shavuot, 18, 71, 198n33; Christian visitors on, 96–97; cross-denominational appeal of, 79–82; flower children of 1860s in, 82–92, 87, 89; opulence and extravagance of, 92–96; ritualizing Jewish religion and, 96–97; teaching Torah in modernity on, 74–78. See also confirmation ceremonies

Shearith Israel, 30, 31–32, 184n33, 184n36

Sisterhood of Personal Service, 130

Sloss, Hattie Hecht, 136

smallpox epidemic, 184n33

Smith, Jonathan Z., 10, 181n32

Solomon, Hannah Greenebaum, 131, 135, 136

Sonneschein, Rosa, 44–45, 125, 139, 189n101, 207n99

South Carolina, 22, 27, 30, 39, 63, 107; Occident and American Jewish Advocate

on, 31–32; prizes and paraphernalia in, 111, 112–13, *113*; *Sabbath School Companion* from, 100–101; Victorian era floral culture in, 87, *87*
The Spirit of Judaism (Aguilar), 197n21
Stahl, Ronit, 172
stereopticon. *See* magic lanterns
subscriptions for Jewish children's periodicals, 107–8
Sunday schools, 6–7, 34, 184n21; congregational Sunday schools, 26–28, 129; contents of, 115–16; educational marketplace and, 100–108; in Iowa, 150, 185n45; Jewish day schools compared to, 169–70, 215n10; NCJW for, 135–40; Reform movement related to, 4–5; in San Francisco, 36, 94, 120, 132, 136–37, 146, 210n60; in UAHC, 186n61; visual stimuli of, 116–17; Wiser on, 1, 4–5, 185n40; women as activists for, 131–35, *133*. *See also specific locations*
supersessionist theology, 125
surveys: of Judaism as religion, 167; by Pew Research Center, 215n10; by UAHC, 13, 34; on women's religion, 12, 13
synagogue choirs, 85
synagogue membership, 19, 183n15, 207n8; American patriotism related to, 10; free classes without, 27–28; priority of, 12, 171
synagogue renovations, 131–32
Szold, Benjamin, 32–33, 63, 193n59, 193n63
Szold, Henrietta, 96, 208n29, 209n42, 210n53; on Torah, 154–55

Talmud, 2, 45, 185n38, 196n11; Bible compared to, 27, 75–76, 77; Torah compared to, 75, 197n18, 197n25
Talmud Torah and Hebrew Institute of New York, 54
Talmud Torahs, 5, 13, 54, 191n23; Benderly and, 169; private tutors or, 21–22

Tanakh (Hebrew Bible), 75, 168, 197n19, 212n32
teacher gender ratio, 182n37
teachers in Israel, 34–35, 41; in Michigan, 37, *37*; in Mississippi, 38–39; in New York, 36, 40
Teachers' Institute, 115–17, 152, 204n60
teaching Torah in modernity. *See* Shavuot
Temkin, Sefton D., 194n81
Temple Beth El (Detroit), 34–35, 37, 41, 43, 76, 86
Temple Beth El (New York), 36
Temple Israel (Boston), 122, 123
Temple Ohabei Shalom (San Francisco), 36
Temple Oheb Shalom (Baltimore), 63
Texas, 40–41, 94, 104, 121
textbooks, 4
theater, 133, *133*; in confirmation ceremonies, 92–93
Torah, 155, 212n32; confirmation ceremony related to, 18; danger of, 154; Talmud compared to, 75–76, 197n18, 197n25
Touro, Judah, 19, 31, 34, 186n46
Touro Synagogue (New Orleans), 94
traditions, 20, 126, 145–46, 207n103
transatlantic Jewish instruction: American publications in, 53; catechisms in, 52, 190n16; contents of, 53–54; European Jewish catechisms in, 52–54, 190n12; Josephinian reforms in, 190n13; production of, 52–53; textbook demands in, 52, 190n13

Union of American Hebrew Congregations (UAHC), 46, 101, 186n61, 212n26; on Americanization, 128–29; HSSUA from, 105; leaflets from, 150–51, 212n26, 212n28; survey by, 13, 34
Union Prayer Book (CCAR), 80
universal religion, Judaism as, 67, 69

Verein, Miriam Frauen, 132

Victorian culture, 45, 86–88, 97

Virginia Sunday school, 28, 184nn35–36

volunteer female teachers, 14, 26–27

Voorsanger, Jacob, 136, 202n14

Warrenton, North Carolina, 53

Washington, George, 9

Weinman, Rose Barlow, 188n89

Weinstein, Esther, 99

Weismann, Jenna, 134

Werner, Julian, 125–26

West Virginia, 89, 89, 94–95, 96–97

Wilson, Edward L., 122

Wilson, Kathleen, 72

Wise, Isaac Mayer, 61, 66, 185n40, 202n14; on Bible history, 77, 197n25; catechism by, 60, 193n50; compensation for, 1, 179n2; education of, 1–2; Eppstein compared to, 67; on flower children of 1860s, 91; on inadequate education, 1, 179n3; *Israelite* from, 99–100; Loewenthal and, 33; on mothers of Israel, 43; Reform movement and, 5; on Sunday School, 1, 4–5, 185n40; on Torah compared to Talmud, 197n25

Wolff, Boanna, 30

women, 14, 26–27; benevolent causes from, 184nn38–40; higher education for, 38, 187n71; Jewish continuity related to, 181n35; as public school teachers, 36–37

women as activists: American Christian women in, 130; children's service from, 132; in Cincinnati, 134–35; in Detroit, 131; fundraising by, 130, 131–32; for Jewish immigrants, 130, 133; in Kentucky, 134–35; male leadership and, 130–31; Sisterhood of Personal Service in, 130; for Sunday schools, 131–35, 133; synagogue renovations from, 131–32; transformation related to, 131, 207n8. *See also* Gratz, Rebecca

women authors, 39, 188n80

women's auxiliaries, 17; men associated with, 184n40; men's auxiliaries compared to, 184n37

women's benevolent organizations, 29–31, 185n40

women's employment, 187n71

women's public leadership, 186n49; displacement of, 14, 35; fundraising fairs and, 187n72

women's religion, 17–18; Conservative and Orthodox congregational schools and, 13; failures of, 6, 12, 13, 180n17; feminization of, 13–15; gender dynamics of, 15–16; men in, 14–15; "mission schools" from, 13; public school education compared to, 15; student gender in, 14, 179n16; surveys on, 12, 13

women teachers, 2; affective skills of, 35; compensation for, 40–41; creativity of, 38–39; graduates as, 37–38

working girls, 137–38

World's Columbian Exposition (Chicago, Illinois), 44, 135, 208n27

Wundt, Wilhelm, 156

Yiddishkeit (Jewish customs and practices), 42

Young Israel (periodical), 100, 105, 106, 201n8, 202n22, 212n28

Young Women's Hebrew Association, 44

ABOUT THE AUTHOR

LAURA YARES is Assistant Professor in the Department of Religious Studies at Michigan State University. Her work focuses on religion, gender, and Judaism, with particular interests in Jewish education.